Minister for Health and Children's Foreword

In every aspect of every individual's life, health is pivotal. It is the key factor in a child's development to adulthood. It is a prerequisite to the achievement of wholeness and fulfilment in adult life. It is central to a contributory and confident later life.

Health is also crucial to Ireland as a nation. Our health care system must reflect our national values: our concerns for equity, our commitment to diversity, our determination to end poverty and disadvantage. It must, as a major employer, provide a context for professionalism, growth and development at every level within the workforce.

Public health systems, worldwide, are experiencing unprecedented pressures in these, the early years of a new century. Those pressures include a quantum leap in available technology, matched by radically different expectations within the population. Our growing population and changing lifestyles create new and different needs.

It is essential, therefore, to inform the long-term development of this massive, complex system, that we have an over-arching Strategy. Such a Strategy empowers Health Boards, institutions, agencies and voluntary organisations to structure their planning in an integrated, streamlined way. In turn, this will make the best of the immeasurable human resource they represent, to share best practice across all disciplines, and to make full and transparent use of the unequalled funding this Government is committing to health.

What distinguishes this Strategy is the unique level of public consultation on which it is based. Individuals, professional groups, disciplines, voluntary organisations and state agencies all contributed significantly to the thinking manifest in the Strategy, and will continue to contribute to the management of the changes they sought. The Strategy, at all points, envisages cross-disciplinary collaboration to achieve new standards, protocols and methods. In setting out an innovative and costed programme of massive change, as Minister for Health and Children, I have at all times stressed the involvement and influence of those who have – often under great financial constraint – constantly delivered care which, in its professionalism and humanity, is second to none.

This is a comprehensive and ambitious Strategy: a blueprint to guide policy makers and service providers towards delivery of the articulated vision. It identifies overarching goals to guide planning and activity in the health system over the next 7-10 years.

I must stress, however, that this Health Strategy is more than a considered, conceptual draft for the long-term future. In the immediate future – indeed, before the end of this year – service deficiencies and waiting lists must be, and are, addressed. Underdeveloped services must be enhanced, and the document makes specific provision for immediate enhancements.

Because of this confluence of long-term strategic planning and shorter-term tactical initiatives, this Strategy will immediately benefit substantial numbers of our people, while allowing us all to observe, gain from, and contribute to, the construction of a health system which, in little more than half a decade, will be immeasurably improved and visibly different, while retaining the best of what was achieved in the last century.

Micheál Martin

Micheál Martin, T.D.
Minister for Health and Children

Acknowledgements

The Health Strategy *Quality and Fairness: A Health System for You* is the result of many months of hard work by the Department of Health and Children, the health boards and many others with an interest in health.

It would not have been possible to bring the work to completion without the excellent input of the individuals, groups and organisations who participated so positively in the National Consultative Forum on the Health Strategy. The Forum was divided into a series of sub-groups to allow detailed consideration of key issues. The energy and enthusiasm of the chairpersons of these sub-groups, and the commitment of all who took part, added greatly to the deliberations on the direction of the Strategy.

The Department received some 1,500 written submissions from individuals and over 300 from organisations. The messages from the submissions helped sharpen our understanding of the concerns about health and the strategic direction that is required for the future. They reflected both the complexity of the policy questions being considered and the breadth of the consultations undertaken in preparing the Strategy. The outcome of the consultation process is being published as a separate document, *Your views about health*.

Work on the Strategy benefited greatly from the input of an international panel and also from the working of an inter-departmental group which focused on how best to address issues beyond the health services that affect our health and well-being. The contribution made by the various working groups within the Department and by staff more generally in both the Department and the health boards was also significant.

Finally, sincere thanks are offered to the members of the Steering Group who led the development of the Strategy and to the Project Team who drafted the document.

Michael Kelly
Secretary General

Quality and Fairness

A Health System for You

Health Strategy

**DEPARTMENT
OF HEALTH AND
CHILDREN**
AN ROINN
SLÁINTE AGUS LEANAÍ

Taoiseach's Foreword

Over the last few years, the largest ever expansion in health funding has been accompanied by an unprecedented series of studies and detailed investigations into all aspects of our health system. These have provided the essential building blocks for a comprehensive plan to develop and reform services which can meet the needs of Irish society today and across the next decade.

There is no denying the fact that our health system has many problems. These must and will be addressed – but there is no 'quick-fix' which can achieve what we all want, the highest quality of care for all.

This Strategy outlines a programme of investment and reform, starting immediately and stretching across the next decade. It sets clear priorities but also involves all elements of the system.

It is a highly ambitious and challenging agenda for change. With effective reform, and fully utilising the expertise of what is the largest professional workforce in the country, the unprecedented levels of investment which have been committed to our health services can deliver major improvements in services throughout the country.

For all parts of the system, from Government down, implementation will require an effective partnership with people willing to work together and, where necessary, change the way business is currently done.

On behalf of the Government I would like to thank the thousands of people who participated in the work of developing the Strategy. I have no doubt that the same spirit of openness and commitment will be seen as we all move forward to bring about the future which the Strategy is pointing us towards.

Bertie Ahern, T.D.
Taoiseach

Members of the Steering Group

Mr. Michael Kelly (Chair)	Secretary General	Department of Health and Children
Mr. Frank Ahern	Director	Department of Health and Children
Mr. Paul Barron	Assistant Secretary	Department of Health and Children
Mr. Donal Devitt	Assistant Secretary	Department of Health and Children
Mr. Denis Doherty	Chief Executive Officer	Midland Health Board
Mr. Tony Enright	Assistant Secretary	Department of Health and Children
Ms. Deirdre Gillane	Policy Advisor to the Minister	Department of Health and Children
Mr. Pat Harvey	Chief Executive Officer	North Western Health Board
Dr. Jim Kiely	Chief Medical Officer (CMO)	Department of Health and Children
Mr. Michael Lyons	Area Chief Executive	East Coast Area Health Board
Mr. John Thompson[1]	Principal Officer	Department of Finance
Mr. Peter MacDonagh	Policy Advisor to the Taoiseach	Department of the Taoiseach
Mr. Tom Mooney	Deputy Secretary	Department of Health and Children
Mr. Donal O Shea	Regional Chief Executive	Eastern Regional Health Authority
Dr. Sheelagh Ryan	Chief Executive Officer	Western Health Board
Mr. Dermot Smyth	A/Assistant Secretary	Department of Health and Children
Ms. Frances Spillane	Director	Department of Health and Children

1 Mr. John Thompson was replaced by Mr. Joe Mooney

Members of the Project Team

Ms. Frances Spillane (Chair)	Director	Department of Health and Children
Mr. Vincent Barton[1]	Principal Officer	Department of Health and Children
Mr. Tom Beegan	Deputy Chief Executive Officer	South Eastern Health Board
Ms. Elizabeth Canavan	Assistant Principal Officer	Department of Health and Children
Dr. John Devlin	Deputy CMO	Department of Health and Children
Ms. Mary Dowling	Assistant Principal Officer	Department of Health and Children
Ms. Maureen Flynn	Nurse Research Officer	Department of Health and Children
Ms. Deirdre Gillane	Policy Advisor to the Minister	Department of Health and Children
Dr. Tony Holohan	Deputy CMO	Department of Health and Children
Dr. Kevin Kelleher	Director of Public Health	Mid-Western Health Board
Ms. Siobhán Kennan	Assistant Principal Officer	Department of Health and Children
Mr. Fergal Lynch	Principal Officer	Department of Health and Children
Dr. Ambrose McLoughlin	Deputy Chief Executive Officer	North Eastern Health Board
Mr. Kevin McCarthy	Assistant Chief Executive	East Coast Area Health Board
Mr. Seamus Molloy	Assistant Principal Officer	Department of Health and Children

1 Until end March 2001

Secretariat

Ms. Aodhín Delaney	Librarian	Midland Health Board
Ms. Marian O'Toole	Executive Officer	Department of Health and Children
Mr. Michael Smith	Assistant Principal Officer	Department of Health and Children

Specialist Registrars in Public Health Medicine, Dr. Joan O'Donnell, Dr. Tom O'Connell and Dr. Emer Feely assisted the Project Team during their placement in the Department.

The Project Team was also supported by the staff of the Change Management Unit of the Department of Health and Children

Members of the Inter-departmental Group

Mr. Michael Kelly (Chair)	Secretary General	Department of Health and Children
Mr. Seán Aylward	Director General	Irish Prisons Service
Mr. Peter Baldwin	Assistant Secretary	Department of Education and Science
Mr. Jim Beecher	Assistant Secretary	Department of Agriculture, Food and Rural Development
Mr. Brian Brogan	Assistant Principal Officer	Department of Health and Children
Mr. Gerry Daly	Assistant Secretary	Department of Social, Community and Family Affairs
Dr. John Devlin	Deputy CMO	Department of Health and Children
Ms. Mary Doyle	Assistant Secretary	Department of the Taoiseach
Mr. Chris Fitzgerald	Principal Officer	Department of Health and Children
Ms. Deirdre Gillane	Policy Advisor to the Minister	Department of Health and Children
Mr. Seán Gorman	Assistant Secretary	Department of Enterprise, Trade and Employment
Mr. Con Haugh	Assistant Secretary	Department of Tourism, Sport and Recreation
Ms. Siobhán Kennan	Assistant Principal Officer	Department of Health and Children
Mr. Fergal Lynch	Principal Officer	Department of Health and Children
Dr. Tom O'Connell[1]	Specialist Registrar	Department of Health and Children
Mr. Tom O'Mahony[2]	Assistant Secretary	Department of the Environment and Local Government
Mr. Michael Smith (Secretary)	Assistant Principal Officer	Department of Health and Children
Ms. Frances Spillane	Director	Department of Health and Children
Mr. John Thompson[3]	Principal Officer	Department of Finance

1 Dr. Tom O'Connell was replaced by Dr. Emer Feely

2 Ms. Rhíona Ní Fhlanghaile acted as alternate for Mr. Tom O'Mahony

3 Mr. Fred Foster acted as alternate for Mr. John Thompson

Chairs of the Forum Sub-groups and Informal Working Groups

Ms. Jacqueline Crinion	Management Development Specialist	Office for Health Management
Mr. Michael Dempsey	Managing Director	Bristol Myers Squibb
Professor Andrew Green	National Centre for Medical Genetics	Our Lady's Hospital for Sick Children, Crumlin
Ms. Maureen Lynott	Management Consultant	
Professor Geraldine McCarthy	Head of the Department of Nursing Studies	University College Cork
Mr. Tom Mooney	Deputy Secretary	Department of Health and Children
Professor Michael Murphy	Dean of the Medical School	University College Cork
Professor Ivan Perry	Professor of Epidemiology and Public Health	University College Cork
Mr. Dermot Smyth	A/Assistant Secretary	Department of Health and Children
Ms. Frances Spillane	Director	Department of Health and Children
Professor Jane Wilde	Director	Institute of Public Health in Ireland

Members of the International Panel

Professor Richard Alderslade	Regional Adviser	WHO Regional Office for Europe
Dr. Charlotte Dargie	Senior Research Associate	Judge Institute of Management Studies, University of Cambridge (UK)
Dr. Judith Kurland	Regional Director	Department of Health and Human Services (USA)

Table of Contents

The Vision

A health system that supports and empowers you, your family and community to achieve your full health potential

A health system that is there when you need it, that is fair, and that you can trust

A health system that encourages you to have your say, listens to you, and ensures that your views are taken into account.

Introduction

Introduction

Why a new Strategy?

Over the last four years health services in Ireland have benefited from the largest ever sustained increase in funding. Facilities are being developed and refurbished, more staff are being hired and the number of people benefiting from health services has increased substantially.

A lot has been achieved, but a lot remains to be done. Very clear deficiencies in services remain which must be addressed. There are unacceptably long waiting times in various parts of the system, important services remain underdeveloped and major demographic challenges must be addressed. By doubling health funding over the last four years, the Government has moved the debate on health funding from resources alone to both resources and reform.

A wide range of issues must be addressed – encompassing everything from more effective preventive work through to the development of major acute facilities. This requires a comprehensive blueprint for developments, setting out core principles for the whole system and detailed plans for development and reform. This is why a wide-ranging and ambitious Strategy is required.

For the Strategy to work it must be based on a foundation of solid research and evaluation. This Strategy marks a decisive move away from a short-term and limited approach to planning. An unprecedented series of detailed studies of fundamental issues has been undertaken. These include:

- The first ever detailed audit of value for money within the system;

- A comprehensive review of the existing and future demand for acute hospital services;

- Extensive work on projecting the likely need for different services over the next decade; and

- A blueprint for the future of nursing as set out in the Commission on Nursing.

In addition, the Government believes that the public and people working within the health system need to have their say. As a result, the largest consultation process ever undertaken in the preparation of a strategy was implemented. Over 1,800 submissions have been considered, and these were fed directly into the work of those drafting the Strategy.

Setting a new vision

The agenda being set in this Strategy document involves organising the future health system around a new vision:

A health system that supports and empowers you, your family and community to achieve your full health potential

A health system that is there when you need it, that is fair, and that you can trust

A health system that encourages you to have your say, listens to you, and ensures that your views are taken into account.

A number of principles is put forward in support of this vision. These are concerned with:

- equity and fairness

- a people-centred service

- quality of care

- clear accountability.

Flowing directly from these principles are specific actions which have the capacity to deliver the highest quality of care and support to all people. Key examples of this include:

- Primary care services will undergo major development to deliver an integrated community-based service accessible to all on a round-the-clock basis;

- Acute hospital care will be developed and reformed through the creation of 3,000 extra hospital beds for public patients and a range of other measures which will ensure that no public patient will wait longer than 3 months from the date of referral for the scheduling of treatment.

- Continuing care services will undergo a sustained expansion for people with disabilities and older people.

- National treatment protocols will be put in place to ensure that all patients receive a uniformly high quality of care.

- The planning and funding of acute hospital services will be reformed.

- Funding will be more directly linked to service levels and there will be much greater transparency in the planning, funding and delivery of services.

Resourcing health

This Strategy outlines the largest concentrated expansion in services in the history of the Irish health system. Across the full range of care areas, a vision is set out for how the system can develop immediately and over the next decade to deliver high-quality care for all. Proposals are based on detailed research and expert input addressing system-wide as well as programme-specific issues.

The Strategy implies a major increase in the level of health funding. The single most important part of ensuring that this funding can be provided in the coming years is to ensure that we have an economic and fiscal situation which is capable of sustaining such increases. In previous years, Ireland may have had higher percentages of spending on health as a proportion of GNP, but the level of funding was dramatically lower. It is the economic and fiscal policies of recent years which have made possible an unprecedented expansion in health funding.

Over recent years health has been by far the largest beneficiary of new resources available for public services. The Government is committed to keeping health as a key priority area. It is equally committed to working to protect Ireland's economic and fiscal situation, as the key prerequisite to providing the funding required to implement the Strategy.

A full range of options for funding methods has been considered in the preparation of this Strategy. Having considered the alternatives, it is clear that none would deliver significant improvements over the present tax-based method, while each would undermine the ability of the system to deliver the expansion of capacity required both immediately and across the next decade. In addition, the reforms to the current funding system outlined in this Strategy will address clear deficiencies without diverting resources away from the needs of core services.

Implementation

Implementation will require a significant programme of development and growth, reform and modernisation. This programme will be led by the Department of Health and Children, reporting through the Minister to a special sub-committee of the Cabinet. The action programme outlined at Chapter 7 shows how clear leadership, consistent effort and wide collaboration will be required for its implementation.

For its part the Government is committed to continuing to give health the highest priority over the coming period. It anticipates a similar level of commitment from those working in the health system and looks forward to a successful partnership in delivering better health services and improved health outcomes for the population in the years ahead.

CHAPTER 1

New vision, new horizons

Introduction

This Strategy is centred on a whole-system approach to tackling health in Ireland. It goes beyond the traditional concept of 'health services'. It is about developing a system in which best health and social well-being are valued and supported. At its widest limits this system does not just include the services provided under the auspices of the Minister for Health and Children. It includes both public and private providers of health services. It includes every person and institution with an influence on or a role to play in the health of individuals, groups, communities and society at large. In describing the strategic direction for the future, this Strategy incorporates many strands of activity within a shared vision in order to deliver a healthier population and a world-class health system.

Health – a definition

The concepts of health and social gain introduced in Shaping a healthier future, the 1994 Strategy, are key to this Strategy also.

Health gain is concerned with health status, both in terms of increase in life expectancy and in terms of improvements in the quality of life through the cure or alleviation of an illness or disability or through any other general improvement in the health of the individual or the population at whom the service is directed.

Social gain is concerned with broader aspects of the quality of life. It includes, for example, the quality added to the lives of dependent elderly people and their carers as a result of the provision of support services, or the benefit to a child of living in an environment free of physical and psychological abuse.

This Strategy adopts the definition of 'health' used by the World Health Organisation:
'a complete state of physical, mental and social well-being and not merely the absence of disease or infirmity' …
'a resource for everyday life, not the objective of living; it is a positive concept emphasising social and physical resources as well as physical and mental capacity.'

Linking the factors that determine health

To develop an effective health system, the determinants of health, that is the social, economic, environmental and cultural factors which influence health, must be taken into account. The diagram below sets out these factors.

Figure 1 **Determinants of Health**

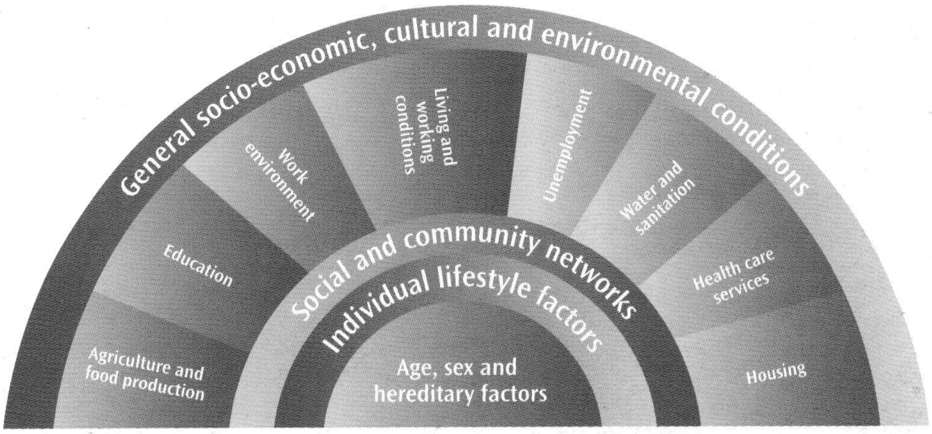

- Age, sex, and hereditary characteristics inherited from parents are the basic determinants of health status. These are factors over which individuals have no control.

- Important foundations of adult health are also established in prenatal life and early childhood. Slow growth and lack of emotional support during this period raise the lifetime risk of poor physical health and reduced physical, cognitive and emotional functioning.

- Social and community networks, including families, have a considerable role to play in the health of individuals. It is often through local structures that services are delivered or that individuals and communities get information about health and health services and get the support they need to take an active role in improving their own health.

- Other determinants of health include education, employment, housing, work environment, agriculture, food production, water and sanitation, and health services. These factors are described as socio-economic, cultural and environmental conditions and they affect an individual's social and educational pathway through life.

Achieving full health potential does not depend solely on the provision of health services. Many other factors, and therefore, many other individuals, groups, institutions and public and private bodies have a part to play in the effort to improve health status and achieve the health potential of the nation. One aim of this Strategy is to ensure that health is given priority across all the sectors with a role to play in improving health status.

Making the right choices

People's lifestyles, and the conditions in which they live and work, influence their health and how long they live. The individual's ability to pursue good health is influenced by his or her skills, information and economic means. Most people have a basic understanding of the positive and negative effects which lifestyles can have on their health. With the proper information and support, they can control many factors which influence their health and take greater personal responsibility for their own health and well-being.

The health system must focus on providing individuals with the information and support they need to make informed health choices.

Emphasising the non-medical aspects of achieving full health potential

The definition of health used in this Strategy places a value on quality of life; the emphasis will not be on medical status alone. The health system in Ireland encompasses both health and personal social services and these must be accessible and well co-ordinated. This means reaching out to groups and individuals to ensure they can understand their entitlements and access the services they need. It also means recognising the formal and informal roles of family and community in improving and sustaining social well-being in society.

Addressing quality of life issues must be a central objective of the Health Strategy.

Viewing health expenditure as an investment

This Strategy recognises the value of investment in health, the benefits to be gained in, for example, overall economic development; and the potential to contribute to societal well-being by focusing on people's ability and willingness to work together for mutual benefit.

Much of the public debate about health services is focused on the increased cost involved. While there are valid concerns about the growth in health spending, both national and international, the proper context for this debate is one which views health spending as an investment delivering benefits as well as accruing costs.

Apart from the social value of improved health and well-being, better health also brings more direct economic benefits. For example, lower absenteeism rates should lead to increased productivity in the economy. Increased life expectancy and reduced premature mortality can lead to a longer span of productive working life in the formal economy or in other ways, for example, through family caring or through participation in community or voluntary activity. Also, good quality health infrastructure is likely to be an important factor in improving the attractiveness of particular locations in the context of spatial planning or industrial and commercial development.

The debate about health spending must recognise the social and economic value which accrues from investment in health and personal social services.

Developing the Strategy document

Purpose

This Strategy is a blueprint to guide policy makers and service providers in achieving the vision of a future health system. It identifies overall national goals to guide activity and planning in the health system for the next 7-10 years. It also describes how the Government, the Minister and the Department of Health and Children will:

- work with everyone in the health system who has a role to play in improving health

- engage with the wider community to improve health

- evaluate services so that resources are used to best effect

- reform the way we plan and deliver services within the system

- modernise and expand health and personal social services through focused investment

- support the development and contribution of people who work in the health system.

Principles

Four principles guided the development of the Strategy: **Equity, People-centredness, Quality** and **Accountability**.

Equity

Everyone should have a fair opportunity to attain full health potential and, more pragmatically no-one should be disadvantaged from achieving this potential, if it can be avoided. Inequity refers to differences in health which are not only unnecessary and avoidable but, in addition, are considered unfair and unjust (Health 21, WHO).

Equity means that:

- *health inequalities are targeted*

- *people are treated fairly according to need.*

17

People from the lower socio-economic groups suffer a disproportionate burden of ill-health. The equity principle recognises that social, environmental and economic factors including deprivation, education, housing and nutrition affect both an individual's health status and his or her ability to access services. The equity principle underpins the National Development Plan and the need to address health inequalities in more radical ways than in the past was highlighted in the 1999 Report of the Chief Medical Officer.

Access to health care should be fair. The system must respond to people's needs rather than have access dependent on geographic location or ability to pay. A perceived lack of fairness and of equal treatment are central to many of the complaints made of the existing system. Improving equity of access will improve health by ensuring that people know what services they are entitled to and how to get those services and that there are no barriers, financial or otherwise, to receiving the services they need.

Equity will be central to developing policies (i) to reduce the difference in health status currently running across the social spectrum in Ireland; and (ii) to ensure equitable access to services based on need.

People-centredness

Ireland's future health system must become one that helps you be healthier, that is fair, that you can trust, and that is there when you need it.

The way health and social services are delivered in the system must also be personalised. Individuals differ in a great many ways, including their knowledge of and ability to understand the system and/or their own health status. Individuals have different needs and preferences. Services must adapt to these differences rather than the individual having to adapt to the system. This means that:

A people-centred health system:

- *identifies and responds to the needs of individuals*

- *is planned and delivered in a co-ordinated way*

- *helps individuals to participate in decision-making to improve their health.*

- services must be organised, located and accessed in a way that takes greater account of the needs and preferences of the community they serve

- health and social systems must be able to accommodate differences in patient preference and encourage shared decision-making

- consumers are given greater control, but also greater responsibility, for their own health

- consumers need access to high-quality information on health to fully benefit from health and social systems and to participate in decisions relating to their health. Readily available information stimulates self-help and informed choice

- increased involvement of consumers as partners in planning and evaluation is an important component in promoting openness and accountability.

The 'people-centred' health-care system of the future will have dynamic, integrated structures, which can adapt to the diverse and changing health needs of society generally and of individuals within it. These structures will empower people to be active participants in decisions relating to their own health.

Quality

Gaining people's trust in a health system is about guaranteeing quality. People want to know that the service/care they are receiving is based on best-practice evidence and meets approved and certified standards. Improving quality in the health system requires implementation of internationally-recognised evidence-based guidelines and protocols, and on-going education and commitment from health-care institutions and professionals. Trust requires that deficiencies in the system are identified, corrective actions taken and future progress monitored.

Setting and meeting standards is not enough. The development of a quality culture throughout the health system can ensure the provision of homogeneous, high-quality, integrated health-care at local, regional and national level. This involves an inter-disciplinary approach and continuous evaluation of the system using techniques such as clinical audit. It also means that information systems must have the capacity to provide feedback to health providers and consumers on the quality of care delivered and received.

Quality in health means that:

- *evidence-based standards are set in partnership with consumers and are externally validated*

- *continuous improvement is valued.*

Quality was one of the three main principles underlying the 1994 Health Strategy. To date many quality initiatives have been undertaken, although not necessarily as part of an overall co-ordinated plan. It is time now to embed quality more deliberately into the health system through comprehensive and co-ordinated national and local programmes.

Accountability

Measuring the costs and quality of services, managing capital resources, co-ordinating services and managing human resources, have become increasingly complex at all levels within modern health-care organisations. Budgetary controls have improved in recent years. This progress must continue and extend to wider organisational accountability. Better planning and evaluation models must demonstrate that available resources are used as efficiently and effectively as possible. Strengthening and clarifying accountability and measurement mechanisms will require action on a number of fronts.

In addition, professionals now practise in a more demanding environment. Evidence-based guidelines, tighter professional standards, the requirements of health-care organisations, and patient rights and expectations all add to these demands. This is another aspect of accountability which must be supported and strengthened.

Accountability means

- *financial*

- *professional and*

- *organisational accountability is strengthened for better quality, efficiency and effectiveness*

Accountability, encompassing financial, organisational and professional responsibilities, will be underpinned in the formulation of the Strategy.

Consultation process

The Government undertook an unprecedented consultation process to help it devise this new Health Strategy. Deepening an understanding of the difficulties people face in achieving better health status has been essential to planning improvements. An emphasis was also placed on cross-sectoral issues which affect people's health status. The role of an inter-departmental network and linkages with work on the National Anti-Poverty Strategy health targets were vital. Details of the approach taken are outlined in Appendix 1. Full details of feedback from the consultation will be published separately.

Structure of the document

The Health Strategy is divided into three main parts. In the remaining chapters of Part 1, the health of the nation (Chapter 2) and the current health system (Chapter 3) are examined and explained. This analysis provides the signposts for the overall national goals of the Strategy and identifies priority areas requiring development and reform within the system.

Part 2 of the Health Strategy sets out the priority goals and the means of achieving them. Chapter 4 outlines the national goals for the next 7-10 years and elaborates on the detailed actions required to reach them. Chapter 5 analyses how the system needs to be developed and reformed in order to deliver the national goals, and outlines the essential actions under six frameworks for change. Chapter 6 describes the implications of the Strategy for specific groups of the population.

In Part 3 the programme for implementing the Health Strategy is described. This includes a detailed action plan listing strategic actions with targets and timeframes (Chapter 7). In addition, a programme for monitoring Health Strategy implementation and evaluating the outcomes on an ongoing basis is set out in Chapter 8.

CHAPTER 2

Understanding our health

Defining health

This Health Strategy is concerned not only with illness, and the health services, but also with the role of other sectors in keeping people healthy. It also recognises the impact that being less healthy, being ill or having a disability may have on the quality of life of individuals, their families, their community and society in general.

Measuring our health – health status indicators

Although 'health' goes beyond 'the absence of disease or infirmity', for practical purposes population health is frequently measured by health indicators derived from life expectancy, mortality and morbidity statistics. While this presents a limited picture, it is of value in describing population trends over time and making comparisons with other countries. This section considers life expectancy, mortality and certain morbidity trends in Ireland and makes comparisons with European Union (EU) countries.

Life expectancy

Life expectancy at birth has substantially increased for Irish women and men over the past four decades although life expectancy is still poorer for men. At the same time, life expectancy in Europe has increased at a greater rate (Figures 2.1 and 2.2).

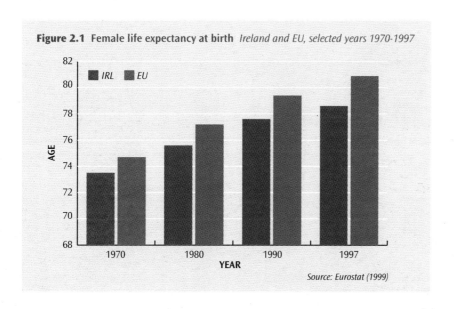

Figure 2.1 Female life expectancy at birth *Ireland and EU, selected years 1970-1997*

Source: Eurostat (1999)

Figure 2.2 Male life expectancy at birth *Ireland and EU, selected years 1970-1997*

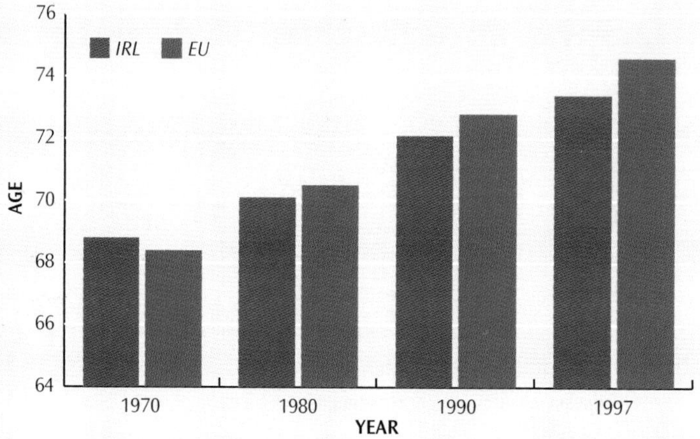

Source: Eurostat (1999)

Life expectancy has also increased in older age groups. However, this increase is relatively small. For example, the increase between 1970 and 1997 was only 1.7 years for males and 2.5 years for females. Despite improvements, Irish life expectancy at age 65 years was still the lowest of all 15 EU countries in 1997.

Improvements in life expectancy in Ireland reflect the lower mortality rates seen in infants and young children over recent years. These increases in life expectancy at birth contrast with the relatively small increases for older people for whom the prevention and management of chronic conditions continue to represent a major challenge.

Infant mortality

Infant mortality measures deaths in children under one year of age per one thousand live births and is a reliable indicator of a nation's health. Figure 2.3 highlights the continuing progress made over the past two decades.

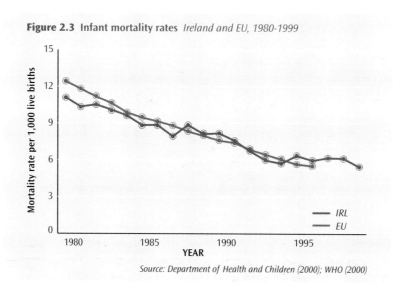

Figure 2.3 Infant mortality rates *Ireland and EU, 1980-1999*

Source: Department of Health and Children (2000); WHO (2000)

The perinatal mortality rate, defined as stillbirths and deaths of infants aged under one week per thousand total births, has also decreased. Like general mortality rates, the rate of perinatal mortality remains higher than the EU average.

Major causes of mortality

Circulatory disease and cancer account for nearly 65 per cent of deaths every year in Ireland (Figure 2.4). The relative contribution of cancer to overall mortality has been increasing in recent decades. For example, cancer accounted for only 11 per cent of overall mortality in 1950 compared with 25 per cent in 1999. This pattern is likely to continue in future years on account of current population trends. The major causes of premature mortality in 1999 are illustrated in Figure 2.5 where it can be seen that over 60 per cent of deaths are due to cancer or cardiovascular disease and 16 per cent to injury/poisoning.

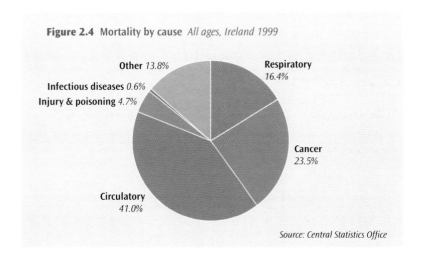

Figure 2.4 Mortality by cause *All ages, Ireland 1999*

Other *13.8%*
Infectious diseases *0.6%*
Injury & poisoning *4.7%*
Respiratory *16.4%*
Cancer *23.5%*
Circulatory *41.0%*

Source: Central Statistics Office

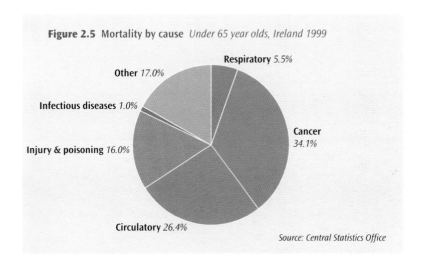

Figure 2.5 Mortality by cause *Under 65 year olds, Ireland 1999*

Other *17.0%*
Respiratory *5.5%*
Infectious diseases *1.0%*
Injury & poisoning *16.0%*
Cancer *34.1%*
Circulatory *26.4%*

Source: Central Statistics Office

As described in the following pages, it is clear that with the exception of cerebrovascular disease (stroke), the differences between Irish and EU mortality rates are considerable. The contribution of these diseases to premature mortality has already been highlighted. In addition, as our population ages it is likely that cancer morbidity will increase.

Many deaths caused by cancer, circulatory diseases and injury are preventable

Cardiovascular disease

Cardiovascular disease, which includes coronary heart disease, stroke and disorders of blood vessels, is the single most important cause of mortality in this country and a major cause of premature mortality for many. Other people with cardiovascular disease suffer chronic ill-health and reduced quality of life. While it is probable that the target set in the 1994 Health Strategy to reduce premature mortality from cardiovascular disease by 30 per cent will be met, Figure 2.6 illustrates the scale of the problem in Ireland. While ischaemic (coronary) heart disease death rates for the total population continue to fall, the large differences between Irish and EU rates remain.

A high percentage of cardiovascular mortality and morbidity is preventable.

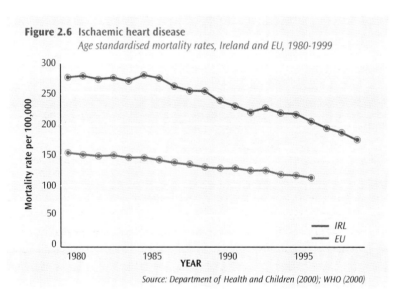

Figure 2.6 Ischaemic heart disease
Age standardised mortality rates, Ireland and EU, 1980-1999

Source: Department of Health and Children (2000); WHO (2000)

For strokes, the situation is more encouraging where the once high mortality rate has been reduced considerably and Irish rates are similar to the EU average (Figure 2.7).

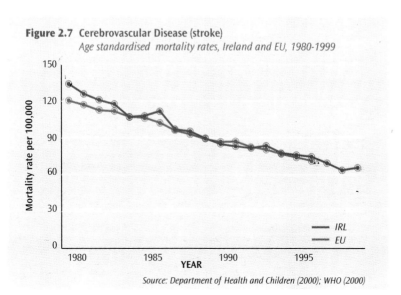

Figure 2.7 Cerebrovascular Disease (stroke)
Age standardised mortality rates, Ireland and EU, 1980-1999

Source: Department of Health and Children (2000); WHO (2000)

Cancer

Approximately 21,000 new cases of cancer are recorded annually. One in three individuals will develop cancer in the course of their lifetime but not all will die from the condition.

Cancer is more common in older people (Figure 2.8). As our population gets older, we can expect more cases of cancer.

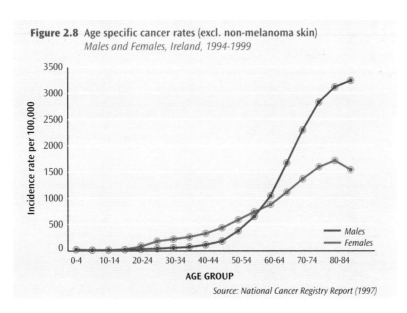

Figure 2.8 Age specific cancer rates (excl. non-melanoma skin) *Males and Females, Ireland, 1994-1999*

Source: National Cancer Registry Report (1997)

Cancer is the second most frequent cause of death and represents a major burden for individual sufferers, their families, and the health system. Since 1994, mortality rates have been reduced. However, when compared to the EU, there is scope for improvement (Figure 2.9). Seven thousand cancer deaths occur annually in Ireland, of which lung cancer is the most common (Figure 2.10). Other common killers include colorectal cancer, prostate cancer in men, and breast cancer in women. A range of preventive initiatives in terms of screening and tackling environmental factors can reduce risk.

It is estimated that around 30 per cent of all cancers are due to smoking.

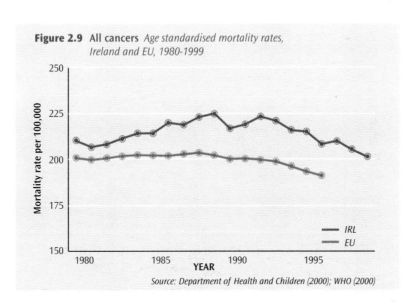

Figure 2.9 All cancers *Age standardised mortality rates, Ireland and EU, 1980-1999*

Source: Department of Health and Children (2000); WHO (2000)

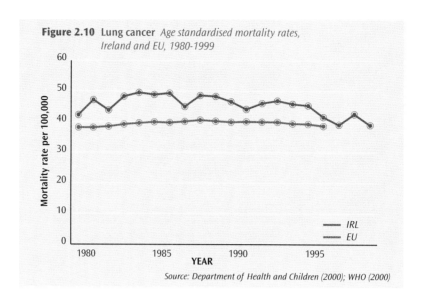

Figure 2.10 Lung cancer *Age standardised mortality rates, Ireland and EU, 1980-1999*

Source: Department of Health and Children (2000); WHO (2000)

Injury/Poisoning

The most common causes of injury-related deaths are road traffic accidents and suicides, followed by falls, poisoning and drowning. The European Home and Leisure Accidents Surveillance System (EHLASS) Report for Ireland (1998) demonstrated that 10 per cent of accidents require hospitalisation. The Hospital In-Patient Enquiry system (HIPE) demonstrates that accidental falls are the most common type of injury requiring hospitalisation (Health Statistics, Department of Health and Children, 1999).

Every year, approximately 1,500 Irish people die from injuries. While mortality from road traffic accidents has been gradually declining, between 400 and 500 people die on Irish roads annually. There is also evidence of an increase in the number of road traffic accidents in recent years. Together, these data suggest that more people are surviving their injuries. It is worth noting that injuries represent a larger burden on the health system than many other health problems and the financial and social costs are high – in terms of potential years of life lost in those aged under 65, injuries are more significant than either cancer or cardiovascular disease.

Figure 2.11 shows the rate of self-injury and suicide in Ireland between 1980 and 1998. Both have been increasing steadily since 1980 although increased reporting may be affecting the overall trends shown by the data.

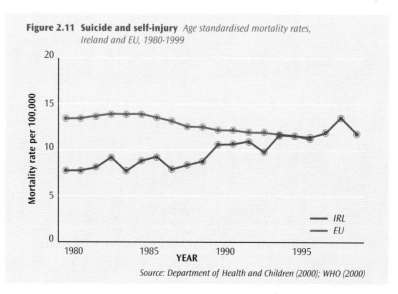

Figure 2.11 Suicide and self-injury *Age standardised mortality rates, Ireland and EU, 1980-1999*

Source: Department of Health and Children (2000); WHO (2000)

Injuries are a common cause of premature mortality and a significant cause of morbidity.

This area has been somewhat neglected as a focus for policy development because of the view that accidents are unpreventable random occurrences. In fact, there is wide scope for prevention.

Life expectancy in Ireland is increasing, but not as fast as in the EU.
Life expectancy is poorer for males than females.
The gap in life expectancy between Ireland and the EU is widening.
Life expectancy for older people has shown only modest improvement.

Infant mortality rates are falling but are still higher than in the EU.
General mortality rates due to cardiovascular disease and cancer are still above EU levels.
Due to demographic change in Ireland, cancer rates are likely to increase in future years.

Injuries represent a significant financial and social burden on the community and the health system.

Many deaths caused by cancer, circulatory diseases and injury are preventable.

Health and lifestyle

Lifestyle choices directly influence our physical and mental well-being. Two national surveys of health-related behaviours among adults, The National Health and Lifestyle Survey (SLÁN), and among school-going children, Health Behaviour in School-Aged Children (HBSC), have established baseline information on lifestyle behaviour in Ireland. The European Community Household Panel Survey also provides information on self-reported health status.

In these surveys, most Irish adults reported excellent or very good health. This was higher for non-smokers. The vast majority of children perceived themselves as healthy. However, despite this good overall message, there are disturbing findings relating to smoking, drinking, healthy eating and physical activity (Figure 2.12).

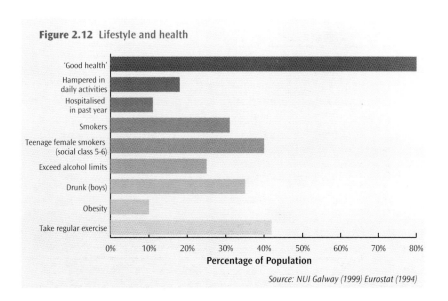

Figure 2.12 Lifestyle and health

Source: NUI Galway (1999) Eurostat (1994)

- One in three adults smoked. Rates among younger women were now similar to younger men.

- Adults in lower social groups smoked more. The growing popularity of smoking among girls from lower social groups was a particular cause for concern.

- Most adults drank alcohol, with approximately one in four exceeding the recommended weekly limits of sensible alcohol consumption.

- It was encouraging that the vast majority of adults and children were not involved in substance abuse. However, males under the age of 35 years living in urban locations were most likely to have used drugs of some type.

- Thirty-two per cent of adults were overweight; 10 per cent obese. Many adults and children did not adhere to the national healthy eating guidelines, this being more evident in social classes five and six.

- Two in five Irish adults engaged in some form of regular physical activity. Adults were less likely to exercise with age and almost one third of those over 55 years did not exercise at all in a typical week.

- Most children participated in vigorous exercise, with higher rates in boys and younger children.

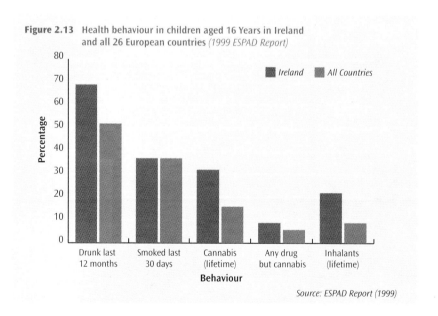

Figure 2.13 Health behaviour in children aged 16 Years in Ireland and all 26 European countries *(1999 ESPAD Report)*

Source: ESPAD Report (1999)

HBSC survey results indicate that the percentage of Irish students who had experimented with each of a range of substances was higher than that of the EU average, particularly in relation to cannabis, although it has declined since the 1995 figure. Results also indicate that the consumption of alcohol is becoming more regular within younger age groups in children, 35 per cent of boys compared with 24 per cent of girls reported that they were drunk on at least one occasion and 20 per cent of 15-17 year olds reported having been drunk more than ten times.

The data highlight areas of concern including levels of smoking, alcohol intake, unhealthy diet and sedentary lifestyles in many young people as well as the social variations in health and lifestyle behaviours between the lower and higher socio-economic groups. Healthy lifestyle has a major role to play in the improvement of an individual's health status.

Lifestyle influences future health.

A significant proportion of Irish adults and children live unhealthy lifestyles.

If the trends in smoking, alcohol consumption, diet and lifestyles are not reversed, this is likely to continue to lead to many avoidable deaths in future years.

Inequalities in health status

Inequalities in health can exist for a variety of reasons, including geographical location, gender, age, ethnicity, hereditary factors and socio-economic status. Poverty, unemployment, education, access to health services and environmental factors including housing and water quality, all play important roles in determining the health of individuals. Disparities in health status within the population lead to consideration of the links between socio-economic factors and health. There are clear occupational class gradients in mortality.

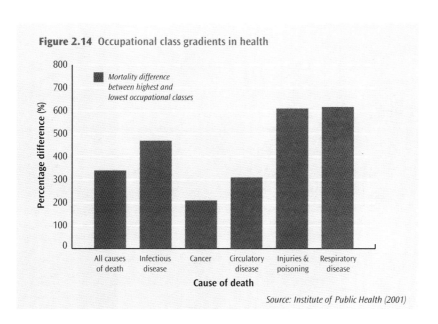

Figure 2.14 Occupational class gradients in health

Source: Institute of Public Health (2001)

- The Institute of Public Health (2001) has demonstrated that there was more than a three-fold difference in the age-standardised death rates between men in the lowest and the highest socio-economic groupings during the period 1989-1998. The strong impact of occupational class was evident for nearly all of the major causes of death (Figure 2.14). When the lowest occupation class is compared with the highest occupational class there are major differences in mortality

- A Trinity College study on health inequalities demonstrated significantly higher mortality in semi-skilled and unskilled manual workers (TCD, 2001). This study showed that low birth weight was more likely in the unskilled manual and unemployed socio-economic group

- The ESRI (Nolan, 1994) has demonstrated that perinatal mortality and low birth weight are associated with socio-economic background

- Health inequalities are also evident in non-fatal but chronic disabling conditions. Psychiatric admissions can be used as an indicator of mental health and are more likely to be seen in the lower socio-economic groups (TCD, 2001). A recent ESRI study demonstrated that health status varies across occupational groups (Nolan, 2000). Adults in the lowest socio-economic group were twice as likely to report a long-standing illness as those in the highest socio-economic group (Nolan, 1994).

- One group at significant disadvantage in health status is the Traveller community. The Travellers' Health Status Study demonstrated that life expectancy at birth for Traveller men was 9.9 years less than for settled men and 11.9 years less for Traveller women than for settled women.

Other lifestyle factors and geographic location may also have an underlying socio-economic link. For example:

- The findings of the National Health and Lifestyle Survey (SLÁN) regarding significantly less healthy lifestyles among lower socio-economic groups than those in higher socio-economic groups, have already been referred to

- The figures that follow show the age-standardised death rates for all causes (Figure 2.15), circulatory diseases (Figure 2.16) and cancer (Figure 2.17), respectively, per 100,000 population by county. While there are differences between health boards for certain health indicators, there are, however, no consistent trends. This is in contrast to the analysis of smaller, more discrete geographic areas where it is possible to identify lower health status, including low birth weight and increased overall mortality. These 'black spots' are generally in socially deprived areas.

Figure 2.15 Standardised death rate per 100,000 population
All causes, Ireland by county, 1995-1999

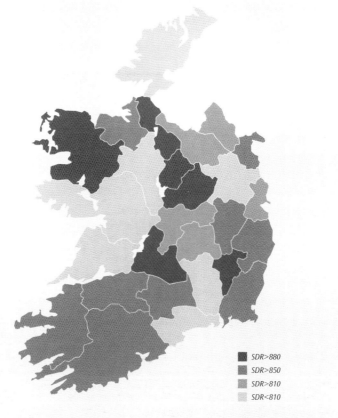

SDR>880
SDR>850
SDR>810
SDR<810

Source: Department of Health and Children (2000)

Figure 2.16 Standardised death rate per 100,000 population
All crculatory diseases, Ireland by county, 1995-1999

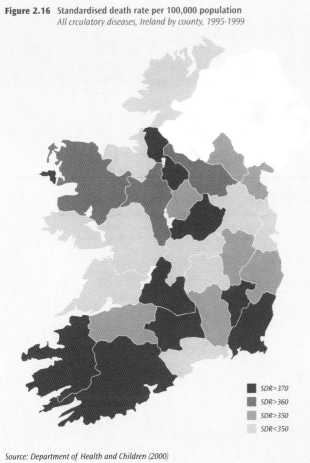

SDR>370
SDR>360
SDR>350
SDR<350

Source: Department of Health and Children (2000)

Figure 2.17 Standardised death rate per 100,000 population
All malignant neoplasms, Ireland by county, 1995-1999

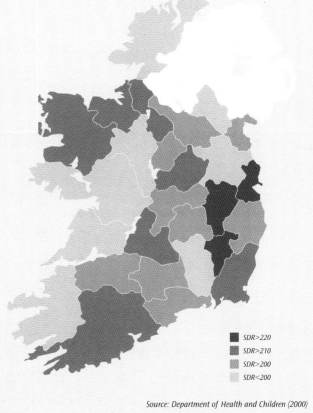

SDR>220
SDR>210
SDR>200
SDR<200

Source: Department of Health and Children (2000)

There is now strong and consistent evidence of a relationship between health and socio-economic status in Ireland.

This is an important consideration in addressing the overall health of the population.

Effective action will require a multi-sectoral approach.

Measuring the impact of ill-health and disability

Overall indicators of life expectancy and mortality provide a limited picture of ill-health in a community. This is because they tell us only about fatal conditions; whereas a great deal of chronic ill-health is caused by non-fatal disease. There are considerable gaps in information related to morbidity which result in a somewhat limited picture of the health of the population, particularly in relation to the occurrence of particular illnesses and to quality of life issues. Information from out-patient and primary care services is limited. Data on mental health and chronic disease are also incomplete.

However, the social cost of some non-fatal illnesses such as those caused by accident or injury is self-evident, as is the burden that illnesses such as cancer can place on sufferers and their families during their lifetime. In this section some further aspects of the nation's 'health' are dealt with – the degree to which mental ill-health and disabilities place a demand on individuals and the health system in Ireland.

Mental health

Mental health is recognised increasingly as a major challenge facing health services in the twenty-first century. Comprehensive data on community mental health services are not currently available, but detailed information on in-patient mental services is available from the National Psychiatric In-Patient Reporting System (NPIRS).

Figure 2.18 Number of psychiatric admissions by diagnosis
Irish population aged over 16 Years, 1999

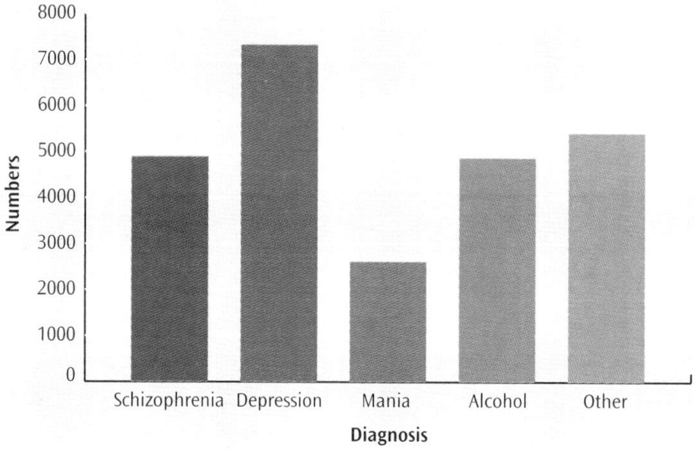

Source: Health Research Board (1999)

In 1999, there were 25,062 admissions to Irish psychiatric hospitals of people aged 16 years or older, which is a rate of 930 per 100,000 population (Figure 2.18). Of these, 7,105 (28 per cent) were first admissions.

First admission rates have shown little change over the past 35 years, whereas all admission rates have increased by almost half. Lengths of stay in hospital have decreased, illustrating a different manner of using hospital beds, moving towards more frequent crisis intervention usage or short in-patient treatment combined with more extensive community-based care.

More than one in four adults will suffer from mental illness at some point during their lives. Twenty-five per cent of families are likely to have at least one member who suffers from mental illness. The WHO has estimated that, globally, approximately 20 per cent of all patients seen by primary health-care professionals have one or more mental disorders. In Ireland, it has been estimated that 10 per cent of the general population suffers from depression and 1 per cent from schizophrenia.

It is likely that the numbers of people presenting to the mental health services for treatment will increase in the coming years, due in part to the modernisation of the services and the reduction in the stigma associated with their use. The ageing population and the increasing incidence of social problems, such as drug abuse and family breakdown, are also likely to contribute to increasing demands on the services in the future.

Intellectual disability

With improvements in child health services over recent decades, a larger number of children with intellectual disability are now reaching adulthood. The recently established National Intellectual Disability Database provides a profile of the Irish population with intellectual disability (Figure 2.19).

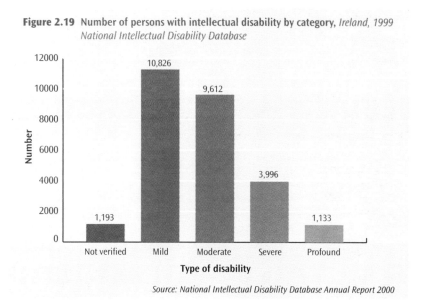

Figure 2.19 **Number of persons with intellectual disability by category,** *Ireland, 1999*
National Intellectual Disability Database

Source: National Intellectual Disability Database Annual Report 2000

Thirty-four per cent of people on the database were aged 19 years and under, thirty per cent were aged between 20 and 34 years, twenty six per cent are aged between 35 and 54 years, and ten per cent were aged 55 years or over.

The prevalence of intellectual disability may increase in coming years due to the steady increase in maternal age and recent advancements in neonatal care which increase the survival prospects of babies at risk of intellectual disability.

Physical and Sensory Disability

The Health Research Board is developing a National Physical and Sensory Disability Database, which will provide a profile of the current population of people with a disability. It will also help in monitoring demographic changes, as well as enhancing service planning by recognising the needs of individuals, their families and service providers.

There are considerable numbers of people with chronic illnesses or disabilities which affect their social well-being.

Improving information about service needs is a priority.

In extending existing services and developing new services, the focus must be on responding to identified needs in a holistic way and maximising the opportunity for individuals to achieve their full health potential.

Summary of key messages

Action to increase life expectancy and achieve better health for everyone must be a priority. This involves taking intersectoral action on lifestyle and environmental factors as key determinants of good health.

There is a need to take more deliberate and assertive action in addressing health inequalities. Trends indicate that without decisive intervention, the gap in health between the rich and the poor will continue to widen. The Health Strategy must prioritise supporting the disadvantaged to improve their health status.

The quality of life aspect of health needs to be highlighted. An increased understanding and awareness of the impact certain illnesses have on quality of life needs to be developed. This will involve creating a supportive environment to maximise social well-being for vulnerable groups.

CHAPTER 3

The health system explained

Introduction

Chapter 2 sets out a clear message about making Ireland a healthier nation and making sure that good health is enjoyed more equally across society. The Irish health system, like all systems, has particular features which influence the way it is structured and the volume and quality of services it provides. These features affect the experiences of people who require services. In this chapter, the degree to which the current system adequately provides equitable, people-centred, quality and accountable health and personal social services in Ireland is considered.

To begin, key features of the system are outlined as a context for the Health Strategy. There is a critical assessment of the strengths of the system that will support strategic goals; and what weaknesses may hinder achieving them. The opportunities and threats that will influence the achievement of goals in the years to come are outlined. In conclusion, key goals to complement those identified in Chapter 2 are outlined. The changes and development required within the health system to match a new strategic direction are also established.

The health system – facts and figures

A number of important characteristics underpin the structure of the Irish health system and influence the way it works. Some of the system's defining features are outlined below.

Organisational structures

The Government, the Minister for Health and Children and the Department are at the head of health service provision in Ireland. The Department's primary role is to support the Minister in the formulation and evaluation of policies for the health services. It also has a role in the strategic planning of health services in consultation with health boards, the voluntary sector, other government departments and other interests. The Department has a leadership role in areas such as equity, quality, accountability and value for money.

The health boards, established under the Health Act, 1970 are the statutory bodies responsible for the delivery of health and personal social services in their functional areas. They are also the main providers of health and personal social care at regional level. Health boards are composed of elected local representatives, ministerial nominees and representatives of health professions employed by the board. Each health board has a Chief Executive officer (CEO) who has responsibility for day-to-day administration and is answerable to the Board. The Health (Amendment) (No. 3) Act, 1996 clarified the respective roles of health boards and their CEOs by making boards responsible for certain reserved functions relating to policy matters and major financial decisions and CEOs responsible for executive matters.

'...To protect, promote and restore the health and well-being of people by ensuring that health and personal social services are planned, managed and delivered to achieve measurable health and social gain and provide the optimum return on resources invested.'

Department of Health and Children Mission Statement

In addition, many other advisory, executive agencies and voluntary organisations have a role to play in service delivery and development in the health system. Figure 3.1 outlines the overall structure. A list of the main health service organisations is contained in Appendix 2.

Figure 3.1 Structure of the health system in Ireland

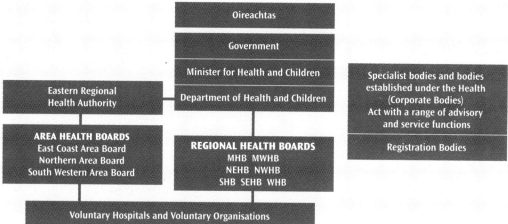

Population distribution

The Central Statistics Office estimated Ireland's population at 3,838,900 in April 2001. This estimate is based on the last census carried out in 1996. The population in 1996 was 3,626,087. The distribution of the population across board areas at that time was as follows:

Table 3.1: **Distribution of population between health boards – 1996 Census**

Health Boards	Numbers	%
Eastern Regional Health Authority and Area Health Boards	1,295,939	35.7
Midland Health Board	205,542	5.7
Mid-Western Health Board	317,069	8.7
North-Eastern Health Board	306,155	8.4
North-Western Health Board	210,872	5.8
South-Eastern Health Board	391,517	10.8
Southern Health Board	546,640	15.1
Western Health Board	352,353	9.7
TOTAL	3,626,087	100.0

Source: Central Statistics Office

Human resources

Some 81,500 people work in the public health sector, making health one of the largest public service employers. Significant growth in employment has happened in recent years, particularly in the year 2000. The employment level in the public health service agreed for 2001 is 86,500. Table 3.2 shows the numbers (whole-time equivalents) (WTEs) employed in 2000. In line with population distribution, the greatest number work in the Eastern Regional Health Authority area and the least in the Midland Health Board region.

Table 3.2: **Numbers in employment (WTEs) by employer**

Employer	Total	%
Eastern Regional Health Authority and Area Health Boards	11,131	14
Midland Health Board	4,100	5
Mid-Western Health Board	5,004	6
North-Eastern Health Board	5,147	6
North-Western Health Board	5,349	7
South-Eastern Health Board	7,318	9
Southern Health Board	8,449	10
Western Health Board	7,305	9
Total Health Board	53,804	66
Total Mental Handicap Homes	8,041	10
Total Voluntary Hospitals	19,668	24
TOTAL	81,513	100

Source: Department of Health and Children

Table 3.3: **Staff breakdown by grade in public health services - 2000**

Grade		2000
Maintenance/Technical		1,533
Management/Administrative		12,366
Of which (estimate):		
- Frontline (64%)	7,914	
- Legal/FoI (5%)	618	
- IT/Payroll/HR (17%)	2,103	
- Admin support (11%)	1.360	
- Services managers (3%)	371	
Medical/Dental		5,698
Nursing		29,177
Paramedical		7,613
Support Services		25,126
TOTAL		81,513

Source: Department of Health and Children

Table 3.3 shows the number of staff employed in the public health services in 2000. The number has increased from 68,000 in 1997 to 81,500 in 2000. There were significant increases in paramedical and support staff, reflecting substantial investment in a range of services such as childcare and disability. There was also a large growth in frontline clerical and administrative staff who support doctors, nurses and other health professionals by relieving them of administrative work and allowing them to concentrate on their professional tasks. Of all staff classified as management/administrative, it is important to note that nearly two-thirds are involved in front-line services for patients, and that a further 5 per cent deal with legislative and information requirements such as Freedom of Information and registration of births, deaths and marriages while others carry out key functions such as service planning and auditing.

Pay costs and remuneration

Pay costs account for some 70 per cent of current spending on health and personal social services. For planning purposes, when calculating the full pay costs of health professionals, an average of £40,000 (€50,790) per professional is used. For all health service staff in health boards, the average pay in 2000 was in the region of £24,500 (€31,108). Some examples of average pre-tax pay for selected grades in the health services are set out below.

- A staff nurse at the maximum of the scale with standard premium pay and no overtime pay earned about £31,000 (€39,362).

- The pay of a therapy professional (e.g. physiotherapists, speech and language therapists, occupational therapists) at the mid-point of the scale is £25,218 (about €32,000).

- The average earnings of a basic grade radiographer (inclusive of on-call allowances) are in excess of £35,000 (€44,440).

- The average clerical salary, based on grades III to VII, is £19,402 (€24,635).

- A hospital consultant earns an average of some £100,000 (€126,974) per annum in the public health service, excluding on-call or call-out arrangements which can vary from post to post. This also excludes private earnings for consultants engaged in private practice.

- While the basic pay for a non consultant hospital doctor at senior house officer grade is less than £30,000, (€38,092) the average earnings – including on-call – are in the region of £60,000 (€76,184) per annum. A specialist registrar would earn an average of £80,000 (€101,579) per year.

- The average payment per general practitioner in the General Medical Services (GMS) Scheme in 2000 was £72,700 (€92,310), including allowances.

Funding

In Ireland public funding makes up approximately 78 per cent of all the money spent on health care. Private funding, through insurance arrangements, makes up approximately another 8.5 per cent of funding. The balance is what individuals pay in 'out-of-pocket' expenses; for example the fees non-medical cardholders pay for general practitioner (GP) and other therapy services.

The public money spent on health comes from funds raised primarily through general taxes. The money raised is allocated to the Department of Health and Children and, in turn, to the regional health boards and the Eastern Regional Health Authority. The boards provide many services themselves and use some of the monies to pay other health service providers (such as health agencies, voluntary hospitals or voluntary bodies) who provide health and personal social services in their region. The total amount of money spent on health in 2001 (excluding capital funding) will be in excess of £5.3 billion, more than double the amount spent in 1997. More than half of the additional money invested in the last five years has been directed to continuing care services, i.e. services for people with disabilities, older people and children. Figure 3.2 shows the breakdown of this expenditure for the year 2001.

Figure 3.2 Health expenditure 2001, by programme

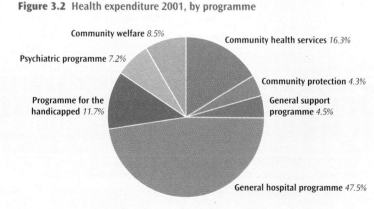

Source: Department of Health and Children

Table 3.3 shows per capita spending on health services in Ireland from 1990-2001 and compares it with average spending per head for EU countries.

Table 3 Per capita health spending 1990-2001 in EU countries: US$(PPP Terms)

	1990	1991	1992	1993	1994	1995	1996	1997	1998	1999 est	2000 est	2001 est
Average per year for EU minus Ireland (OECD data – 1990-1998)	1223	1299	1402	1454	1506	1634	1708	1714	1780	1880	1986	2097
Ireland's Health Expenditure (see footnote)	756	852	1008	1048	1164	1253	1265	1399	1457	1554	1714	2109

Note: The above figures for total expenditure on health for 1999-2001 are estimated by the Department of Health and Children using mean average growth rate trends in spending on health services. The figures for Ireland take account of estimated expenditure on private health care and have also been adjusted to take account of Central Statistics Office projections in population. Comparable figures are not available in regard to health care spending in other EU countries after 1998. Account has also been taken of personal social services spending in this country for 1990-2001; these are not regarded uniformly throughout OECD as health spending. However, there has been a significant level of investment in recent years in the area of personal social services in Ireland and the reduction applied to the period 1999 – 2001 reflects the increased level of investment for that period. In order to obtain international comparisons on health spending, the personal social services element of Irish health spending has been excluded.

Eligibility for services

Any person, regardless of nationality, who is accepted by the health boards as being ordinarily resident in Ireland, is eligible* for health and personal social services. About one-third of the population hold medical cards which entitle them to receive services free of charge. Non-medical cardholders are entitled to some services free of charge. Effectively, everyone has coverage for public hospital services with some modest charges, and some personal and social services, but only medical card holders have free access to most other services (including general practitioner services).

Under the Health Act 1970 eligibility for medical cards is based on a notion of 'hardship'. In today's terms, 'hardship' is defined by income guidelines drawn up by the health board CEOs, which are used as a means test to determine eligibility. These guidelines are revised annually. Health board CEOs also have discretionary powers to award a medical card on hardship grounds even when a person's income exceeds the guidelines.

A number of other schemes govern eligibility for services for certain groups of the population. These include the Long-Term Illness Scheme; Infectious Diseases Regulations; Maternity and Infant Care Scheme; School Medical Service; Public Dental Service; Nursing Home Subvention Scheme; preventive services (such as primary immunisation schemes and child health clinics) and early detection services (such as the National Breast Screening Programme).

The public/private mix

The private sector makes an important contribution to service needs which must be harnessed to best effect for patients. One of the key concerns of the Health Strategy is to promote fair access to services, based on objectively assessed need, rather than on any other factor such as whether the patient is attending on a public or private basis. This is of particular concern in the area of acute hospital services. The current mix of public and private beds in the public hospital system is intended to ensure that the public and private sectors can share resources, clinical knowledge, skills and technology. This mix raises serious challenges, which must be addressed in the context of equity of access for public patients.

* To be eligible means that a person qualifies to avail of services, either without charge (full eligibility) or subject to prescribed charges (limited eligibility).

Strategic development of services

In recent years a planned and strategic approach to the health services coupled with the most significant programme of investment in health care ever undertaken (which has seen spending on health care services increase from £2.7bn in 1997 to more than £5.3bn in 2001) has resulted in a number of significant advances in health and personal social services.

This approach is underpinned by the publication and implementation of a number of important strategies, including the following:

The National Cancer Strategy (1996) which aims to reduce the incidence of cancer and improve services for those with cancer by providing for additional capacity and location of services as well as the introduction of comprehensive screening programmes.

The Cardiovascular Strategy (1999) which aims to reduce the incidence of heart disease through co-ordinated multi-sectoral action at national, regional and local level as well as improve the provision of services for people requiring cardiac care.

The National Health Promotion Strategy (2000-2005) which aims to raise public awareness of the numerous determinants of health through multi-sectoral action.

The National Children's Strategy (2000) which sets out a ten-year plan to improve the quality of all services to children through coordination and planning at national and local level.

The National Drugs Strategy (2001-2008) coordinated by the Department of Tourism, Sport and Recreation, which sets out a series of objectives and actions for a number of government departments and agencies to help prevent as well as tackle drug abuse.

The following table sets out some of the many service developments in recent years. More comprehensive data are available on the Department's website.

Figure 3.3 Key service developments in recent years

Acute hospital services: Tallaght Hospital, Dublin opened in 1998. In addition, there were major hospital developments at St James's Hospital, St Luke's Hospital, Dublin; University Hospital, Galway; Regional Hospitals in Limerick and Galway; and Longford-Westmeath Hospital, Mullingar. The number of consultants increased from 1,170 in 1993 to 1,560 in 2000.

As illustrated below, there has been a continuing substantial increase in day cases and a steady rise in in-patients treated since the mid 1980s. This is in spite of a constant number of acute hospital beds since 1991.

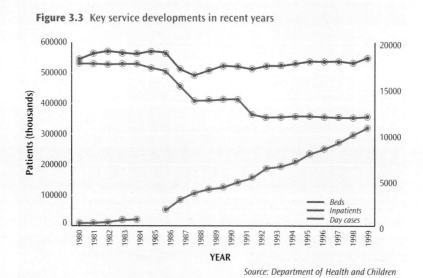

Figure 3.3 Key service developments in recent years

Source: Department of Health and Children

The waiting list initiative has funded a large number of elective procedures and has enabled thousands of patients to receive treatment more quickly than would have been possible otherwise. Waiting times have been reduced substantially in a number of specialties. For example the number of adults waiting for longer than 12 months for cardiac surgery has reduced from 587 to 190 between June 2000 and June 2001; the number of children waiting for longer than 6 months for cardiac surgery has reduced from 66 to 10 in the same period.

Services for people with an intellectual disability: Between 1996 and the end of 2001, additional investment will have led to the creation of an additional 1,650 residential places, 2,300 day places, and a 70 per cent increase in respite care places. The number of people with intellectual disability cared for in psychiatric hospitals is now just below 600, down from 970 in 1996.

Services for people with a physical or sensory disability: Since 1997, developments include an additional 150 residential and respite places, 400 day care places, community/home support services as well as additional occupational therapy, speech and language therapy and physiotherapy services. The National Physical and Sensory Disability Database will enable service requirements on a national basis to be identified.

Services for older persons: New investment since 1997 has resulted in the creation of an additional 400 places in community nursing units and over 1,000 day places. The medical card scheme has been extended to people aged 70 years and older. The provision of these additional facilities, together with the introduction of the Nursing Home Subvention Scheme in 1993, has resulted in a significant expansion in the range of services available for older people with a consequent improvement in the quality of life for a great number of them.

Services for children: The Child Care Act, 1991 has been fully implemented. Since 1997, over £92million has been invested to create the infrastructure necessary to support expansion of services, including additional personnel at all professional levels. Recent developments in the child protection services include the ongoing implementation of Children First-national guidelines for the protection of the welfare of children, and an increase in the provision of high support and special care places from 17 in 1996 to 83 with plans for a further 56 places nationwide. Family support service developments include the establishment in 17 pilot sites of Springboard, a community-based early intervention initiative to support families. Developments in the child health services include the ongoing implementation of a range of immunisation programmes and the implementation of the Best Health for Children report to assist each child to reach his or her best health and well-being potential.

Services for people with mental illness: The mental health services have continued to progress towards a more community-oriented service, with a corresponding reduction in the numbers of long-stay patients in psychiatric hospitals. Forty-three per cent of all acute admissions are now made to units attached to general hospitals, compared to less than one third of admissions in 1994. Since 1994, new acute psychiatric units have been opened in general hospitals in Dublin, Navan, Tallaght, Cork city and Bantry. Further units will be opened shortly. The number of community residences has increased from 368 in 1994 to 402 in 2000 with places increased from 2,685 to 2,993 in the same period.

Significant progress has also been made in the development of specialist psychiatric services for children and older people. Now, all health boards have approval for at least two consultant-led teams in child and adolescent psychiatry and at least one consultant led team in the psychiatry of old age. Services for prisoners and the homeless have also been developed since then.

Carers: New developments include additional funding for respite care for carers, carer support groups, training of carers and home care support services, as well as additional community support services for older people and their carers.

Health promotion: The wide range of health promotion initiatives including initiatives on anti-smoking, alcohol consumption, nutrition and diet, exercise, as well as other measures to promote healthy lifestyle choices.

Dental services: The 1994 Dental Treatment Services Scheme provided for free basic dental services for over 1 million adult medical card holders; eligibility for public dental services has been extended to all children under 16 years.

The health element of the National Development Plan 2000-2006 (The Health Capital Strategy) provides for substantial capital investment in the infrastructure of the health system on a phased basis. It includes commitments to funding for general hospitals, services for older people, mental health services, services for persons with disabilities, primary care, child care and information and communications technology. A fundamental objective of the National Development Plan is to equalise investment between the acute and non-acute hospital services by the end of the period of the plan. The commitments to funding contained in the plan will have significant impact on the capacity of the health system in the years to come.

Strengths of the health system

Health as a priority

Health has remained high on the public agenda, reflecting ongoing public and political attention. In a time of economic growth and prosperity, health is seen as an area for additional investment and this is already reflected in Government spending priorities in recent years. It is clear from the consultation process that health is a priority issue for the general population. The level of response to the call for submissions was relatively high-particularly from individuals. There is evidence from this process of considerable support, both within and outside the health system, for the prioritising of investment in a high-quality, properly resourced health system.

Local structures

As outlined earlier, the principal executive agencies delivering health services are the regional health boards, which have been in place now for some thirty years. The range and diversity of health services touch on every community. Ensuring that these services are effective and responsive requires delivery structures that are close to the communities. By organising the ten health boards on a regional basis the system has shown a clear capacity to develop and oversee rapidly developing services.

Skilled workforce

The health service has a highly committed and dedicated workforce and this has enabled very significant developments in health and social services to be undertaken. The ability to deliver a high-quality service is greatly supported by the knowledge, skill and attitude of the workforce within the health system, the high-quality training that professionals receive, and their enormous commitment to the health and welfare of their patients and clients.

Since 1994, there have been considerable advances in the area of human resource management and staff development.

- The Health Services Employers Agency was established in 1996. The Agency advises, supports and provides industrial relations negotiation services to health service employers. It has an important leadership role in developing human resource management policies for the effective management of people in the health system.

- The Office for Health Management was established in 1997 to facilitate management development in the Irish health services. The Office seeks to achieve this through developing managers and promoting a positive managerial ethos throughout the health and personal social services.

- The establishment of the Health Services National Partnership Forum in 1999 also underlines how the role of staff at all levels has been extended beyond the basics of service delivery to finding solutions to shared concerns in the workplace.

In the meantime, new challenges have also arisen for both managers and staff. The most recent national agreements with the social partners have strengthened the general commitments given in 1994 to planning workforce needs, and developing managers, training and education. Several policy documents have already been prepared to guide and support these developments.

Improved strategic planning in the health system

The 1994 Strategy *Shaping a healthier future* redefined the roles of health providers and the Department of Health and set out a strategic approach to improving health status and developing service provision. It addressed the strands of legal and financial accountability arrangements, together with organisational and management reform.

Legislation, including the Health (Amendment) Act, 1996, subsequently underpinned the implementation of financial and organisational accountability within the health system. This was an important milestone in achieving greater accountability regarding expenditure and levels of indebtedness. The adoption of service plans, annual reports and annual financial statements are now deemed reserved functions of each health board and are vital tools in the planning process at regional and national level.

This kind of strategic planning and building up of the planning system has been described as 'very innovative for the period', and 'an enormous advancement for planning and policy development'. It provides a sound framework for planning and implementing strategic policy objectives. It also creates the conditions in which additional investment can be aimed at specific programmes and the outcomes of investment can then be demonstrated more explicitly.

The voluntary/statutory interface

Co-operation between statutory and voluntary providers allows for a more responsive and dynamic approach to meeting needs. There have been changes in the profile of activity and funding arrangements in recent years. A framework for more formal service agreements between voluntary and statutory providers has been developed in some areas. There continues to be a very strong and diverse role for the community/voluntary sector in the health system. Good relationships and mechanisms for planning and delivering services already exist, and these provide excellent models on which to build. These partnership arrangements are a key strength of the system.

Limitations and shortfalls in the current health system

Equitable access

Two questions emerge from the consultation process and the reports of the Strategy working groups:

- Who should be eligible for specific services?

- Can those eligible actually access these services?

Eligibility

The framework for eligibility should ensure that financial barriers do not adversely affect an individual's opportunity to reach his or her full health potential. The existing schemes which provide for certain services to be delivered free of charge (the most important of which is the medical card scheme) do not adequately reflect the levels at which 'hardship' or financial barriers to accessing the necessary care arise. Emphasis was placed during the consultative process on establishing good health status early in life, with particular importance attached to supporting families with children in this context.

Eligibility arrangements across a range of schemes need to be reviewed to ensure that criteria fully reflect the levels at which barriers to accessing care arise. Investment in the health of children was also identified as a priority.

Access

While individuals may be eligible for services, this does not mean that they will receive the services when they need them or in a reasonable timeframe. The situation is most evident in the hospital system where public patients may have to wait considerably longer than private patients for certain elective (non-emergency) treatment. It also arises where some community-based services are available to public patients in one part of the country but less available in another.

The Strategy must address the 'two-tier' element of hospital treatment where public patients frequently do not have fair access to elective treatment. All patients should have such access within a reasonable period of time, irrespective of whether they are public or private patients. Public patients should also have reasonable access to the range of publicly funded services irrespective of where they happen to live.

Patient focus

In this Strategy, 'people-centredness' has been identified as a key principle. Feedback from the consultation process suggests that patients and clients often have to adapt to the way the system works, rather than the system responding to their needs. The consultation process showed that:

* people want to have a say in matters to do with their treatment

* people want to know what is happening when they have to wait for services and when they are receiving services or treatment

* systems and procedures need to be more user-friendly, taking account of the needs of particular groups

* having to give the same information 'over and over again' is a frustration for patients/clients in the system.

Attitudes of providers to service users were seen, in some cases, as showing a lack of courtesy, sensitivity, flexibility or respect. The question of health-care workers having inadequate time to listen and reassure individuals was also raised, although submissions often recognised that this was due to the pressure experienced by many staff. Much concern was expressed about opening hours and appointment arrangements for out-patient clinics as well as excessive waiting times in Accident and Emergency departments. Submissions argued that patients' loss of time, and how this affects their work and family commitments, are inadequately recognised in the organisation of the system.

Submissions from organisations also identified the need for better mechanisms for consultation with a wide spectrum of interests. This includes local communities, staff, private providers and users, and existing provisions for health board representation and consultation with the voluntary sector. Consultation and participation in decision-making for communities, members of the public, patients, clients, families/carers, providers and service users were also raised in the parallel consultation process on the National Anti-Poverty Strategy and Health.

The health system must become more people-centred with the interests of the public, patients and clients being given greater prominence and influence in decision-making at all levels. This points to a need to empower individuals through:

- improved ways of delivering services that take account of modern social trends and lifestyles

- improved customer care procedures which are sensitive to the needs of particular groups and individuals and ensure the greatest ease of access to information on eligibility for services and where and how to access them

- comprehensive, easily accessible complaints and appeal procedures

- consultation processes that engage the wider community in decisions about the delivery of health and personal social services

- mechanisms that capture customer feedback on a regular basis.

Poor integration of services within the system

Improving 'patient focus' in delivering services was linked to calls during the consultation process for a 'seamless service'. Factors identified as obstacles to integration were the following:

- the type and number of organisations with inadequate linkages between them

- inadequate information technology systems, data and information sharing, which could support integration

- professional barriers and structures that may hinder the integration of services for patients and clients

- job specialisation and the absence of inter-disciplinary teams which result in patient needs not being addressed in an integrated holistic way.

Focus needs to be placed on promoting and facilitating the delivery of health care through inter-professional partnership for the benefit of the patient. For a partnership model to be effective, the old hierarchical thinking in relation to the professions must disappear, along with the turf wars which are a barrier to patient care.

Quote from the public consultation.

The submissions emphasised the need for:

- better linkages and relationships between the key players in the health system across agencies, between community and hospital-based providers and across the voluntary/statutory interface

- better, more integrated information systems

- improved inter-disciplinary team-working at individual team and inter-professional levels

- the development of primary and continuing care on a more integrated basis within the community with more structured links to specialised parts of the health system.

Quality

Quality and continuous improvement must be embedded in daily practice to ensure consistently high standards. The health system does not have the mechanisms and infrastructure to support this adequately at present. Issues raised by the Health Strategy Consultative Forum and departmental working groups included:

- inadequate and poorly integrated information systems to support the measurement of inputs and outcomes on a quantitative or qualitative basis in the health system

- insufficient investment in the development of intellectual and organisational capacity to carry out comprehensive research and analysis of policy options

- lack of an overriding national structure responsible for the development, dissemination and evaluation of the impact of agreed national quality protocols and standards

- a lack of mechanisms between employers and professional regulatory bodies for identifying the scope of and boundaries between the role of the regulators to assure individual competence and that of the employers to manage performance at work

- concerns about a 'blame' culture in which quality audits and evaluations make individual practitioners feel isolated and vulnerable.

High-standard, well-integrated and reliable information systems are central to quality. While a number of good information systems exist or are being developed, the ability to identify health needs or to evaluate equity, efficiency, effectiveness and overall quality of health services is limited. This is due, in part, to inadequacies in the availability, quality and integration of health information systems.

A number of steps will be required to support and develop the quality agenda. Prioritising investment in information systems will be a pre-requisite to the planned shift to an evidence-based approach to decision-making at all levels – policy, clinical or managerial – in the health system.

Configuration, capacity and funding of the health system

The consultation process showed that people understood the breadth of health and personal social services and had clear views on the priorities for change.

Table 3.4: **Consultation process: proposals for change**

	Public: % of proposals for change in each area
Meeting special needs*	23%
Community services	18%
Acute care (hospitals)	15%
Health promotion	13%
Equity, eligibility and entitlements	10%
Quality systems	7%
Improving people's experiences of health services	5%
Other	9%
Total	100%

* including older people; people with learning, physical or sensory disabilities; people with mental health difficulties

Organisations also identified particular areas or groups for special attention: 43 per cent of submissions referred to acute hospital care; 31 per cent to community services and 60 per cent to special needs groups such as older people (15 per cent); people with mental health problems (13 per cent); people with physical and sensory disabilities (10 per cent) and people with learning disabilities (7 per cent). The priority given to the development of services for particular types of care and care groups was of particular concern in drafting the Health Strategy.

Configuration of services

The consultation process pointed to the need for more care in the community and identified many services that require to be developed in a cohesive way. The public demand is for services closer to home which can be more easily accessed when needed. Accordingly, radical reconfiguration of the whole primary care structure is central to the Strategy. This will require a stronger emphasis on the community setting and emphasises the vital role individuals, families, communities and other sectors have in helping everyone to achieve their full health potential.

Capacity/service development issues

Figure 3.3 shows the considerable development that has taken place across a range of services in recent years. However, deficiencies remain and these need to be addressed as part of the Health Strategy.

Acute hospital services

Acute hospital services form a vital part of the health system. Despite considerable reductions in acute hospital bed numbers in the late 1980s and early 1990s, the level of services to patients increased significantly. Taken together, in-patient and day case activity in hospitals has increased by 21 per cent since 1995, an annual average increase of 4.2 per cent. However, this has imposed serious strains on hospital staff, facilities and services.

The consultation process highlighted problems of capacity, waiting times for some specialties and in out-patient departments, and frequent cancellation of non-emergency treatment.

The Health Strategy must address the problems in acute hospital services. This will require:

- continued investment to increase the number of beds in the system

- a stronger planning and decision-making framework in regard to the distribution of hospital beds, geographically and by specialty

- new initiatives to make access for public patients fairer, waiting times shorter and services more streamlined.

Developments for particular care groups

As mentioned earlier the needs of a number of specific groups received particular prominence during the consultation process. Older people and people with disabilities, including mental illness, were mentioned in a great many submissions, both from individual members of the public and from organisations.

In the case of older people, the emphasis was largely on improving the quality of life for older people. Supporting their carers, especially family carers, was an important concern. Providing improved assessment, community support services and rehabilitation in order to enable older people to remain in their own homes or community for as long as possible was also mentioned, as well as many proposals on the availability, cost and quality of long-term residential care.

In relation to special needs there were similar proposals for increased community support and respite places, as well as proposals relating to advocacy for vulnerable groups; greater education for health-care workers and the public about the needs of people with disabilities and mental illness; and many proposals for the development of specific specialised services in these areas.

Funding

There has been extensive debate about funding the health system. Despite considerable investment in recent years, two problems remain in the current system of funding. Firstly, the perceived inflexibility and uncertainty of the current allocation system, which is centred on the annual Estimates and Budgetary cycle, has been raised in submissions as a weakness, given the need for longer-term planning.

Secondly, despite increased investment levels in recent years, the levels of funding were considered in many submissions to be inadequate to support current needs. The concerns about capacity and the configuration of services underline the need for ongoing capital investment, expansion in acute hospital services and substantial strengthening of primary care and community services.

The Health Strategy must address the need for:

- improved funding arrangements to facilitate the planning process, in order to ensure that funding and service planning are closely linked

- continued investment across a range of specific development programmes.

Human resources

Human resources and management were also raised during the consultation process. It was considered by one of the departmental working groups and a sub-group of the Health Strategy Consultative Forum which stressed the need for an adequate skilled workforce. The lack of availability of adequate numbers of staff in certain professional grades has had a serious impact on service development for a number of years.

A second area of concern was the increasing difficulty for all public sector organisations to compete as employers of choice in the labour market.

A proper human resource plan is needed to support any new health strategy. Strategies may come and go, but the people who are an integral resource to the health system need to be appreciated, developed, motivated and effectively managed with respect and dignity if the desired vision, values, goals and objectives are to become reality.

Quote from the consultation with organisations.

It has become clear that to meet the growing workforce demands and to make the health system an employer of choice the health service must have:

- improved workforce planning and recruitment processes

- greater recognition of occupational health issues

- better human resource management to maximise retention and development of the workforce

- greater use of the partnership model to involve staff more closely in the development and ownership of a people-centred and responsive health system.

Organisational issues

The structure of decision-making, roles and responsibilities within the health system is complex, with many layers and very many intersecting roles. On the role and functions of health boards, the submissions suggested that achieving a balance between national and local decision-making is difficult. The need for greater clarity of levels of decision-making was also raised. This includes the roles played by the boards, the Department of Health and Children and the Department of Finance. Despite improved strategic planning in recent years, deficiencies remain, particularly in the area of acute hospital services where local considerations rather than national evidence-based policies tend to hold sway.

Reports of the departmental working group and sub-group of the Health Strategy Consultative Forum suggested that, in some respects, the health boards operate as separate entities with a resultant lack of consistency in the standard and stage of development of services. Initiatives adopted in one or more boards to apply 'best practice' throughout the system are not always entirely effective. In addition, it is suggested that health boards have not been wholly successful in establishing a regional identity within their functional areas; county loyalties remain as a strong feature. This is seen as having the potential to affect the optimal development of patient-centred services within each health board region as a whole.

Meeting these criticisms will require:

- review of the functions and operations of the Department and Health and Children and health boards, aimed at strengthening strategic planning and effective service delivery respectively

- new mechanisms and structures to support the development and application of national standards for the whole health system

- review of the roles of existing health agencies in light of new strategic goals and objectives.

Opportunities/challenges for the future

In setting out important factors for developing this Health Strategy, it was suggested that a key factor was 'ensuring appropriate responsiveness to unplanned events' (Wiley, 2001). It is not possible to predict 'unplanned' events, but it is possible to look to the future and consider some of the trends that may affect the priorities for the health system and the changing nature or volumes of activity in particular areas.

Demographic patterns

Population trends will have an important impact on the demands and pressures in the health system in the years to come. Population projections for the next 20 years show that not only will the population increase but also the number of older people will form a larger portion of the population (Figures 3.4 and 3.5).

Utilisation of health and personal social services increases with age; not just services specifically for older people, but all services. In addition, Ireland is now moving towards a more multi-ethnic/multi-cultural society. In health, as in other areas of public policy, this brings a need to plan for diversity with a wider range of needs to be addressed – affecting both the health workforce and the patient/client group.

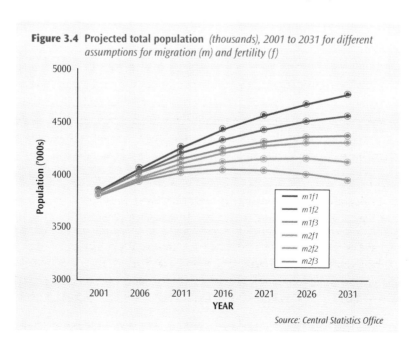

Figure 3.4 Projected total population *(thousands), 2001 to 2031 for different assumptions for migration (m) and fertility (f)*

Source: Central Statistics Office

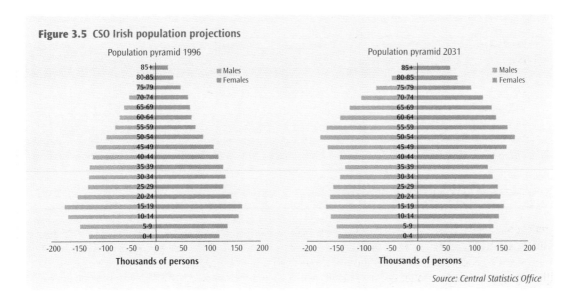

Figure 3.5 CSO Irish population projections

Population pyramid 1996

Population pyramid 2031

Source: Central Statistics Office

The physical environment

Food safety, global warming, a reduction in air quality and availability of housing, are all areas of growing public concern. Trends in the area of food production, many brought forward by the commercial pressures to intensify production, raise questions about food safety and the transference of disease from animals to humans. The continuing pressures on the environment affecting water and air quality are concerns that are shared globally.

The importance of fostering and maintaining links with international organisations in order to anticipate, manage and protect against risks emerging from changes in the physical environment will be emphasised in the Health Strategy.

Science and technology

For many people, science and technology hold the potential for wonderful opportunities for the future. Cures for potentially fatal disease, other more advanced diagnostics, biotechnology applications, tissue engineering, imaging capacity and advances in drug development all hold the possibilities of lengthening life and improving its quality. Developments in these areas also suggest that in the future there will be a greater emphasis on the possibilities for prevention and a much more intensive approach to preventive medicine.

Information technology advances are also likely to revolutionise care. These advances include a variety of patient care databases; opportunities to share and work to standardised evidence-based protocols and decision-support systems; and the possibility of remote consultations through telemedicine.

On the other hand, these advances may also present potential threats. The availability of new treatments and technologies may bring greater demands for new services, some with major ethical implications. The problem of infection brought about by increasing antibiotic resistance is becoming more acute and new infectious agents will continue to emerge. Increased international travel and migration will pose additional challenges in Ireland.

The Strategy must establish the mechanisms and structures to support the health system in monitoring and evaluating the benefits and risks which technology can bring so that the system can take advantage of benefits and respond quickly to challenges that may arise.

Social trends

Health follows a social gradient: 'poor people get sick more often and die younger'. Chapter 2 has outlined how much wider than health services or genetic endowment are the determinants of health. It has been suggested by the Combat Poverty Agency (CPA) that poverty can reduce the opportunity or the motivation to adopt healthy lifestyles. In addition, poverty can make it more difficult to access or afford adequate or appropriate health care. As acknowledged by the CPA (2001), tackling health inequalities is inextricably linked with poverty. In devising the actions to tackle health inequalities for the Health Strategy, the Department has worked closely with the group working to review the targets for health for the National Anti-Poverty Strategy. The Strategy must also reflect the inter-departmental working required to tackle the link between poverty and the other determinants of health, outside of health service provision.

Quality of life

With rising prosperity, expectations of high quality of life have increased greatly. At the same time, the pressures of modern life are giving rise to more people feeling stressed in their daily lives. Strong social support contributes to health by providing people with emotional and practical resources. However, changes in family structures and community life may mean these supports are less available than in the past. Groups such as the elderly, people with disabilities, people with mental illness, and those with chronic illnesses, expect to be able to enjoy a reasonable quality of life. In the future, services will be planned to meet these expectations and the 'whole person' perspective.

Community and social capital

Many groups have emphasised the impact which changes in the availability of work, workplace practices and employment law have already had on the numbers and structure of the workforce. Greater flexible working and the increase in job opportunities have enabled many more women to take up paid employment.

Commuter towns, where those living in new developments spend their days travelling to a distant employment, may give rise to a loss of 'community' associated with more traditional neighbourhoods. The loss of such community support also has implications for the care of young children and for support for older people.

The evolving body of research on social capital suggests that participation in formal and informal networks such as sporting clubs or basic neighbourhood activity can have a major impact on health status. While the evidence for Ireland is not fully clear, there are indications that these networks are declining in places.

The Health Strategy must take account of the changing role of the family and community and improve supports for community and family participation in voluntary and informal care.

Summary of key messages

The health system has many strengths on which to move forward. In Chapter 2, improving health status, reducing inequalities in health, and addressing quality of life issues are clearly identified. The analysis in this chapter suggests further goals arising from people's experience of interacting with health and personal social services. They can be summarised as follows:

Eligibility, access and equity

- Eligibility and entitlement to services to be clear

- Barriers to accessing services to be removed

- Access to services to be more equitable – the perceived two-tier aspect of health care to be eliminated.

Responsiveness and appropriateness of care

- Investment to be increased

- Patient focus in the planning and delivery of services to be improved

- Better patient information to improve planning of services

- Greater opportunities for the community to participate in the decisions about health services

- Community-based health services to be used more, with a radically strengthened primary care service

- Greater support for formal and informal care given by the community.

Improving system performance

- Standardised quality systems to support best patient care to be developed

- An evidence-based, strategic approach to decision-making to be developed at all levels

- Accountability to continue to be improved.

Meeting these concerns will require changes to the current health system, particularly in

- primary care

- acute hospital services

- funding

- human resources

- organisational structures

- information systems.

CHAPTER 4

National goals

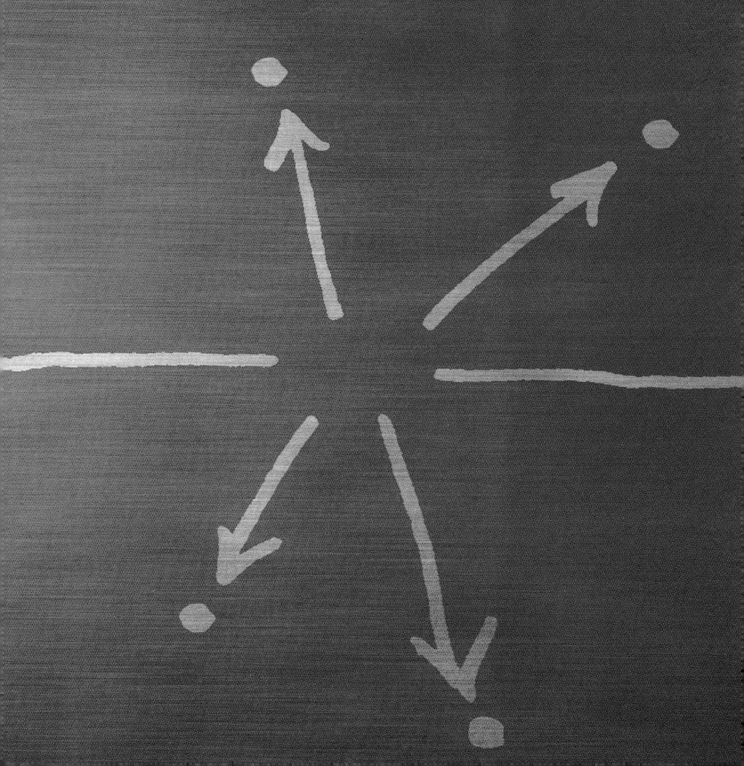

Setting goals for the Health Strategy

Chapter 1 set out a vision of a future health system and the principles to guide everyone working in the system. Towards that vision, this chapter sets out four national goals to encompass the many proposed developments and reforms that emerged from the deliberations of the consultation process and the analysis of the Health Strategy Steering Group. It has not been feasible to include all of the individual ideas put forward during the consultation process. The goals are intended, however, to encompass the major conclusions in terms of overall direction for the future.

The four goals are:

*   **Better health for everyone**

*   **Fair access**

*   **Responsive and appropriate care delivery**

*   **High performance.**

This chapter describes the four goals in detail. Specific objectives and actions to help achieve each goal are also outlined. Implementation of some of these actions will require legislative, organisational and cultural change. The key areas needing reorganisation, reform or development are described in Chapter 5, The Frameworks for Change.

Goals

Objectives

National Goal No. 1:
Better health for everyone
*   The health of the population is at the centre of public policy
*   The promotion of health and well-being is intensified
*   Health inequalities are reduced
*   Specific quality of life issues are targeted.

National Goal No. 2:
Fair access
*   Eligibility for health and personal social services is clearly defined
*   Scope of eligibility framework is broadened
*   Equitable access for all categories of patient in the health system is assured.

National Goal No. 3:
Responsive and appropriate care delivery
*   The patient is at the centre in planning care delivery
*   Appropriate care is delivered in the appropriate setting
*   The system has the capacity to deliver timely and appropriate services.

National Goal No. 4: High performance
*   Standardised quality systems support best patient care and safety
*   Evidence and strategic objectives underpin all planning/decision-making.

National Goal No. 1: Better health for everyone

The first goal is concerned with promoting and improving everyone's health and reducing health inequalities. It is based on the concept of population health, i.e. promoting the health of groups, families and communities, as well as addressing individual health problems. Chapter 2 suggests that, overall, Ireland has a relatively unhealthy population by comparison with other countries at a similar stage of economic and social development. It also demonstrates the importance of the wider determinants of health, highlighted and referred to in the National Health Promotion Strategy 2000-2005. The need for collaborative action from a number of agencies both within and outside of the health system is imperative to achieve and sustain a healthy population. The main conclusions from Chapter 2 lead to the four objectives under this goal.

Objective 1: The health of the population is at the centre of public policy

Health is important for everyone. A large number of agencies, bodies and government departments is involved in promoting good health and treating and supporting those who suffer ill-health or who have a disability. Some of these have a very direct and clear function in the area of health and are part of the health and personal social services. In addition, many agencies and government departments whose role may appear more peripheral or indirect have a vital contribution to make in achieving an integrated strategic approach to promoting and improving the health of the whole population. This objective is concerned with ensuring a joint approach, co-ordinated under one coherent strategy, to maximise the impact on health of existing policies, structures and initiatives. It is designed to ensure that all policy makers, especially those more indirectly involved in the health system, consider the impact that their decisions might have, both directly and indirectly, on the health of the population.

Achieving full health potential does not depend solely on the provision of health services. Many other factors and, therefore, many other individuals, groups, institutions and public and private bodies have a part to play in the effort to improve health status and achieve the health potential of the nation.

Objective 2: The promotion of health and well-being is intensified

People's lifestyles, and the conditions in which they live and work, influence their health and longevity. Most people have a basic understanding of the positive and negative effects lifestyles can have on their health. The reality is that the achievement of health and well-being is not the responsibility of the individual alone. This objective is concerned with providing a supportive environment to help us all make the healthier choice the easier choice and thereby contribute individually to improving overall health status.

- *Life expectancy in Ireland is increasing, but not as fast as in Europe*

- *The gap in life expectancy between Ireland and Europe is widening*

- *General mortality rates due to cardiovascular disease and cancer are still above EU levels*

- *Injuries represent a significant financial and social burden on the community and the health system*

- *Many deaths caused by cancer, circulatory diseases and injury are preventable*

- *If the trends in smoking, alcohol consumption, diet and lifestyles cannot be reversed, this is likely to continue to lead to many avoidable deaths in future years.*

Objective 3: Health inequalities are reduced

As outlined in Chapter 2, the most powerful influences affecting health and the promotion of health are socio-economic factors, in particular poverty. Every major health problem has a significant social gradient, with those at the lowest socio-economic level suffering most ill-health. This is supported by the findings of the first National Health and Lifestyle Survey (SLÁN). There is a need to build on the initiatives set out in the National Health Promotion Strategy, with a special focus on those identified as at risk in order to minimise the gap in socio-economic variations. This objective is about ensuring that disadvantaged groups get the help and support they need to ensure that everyone in society has an equal chance to achieve his or her full health potential.

Objective 4: Specific quality of life issues are targeted

As defined in this Strategy, 'health' is more than simply the absence of illness or disease. It is also about quality of life. Many people with a long-term illness, mental illness, or a disability, have a considerable reduction in their quality of life. In addition, social trends are placing new pressures on individuals and their families. It is clear from the consultation process that actions to improve social gain and quality of life should form part of a coherent health strategy.

Addressing quality of life issues must be a central objective of the Health Strategy

Objective 1: The health of the population is at the centre of public policy

1   Health impact assessment will be introduced as part of the public policy development process

The health impact assessment process identifies the factors which have a potential impact on health. Accordingly, it is a means for all sectors to determine the effects of their policies and actions on health and it has the potential to bring greater transparency to the decision-making process by clarifying the nature of trade-offs in policy.

The Department of Health and Children will develop the 'procedures, methods and tools by which a policy, programme or project may be judged as to its potential effects on the health of the population and the distribution of those effects within the population' (WHO, Regional Office for Europe, 1999) and will have a key role in supporting other departments and agencies in carrying out health impact assessments. In doing so, the Department will have regard to the actions on health impact assessment outlined in the report of the Working Group on the National Anti-Poverty Strategy (NAPS) and Health, due to be published shortly.

Regional-level structures such as local authorities and county development boards with a role in implementing public policy locally will also be asked to consider the impact of their decisions on population health in their area.

2   Statements of strategy and business plans of all relevant Government departments will incorporate an explicit commitment to sustaining and improving health status

The strategic and business planning process, introduced as part of the Strategic Management Initiative, requires every government department to set out its strategic objectives and identify how these objectives will be achieved. The purpose of this objective is to ensure that concern for human health becomes more firmly embedded as a core value at the strategic planning stage for all relevant departments.

3 The National Environmental Health Action Plan will be prepared

The WHO (1999) describes environmental health as comprising 'those aspects of human health, including quality of life, that are determined by chemical, physical, biological, social and psycho-social factors in the environment. It also refers to the theory and practice of assessing, correcting and preventing those factors in the environment that can potentially affect adversely the health of present and future generations'. A proposal for a National Environmental Health Action Plan (NEHAP) was published in 1999. A plan will be prepared and submitted to Government by June 2002 for agreement and publication. Such a plan will be an essential element in helping government departments not directly involved in health services to recognise and assess the potential impact of their policies on the health of the population.

4 A population health division will be established in the Department of Health and Children and in each health board

Department of Health and Children

In the Department, this will bring together a number of existing functions in a more coherent way, to allow for a more focused and integrated approach to delivering on Strategy objectives relating to population health. The division will be responsible for integrating policy development in the following areas:

- Preventive/screening programmes

- Public health

- Environmental health

- Food safety

- Medicines

- Health promotion

- NAPS/social inclusion

- Health impact assessment/health proofing.

This will be addressed in the restructuring of the Department of Health and Children referred to in Chapter 5.

Health boards

In health boards, the new population health function will incorporate and build on the existing public health departments, health promotion units and other relevant areas.

It will strengthen the health boards' role in working with local authorities, schools, colleges, universities, health professions, employers, community groups, voluntary organisations and relevant actions in the private sector to seek ways to promote and improve population health status both locally and regionally.

It will also work closely with the Population Health Division of the Department of Health and Children, particularly in relation to the monitoring and evaluation of regional and local initiatives and the development of appropriate performance targets and indicators.

Objective 2: The promotion of health and well-being is intensified

5 Actions on major lifestyle factors targeted in the National Cancer, Cardiovascular and Health Promotion Strategies will be enhanced

The State has been engaged for a number of years in national strategies to tackle cancer and cardiovascular disease and to promote healthier lifestyles generally. An outline of each of these strategies is included in Appendix 3. Implementing them is essential to tackling improvements in health status and premature mortality. In continuing to implement the National Cancer, Cardiovascular and Health Promotion Strategies, the following actions will be advanced as a priority:

Achievement of the targets set out in the National Health Promotion Strategy (2000-2005) through:

Smoking

- Enhanced health promotion initiatives aimed at addressing the risk factors associated with cancers and cardiovascular disease such as smoking

- Targeting a reduction in smoking for young women.

Alcohol

- Introducing further actions to promote sensible alcohol consumption on the basis of a review of the National Alcohol Policy

- Examining possible further restrictions on the advertising of alcohol.

Diet and exercise

- Continuing action to improve Irish diet so that essential nutrients and energy levels are maintained and fat consumption is controlled

- Continuing measures to promote physical exercise.

6 The Public Health (Tobacco) Bill will be enacted and implemented as a matter of urgency

The Public Health (Tobacco) Bill, 2001 will provide for a new, more comprehensive and strengthened legislative basis for regulating and controlling the sale, marketing and smoking of tobacco products and for enforcing such controls. It will provide for:

- the establishment of the Tobacco Control Agency on a statutory basis

- a comprehensive ban on tobacco advertising (with limited exceptions) and on all forms of sponsorship by the tobacco industry

- the establishment by the Tobacco Control Agency of a register of all retailers selling tobacco products

- ministerial powers to prohibit or restrict smoking in specified places.

7 A reduction in smoking will continue to be targeted through Government fiscal policies

Over recent years the Government has sought to target a reduction in smoking through the largest ever increase in tobacco taxes. In addition, the Government moved to use tobacco taxes directly to help fund the development of health services. A difficulty has arisen where such increases have a direct impact on the Consumer Price Index and lead to demands for compensation. This reduces the ability of the Government to use tobacco revenue to fund health services and reduces the intended financial disincentive.

The Government continues to believe that taxation is an effective means of reducing tobacco consumption and the resulting adverse impact on health status. Decisions must, obviously, be taken in the context of the annual Budgets. Significant progress requires an agreement on the part of the social partners and all concerned to disregard tobacco products as a component part of the inflation figures used to underline wage increases and Budget changes.

8 Initiatives to promote healthy lifestyles in children will be extended

Research shows that unhealthy behaviours adopted in childhood (for example smoking, lack of exercise), have a negative impact on health in later life, particularly where the behaviours are carried on into adulthood.

In schools, the Social, Personal and Health Education (SPHE) programme provides students with a unique opportunity to develop the skills and competence to learn about themselves, to care for themselves and others, and to make informed decisions about their health, personal lives and social development. The SPHE programme will reflect the ethos of the school. To be effective such a programme must be supported by the pillars of the Health Promoting School model: a positive school atmosphere, links to the wider community, a health promoting physical environment, and healthy school policies.

The substance abuse and SPHE programmes in both primary and post-primary schools will be extended to all schools.

9 Measures to promote and support breastfeeding will be strengthened

Breastfeeding of infants and young children provides one of the best opportunities to give children a good start in life. Ireland currently has the lowest breastfeeding rate in Europe. A National Breastfeeding Co-ordinator has been appointed in the Department of Health and Children and a review of the National Breastfeeding policy is currently being undertaken. There are three key areas for action to re-establish a breastfeeding culture in Ireland:

- To generate positive attitudes to breastfeeding by promoting the unique nutritional advantages and the long-lasting health protective benefits of breastfeeding for infants and young children

- To maximise the support for new mothers in the maternity hospitals

- To promote, support, and protect breastfeeding in homes, schools, workplaces and in society generally.

10 A National Injury Prevention Strategy to co-ordinate action on injury prevention will be prepared

Unintentional injuries are a major cause of death, hospital admission and long-term disability in Ireland. Most injuries can be prevented. Injury prevention is a complex task requiring action across many sectors. A co-ordinated plan with a national focus similar to those adopted in the fight against cancer and cardiovascular disease will be developed, with the Department of Health and Children taking a lead role. Such a plan will be particularly relevant to groups such as children, young people (especially young adult males) and older people (over 65) where the incidence of preventable injury is highest.

There are almost 1,500 deaths and 55,000 admissions to hospital for treatment for unintentional injury in Ireland each year.

Quote from the Consultation Process

11 The programmes of screening for breast and cervical cancer will be extended nationally

BreastCheck, the National Breast Cancer Screening Programme, commenced Phase 1 of its Programme in February 2000, offering screening services to all women aged between 50-64 in the Eastern Regional Health Authority, the Midland Health Board and the North-Eastern Health Board areas. The goal of the programme is to reduce breast cancer mortality by 20 per cent in the cohort of women screened between 2000-2010. Phase 1 of the cervical screening programme is currently being implemented in the Mid-Western Health Board. BreastCheck is in consultation with the health boards concerning the provision of additional centres and mobile units to extend the screening programme nationwide. Screening for cervical cancer will also be extended to all areas and the target is to achieve a greater than 80 per cent participation rate by women aged 25-60. The Department's key objective is to ensure that programmes are driven by international quality assurance criteria and best practice and that national coverage will be achieved as soon as possible, having regard to the experience gained in implementing the programmes to date.

12 A revised implementation plan for the National Cancer Strategy will be published

The Department of Health and Children, in conjunction with the National Cancer Forum, will prepare a revised implementation plan which will set out the key investment areas to be targeted for the development of cancer services over the next seven years. This will have regard to existing policies in the areas of symptomatic breast disease and palliative care, the Comhairle na nOspidéal report on haematology services, and the forthcoming recommendations of the Expert Group on the Development of Radiotherapy Services.

Following publication of the national plan, individual health boards, in consultation with the National Cancer Forum, will develop new regional cancer plans which will identify additional requirements for the development of integrated, evidence-based treatment and palliative services for people with cancer. This will enable further expansion of integrated cancer treatment and palliative services rather than disease-or service-specific developments.

13 The Heart Health Task Force will monitor and evaluate the implementation of the prioritised cardiovascular health action plan

This detailed plan is due to be finalised in the coming months by the Advisory Forum on Cardiovascular Health. Its implementation will be monitored by the Heart Health Task Force, with reference to the Health Information and Quality Authority, and it will be evaluated in accordance with the principles set out in *Building Healthier Hearts,* the National Cardiovascular Strategy.

14 Initiatives will be taken to improve children's health

A range of initiatives will be undertaken as follows:

- An integrated national programme for child health will be developed

- National minimum standards and targets for immunisation uptake, surveillance and screening will be drawn up

- Mental health services for children and adolescents will be expanded:

  - Implementation of the recommendations of the First Report of the Review Group on Child and Adolescent Psychiatric Services

  - Development of mental health services to meet the needs of children aged between 16 and 18 (currently being reviewed by the Review Group on Child and Adolescent Psychiatric Services).

15 A policy for men's health and health promotion will be developed

The Health Promotion Strategy identified the development of a national plan for men's health as an important initiative. Recent research (NEHB, 2001) has shown that there is a need to raise awareness about men's health issues and to encourage men to actively seek screening and to seek timely medical help. It is also important to develop models of working which facilitate access to services, and which reflect the particular needs of men. The Department of Health and Children will take the lead role in preparing and driving a policy for men's health in partnership with the health boards and other agencies. Resources will be provided to promote early detection and screening programmes of proven value to men's health in areas such as prostate and testicular cancer.

Men are:

less likely to interpret their symptoms as arising from physical symptoms less likely to develop the confidence to seek preventive help.

Men Talking, North Eastern Health Board, 2001

16 Measures will be taken to promote sexual health and safer sexual practices

The National Health Promotion Strategy sets out, as a strategic aim, the promotion of sexual health and safer sexual practices amongst the population. In order to achieve this aim, an action plan for sexual health will be developed. It will include, through the on-going development of Health Promoting Schools, school-based programmes in schools designed to develop personal skills e.g. Social, Personal and Health Education (SPHE). It will complement the commitment to the full implementation of the recommendations of the AIDS Strategy 2000 (see action 33).

17 Legislation in the area of food safety will be prepared to take account of developments in food safety regulation at national and EU level

Ensuring that the EU has the highest standards of food safety is a key policy priority for the European Commission and the member states, including Ireland. The EU White Paper on Food Safety published in January 2000 outlines an 80-point legislative programme with a timeframe to 2003 for the adoption of new and amending legislation. Ireland will be actively involved in the development of these legislative proposals at EU level and the Department of Health and Children will have responsibility for transposing all food safety related proposals into Irish law.

Objective 3: Health inequalities are reduced

18 A programme of actions will be implemented to achieve National Anti-Poverty Strategy and Health targets for the reduction of health inequalities

In 1997, the National Anti-Poverty Strategy (NAPS) was published. Under NAPS, all government policy is 'poverty proofed' to test if it reduces poverty or has an adverse impact on poorer people. Considerable progress has been made in reducing the level of poverty in Ireland over the intervening years. A commitment to review the NAPS and to set new targets in the areas of health and accommodation/housing was given in the Programme for Prosperity and Fairness.

The Report of the Working Group on NAPS and Health identifies and maps the links between poverty and ill-health and provides the most appropriate framework for concerted action in addressing health inequalities. Four targets which reflect the overall goal of the NAPS health programme, i.e. to eliminate the impact of deprivation and disadvantage on health status, are set out below.

- The gap in premature mortality between the lowest and highest socio-economic groups should be reduced by at least 10 per cent for circulatory diseases, cancers, injuries and poisoning, by 2007

- The gap in life expectancy between the Travelling Community and the whole population should be reduced by at least 10 per cent by 2007

- The life expectancy and health status of Travellers should be monitored so that, by 2003, the existing targets can be reviewed and revised

- By 2007, the gap in low birth weight rates between children from the lowest and highest socio-economic groups should be reduced by 10 per cent from the current level.

The Report of the NAPS and Health Working Group envisages these targets being achieved through a series of actions related to the following:

- increased equity of access to primary health care services

- increased equity of access to public hospital services

- increased access to effective interventions for cardiovascular disease and cancers

- increased equity of access to community supports

- development of an injury prevention strategy

- increasing the income threshold in the guidelines for the medical card, with a view to removing impediments to access to services and taking particular account of the needs of children

- integrating an equality dimension into health and social services

- development of a multi-sectoral approach to health and health impact assessment.

These issues are addressed elsewhere in this Strategy. A key deliverable in relation to NAPS and health will be the putting in place of the indicator and research data needed to monitor and evaluate the NAPS health targets and to review existing targets and set new targets.

19   Initiatives to eliminate barriers for disadvantaged groups to achieve healthier lifestyles will be developed and expanded

Personal and community health is the responsibility not only of government and other providers of health care but also of individuals and communities. Working in partnership with the consumer and community, the following actions will be undertaken to improve the health status of marginalised groups:

- Implementing existing policy on the prioritisation of health promoting activities for vulnerable groups (National Health Promotion Strategy 2000-2005)

- Identifying the barriers to the adoption of healthy lifestyles by those on low incomes and/or with low levels of education and developing effective intervention programmes to overcome those barriers

- Developing initiatives to assess the health information needs of local communities. Once those needs have been identified, information/education and preventive programmes can be developed and sustained locally with community support.

20 The health of Travellers will be improved

The Travellers' Health Strategy will provide a focused plan to improve the health of Travellers and will be implemented over the next seven years.

Travellers' Health Strategy – key elements

- Establishment of active partnerships between Travellers, their representative organisations and health service personnel in the provision of health services

- Provision of awareness training for health personnel in relation to Traveller culture, including Traveller perspectives on health and illness

- Strengthening of Traveller health units comprising health board staff and Traveller representatives, with responsibility for planning and implementing the Strategy in each health board

- Development of initiatives to increase Travellers' awareness of general medical services and to make services more accessible, having regard to the Traveller communities

- Provision of designated public health nurses in each health board to work specifically with Traveller communities

- Replication of the successful 'Primary Health Care for Travellers Project', which established a model for Traveller participation in the development of health services

- Promotion of various 'peer-led' initiatives to strengthen the links between Travellers and various health services

- Establishment of a permanent liaison mechanism between the Department of Health and Children and the Department of the Environment and Local Government, to collaborate in efforts to improve Travellers' living conditions on halting sites.

21 Initiatives to improve the health and well-being of homeless people will be advanced

Detailed strategic plans for homeless adults and young people have been published recently. Initiatives targeting the needs of these groups will be taken in the context of these recently-published strategies.

Homelessness – an Integrated Strategy (2000) – key elements

- Local authorities and health boards, in partnership with the voluntary bodies, will draw up action plans on a county-by-county basis to provide a more coherent and integrated delivery of services to homeless persons by all agencies dealing with homelessness

- Homeless fora, comprising representatives of the local authority, health board and voluntary sector will be established in every county

- Local authorities will be responsible for the provision of accommodation, including emergency hostel accommodation, for homeless persons and health boards will be responsible for the provision of their in-house care and health needs

- Preventive strategies, targeting at-risk groups, are an essential requirement for those leaving custodial or health-related care. Procedures will also be developed and implemented to prevent homelessness among these groups.

The Youth Homelessness Strategy (2001) – key elements

The Strategy provides a strategic framework for youth homelessness to be tackled on a national basis. The goal of the Strategy is 'to reduce and if possible eliminate youth homelessness through preventive strategies and where a child becomes homeless to ensure that he/she benefits from a comprehensive range of services aimed at reintegrating him/her into his /her community as quickly as possible'

- Within three months of the publication of the Strategy, following consultation with relevant statutory and voluntary bodies, each health board will develop a two-year strategic plan to address youth homelessness in line with specific actions required under 12 objectives in three broad categories: preventive measures, responsive services and planning and administrative supports

- A range of other bodies in the public sector, including schools, the National Education Welfare Board, local authorities and the City and County Development Boards will support the actions of health boards and take specific steps themselves

- At national level, given the cross-sectoral dimensions of youth homelessness, the National Children's Office will have lead responsibility for driving and co-ordinating the actions necessary to ensure the successful implementation of the Strategy.

22   Initiatives to improve the health and well-being of drug misusers will be advanced

The National Drugs Strategy (2001) provides a focused plan for the improvement of the health and well-being of drug misusers.

The National Drugs Strategy (2001) – key elements

- Develop a national awareness campaign highlighting the dangers of drugs, the first stage to commence by the end of 2001

- Develop formal links at local, regional and national levels with the National Alcohol Policy by the end of 2001 and ensure co-ordination between the different measures being undertaken

- Have specific actions aimed at younger people that will involve close links between the Department of Education and Science, the Health Promotion Unit of the Department of Health and Children, and health boards

- Have immediate access for drug misusers to professional assessment and counselling by health boards, followed by commencement of treatment as deemed appropriate not later than one month after assessment

- Have access for under-18s to treatment following the development of an appropriate protocol for dealing with this age group

- Increase the number of treatment places for opiate users to 6,000 by the end of 2001 and 6,500 by the end of 2002

- Continue to implement the recommendations of the Steering Group of Prison-Based Drug Treatment Services

- Have in place, in each health board, a service user charter by the end of 2002

- Have in place, in each health board, a range of treatment and rehabilitation options as part of a planned programme of progression for each drug misuser, by the end of 2002.

23   The health needs of asylum seekers/refugees will be addressed

The health system needs to reflect and respond to the increasing diversity in Irish society. Services will be provided in a culturally sensitive way as an integral part of the services being provided to the wider community.

The health boards will also address needs specific to these groups, where mainstream services are unable to meet such needs. This will include the provision of on-site community health services in major accommodation centres for asylum seekers as appropriate.

Seven major new centres are due to be commissioned during 2002. Incremental resources will be provided to support existing community-based services to asylum seekers and refugees to develop on-site services.

24   Initiatives to improve the health of prisoners will be advanced

The Report of the Expert Group on the Structures and Organisation of Prison Health Care Services in Ireland was published in September 2001. This Report makes 43 recommendations. The achievement of the recommendations will require considerable dialogue and negotiation between health care and prison interests. The Department of Health and Children and health boards will work in close collaboration with the Irish Prisons Authority in improving the health of the prisoner population within this framework.

Report of the Expert Group (2001) – key elements

- The overall aim of prison health-care services is to provide a continuum of care to people both in and outside of the prison system. This should be done in conjunction with health agencies

- Prisoners should be designated as a special needs group, in terms of meeting their health requirements

- Developments are needed in relation to areas such as psychiatric services, dental services, communicable diseases, health promotion and training for prison staff

Objective 4: Specific quality of life issues are targeted

25 A new action programme for mental health will be developed

This programme will build on recent initiatives in mental health services, particularly in the areas of attitudes to mental illness, strengthening advocacy for people with mental illness and providing services in areas where gaps have been identified.

Key actions to improve mental health services and promote awareness of mental health

- The Mental Health Commission will be established by end 2001 to begin the implementation of the Mental Health Act, 2001

- A national policy framework for the further modernisation of mental health services, updating Planning for the Future (1984), will be prepared

- Services aimed at specific groups will be further developed including:

  - older people

  - those who would benefit from community-based alcohol treatment programmes

- A report on services for people with eating disorders will be prepared by the Working Group on Child and Adolescent Services.

  - Programmes to promote positive attitudes to mental health will be introduced

  - Independent patient advocacy services will be encouraged and resourced

  - Suicide prevention programmes will be intensified.

26 An integrated approach to meeting the needs of ageing and older people will be taken

In 1996, 402,000 people or 11.5 per cent of the Irish population were aged over 65. By 2031, forecasts suggest that this will have more than doubled to between 837,000 and 858,000 people, representing between 18 and 21 per cent of the population. Many concerns in relation to older people were raised during the consultation process. These included references to the provision of appropriate care and the impact of the continuing attrition of traditional 'community' and neighbourhood on older people's confidence and ability to live independently. The following actions will be pursued:

Key Actions for ageing and older people

- A co-ordinated action plan to meet the needs of ageing and older people will be developed by the Department of Health and Children in conjunction with the Departments of the Environment and Local Government; Social, Community and Family Affairs; and Public Enterprise

- Community groups will be funded to facilitate volunteers in providing support services such as shopping, visiting and transport for older people

- Health boards will continue to take the lead role in implementing the Health Promotion Strategy for Older People, *Adding years to life and life to years* (1998)

- An action plan for dementia, based on the recommendations of the National Council for Ageing and Older People, will be implemented.

27 Family support services will be expanded

The dominant focus in child care services since the early 1990s has been on the protection and care of children who are at risk. More recently, the policy focus has shifted to a more preventive approach to child welfare, involving support to families and individual children, aimed at avoiding the need for further more serious interventions later on. An evaluation of the Springboard Pilot Projects for Children at Risk indicates that the projects have been very successful in keeping vulnerable and at-risk children out of care. These projects will now be mainstreamed and extended throughout the country. Ring-fenced funding will be allocated to health boards for expansion of these and other family support services.

Expansion programme

- Child welfare budgets will be refocused over the next seven years to provide a more even balance between safeguarding activities and supportive programmes

- Springboard Projects and other family support initiatives will be further developed

- Positive parenting supports and programmes will be expanded

- Effective out-of-hours services will be developed in all health board areas as a priority

- Family welfare conferences and other services required to support the Children Act, 2001 will be introduced

- Priority will be given to early intervention for children with behavioural difficulties.

28 A comprehensive strategy to address crisis pregnancy will be prepared

A new statutory agency to combat crisis pregnancy was established in October 2001. The new agency will

- work through education and other programmes to reduce crisis pregnancies

- work to develop and improve the options open to women with a crisis pregnancy and to increase awareness about these

- develop supports for women who have had an abortion.

Health boards already provide some services aimed at supporting women in crisis pregnancies, teenagers who are pregnant, and pregnant women living in poverty. They will work closely with the new agency in developing services to provide increased support at regional and local levels.

29 Chronic disease management protocols to promote integrated care planning and support self-management of chronic disease will be developed

The continuous and co-ordinated care to address the needs of people with particular chronic diseases such as asthma and diabetes is best provided within the primary care system. Patients with chronic illness must be supported and facilitated to participate in planned regular interactions with health-care providers and assisted in becoming the ultimate managers of their own health.

30 An action plan for rehabilitation services will be prepared

Effective rehabilitation draws on a broad range of services to meet the particular needs of patients, with the objective of helping patients return to normal life in the community. There is a shortage of in-patient and community-based rehabilitation services, with the result that acute hospital beds are being inappropriately used for these services. Rehabilitation services have an important role for people with physical disabilities, including the young chronic sick (those requiring constant nursing care or with an acquired brain injury). The action plan will set out a programme to meet existing shortfalls in services and to integrate specialised facilities with locally based follow-up services.

31   A national palliative care service will be developed

Palliative care has an important role in improving quality of life when the medical expectation is no longer cure. The Government committed itself to the development of a national palliative care plan in the Action Plan for the Millennium. The National Advisory Committee on Palliative Care was established in 1999 with a view to preparing a report on the development of palliative care services in Ireland and reported recently.

Report of the National Advisory Committee on Palliative Care (2001) – key elements

- Structured planning and delivery of services

- Specialist palliative care services to be provided in each health board area

- Access to palliative care for people with non-malignant disease

- Palliative care approach to be an integral part of all clinical practice.

32   Entitlement to high-quality treatment services for people with Hepatitis C, infected by blood or blood products, will be assured

Services for persons with Hepatitis C who have been infected by blood or blood products made available within the State will be kept under review, in consultation with the representative groups, services providers and the Consultative Council on Hepatitis C. The aim will be to ensure that the healthcare system continues to respond in an effective and timely manner to the needs of this unique cohort of patients.

33   Resources will be provided to support the full implementation of AIDS Strategy 2000

AIDS Strategy 2000, the report of the National AIDS Strategy Committee (NASC), was published in 2000 and contains recommendations for action in relation to surveillance, education and prevention and care management. The public health services will continue to work in close collaboration with the voluntary sector under the aegis of the National AIDS Strategy Committee to ensure that the recommendations outlined in the Strategy are implemented.

AIDS Strategy 2000 – key elements

- The changing epidemiology of HIV infection and AIDS-related illnesses over the years of the pandemic require new surveillance and clinical management techniques. This includes close monitoring and management of treatment, involving laboratory techniques such as viral load testing and resistance testing.

- HIV/AIDS should now be dealt with in the wider context of sexual health and other sexually transmitted infections.

- There is a need for greater education and awareness of HIV and AIDS, to prevent people becoming infected in the first place. This includes targeted interventions among at-risk groups.

34   Measures to prevent domestic violence and to support victims will continue

Concerns about increasing levels of crime and violence in our society are growing. The links between alcohol and violence are proven. The continued promotion of moderation in alcohol intake as outlined in the National Alcohol Strategy is intended to help reduce crime, lawlessness and violence. Early interventions in schools through Social, Personal and Health Education programmes will also help to encourage civil and non-violent behaviour in adolescents.

The Department of Health and Children will continue to provide funding through the health boards to refuges, rape crisis centres and other agencies in order to support victims of domestic violence. The Department will also continue to work with other Government departments and agencies to combat violence, particularly violence in the home.

35   A national policy for the provision of sheltered work for people with disabilities will be developed

In June 2000 the Government assigned responsibility for vocational training to the Department of Enterprise, Trade and Employment, and rehabilitation training to the Department of Health and Children. There are many people with disabilities who may not have the capacity to work in open employment and for whom some form of sheltered work may be the best option. Employment Challenges for the Millennium – the Report of the National Advisory Committee on Training and Employment – estimated that there are 7,900 people with disabilities working in 215 sheltered workshops. A more structured policy framework covering all aspects of the provision of sheltered work for people with disabilities is required. This should include approved standards and structured support for the establishment and operation of these services.

National Goal No. 2: Fair access

The second goal is concerned with making sure that equal access for equal need is a core value for the delivery of publicly funded services. Access in terms of timing and geographic location are also embraced by this goal.

Objective 1: Eligibility for health and personal social services is clearly defined:

The system of eligibility for services within the health system is complex. Criteria are not always clear-cut and there may be inconsistencies in eligibility for certain services between different health board areas. These problems will be addressed in a review of current legislative provisions and in the preparation of new legislation suited to a modern health system. It is important to note that while the Health Act, 1970 explicitly provides for eligibility[1] for a service, it does not provide that a person is entitled to receive a service. This means that there is currently no statutory framework underpinning access to services within a stated timeframe. In preparing new legislation, the objective will be to move away from the rather theoretical model of 'eligibility', to a system of entitlement to services within a reasonable timeframe.

Eligibility for health services in Ireland is primarily based on residence and means. Health board CEOs have discretionary powers in regard to the medical card scheme. There are also a variety of other schemes which provide eligibility for various services for certain groups of the population.

Objective 2: Scope of eligibility framework is broadened:

The objectives of the various schemes are (i) to provide free medical care for people who are on low incomes; (ii) to provide some monetary relief to those with chronic illness or disability; and (iii) to provide support at particular times for vulnerable groups such as children and older people. The number of people covered by the medical card scheme will be increased significantly. Income guidelines will be extended to cover more people on low incomes and targeted increases will be implemented to ensure that more children are covered. In addition a number of other schemes, including the Maternity and Infant Care Scheme, will be extended.

Eligibility arrangements across a range of schemes need to be reviewed so as to ensure that criteria fully reflect the levels at which barriers to accessing care arise. Investment in the health of children was also identified as a priority.

Objective 3: Equitable access for all categories of patients in the health system is assured:

A core objective of this Strategy is that all people should have access to high-quality services. Many of the areas identified in this Strategy for development and reform concern all groups, irrespective of entitlements. However, it is clear that there are significant inequalities in the system at present which must be addressed, such as unacceptably long waiting times for public patients for some elective hospital procedures.

This Strategy outlines measures to ensure that all public patients can expect the high quality of service within a reasonable period of time. This includes a ten year programme for the largest ever concentrated increase in public acute hospital capacity.

There is also evidence that people have difficulties in obtaining timely, appropriate and user-friendly information about entitlements and how to access services. A more proactive approach to ensuring that people understand their entitlements will be developed. Other issues affecting people's ability to access services, transport to services, opening times, waiting times for appointments and appropriate waiting facilities are also dealt with.

- *All patients should have access to a high-quality service, within a reasonable period of time, irrespective of whether they are public or private patients.*

- *Public patients should also have access to the same range of publicly funded services irrespective of where they happen to live.*

Objective 1: Eligibility for health and personal social services is clearly defined

36 New legislation to provide for clear statutory provisions on entitlement will be introduced

Existing legislation will be reviewed to update and rationalise the framework for entitlement. The objective will be to provide a clear national framework for entitlement to health and personal social services. Guidelines will be published concerning target timeframes for access to various services. The programme of expansion and investment in services outlined in this Health Strategy will allow these timeframes to be reduced on a regular basis. The legislation will include provision for:

- the continuation of two categories of eligibility, i.e. medical card holders and others

- the definition of the full range of health and personal social services:

  - Medical card holders will be entitled to receive services free of charge within the shortest possible timeframe in accordance with need. People with medical cards will be eligible for all publicly funded health and personal social services

  - Non medical card holders will continue to be eligible for a subset of defined core services free of charge and will be subject to charges for the remainder (e.g. hospital and GP services). This will not represent any diminution of current entitlements for this group

- criteria to apply to the discretionary powers of CEOs in granting medical cards

- defined core services, free of charge for all, which will include:

  - childhood immunisations, developmental and school health services

  - The Maternity and Infant Care Scheme

  - specialist mental health services

  - disability support services

  - child care and family support services

  - substance abuse services

  - palliative care services

- a clear framework for financing of long-stay care for older people.

It is recognised that quality care is expensive and that the bulk of the cost of providing a high standard of quality care should be borne by the Exchequer. Nonetheless, it is fair that all those in receipt of publicly provided residential long-term care should make some payment towards accommodation and daily living costs, if they can afford to do so, just as they would if they were living in the community. This principle supports the aim to provide as high quality a service as possible and to make the most equitable use of resources and thus to help maximise the availability of these services.

Where the State encourages participation in evidence-based screening or preventive programmes, the aim will be to provide these free of charge. Such schemes would include preventive programmes and programmes to promote healthy lifestyles, breast cancer and cervical cancer screening programmes, and other screening programmes as the evidence base justifies their introduction.

37 Eligibility arrangements will be simplified and clarified

All groups

The guidelines for entitlement to medical cards will be simplified and clarified. In line with the recommendations of the recent review of the medical card system commissioned by the CEOs under the Programme for Prosperity and Fairness, this will ensure an improved, open and consistent framework for assessing eligibility for medical cards in all parts of the country. The health boards executive (HeBE) will monitor and evaluate medical card guidelines across the country and reduce as much as possible the need to exercise judgement on individual cases outside the guidelines.

Older people

In his report on the Nursing Home Subvention Scheme, the Ombudsman has drawn attention to the uncertainty surrounding the eligibility of older people for long-term residential care. Clarification of entitlement in this regard will be given particular attention in the general review of legislation on entitlement referred to above. Emphasis will also be placed on implementing a standard approach to dependency assessment and the payment of subventions in each area of the country.

People with disabilities

- The forthcoming Disabilities Bill will outline a statutory framework for the assessment of need and provision of services for people with disabilities.

- The Inter-Departmental Working Group examining the feasibility of introducing a Cost of Disability Payment will report during 2002. This will include a review of the wide range of existing allowances and concessions for people with disabilities.

Travellers and homeless people

Health boards will introduce standardised special arrangements regarding medical cards to cater for the needs of Travellers and homeless people.

Objective 2: Scope of eligibility framework is broadened

A number of measures are proposed to improve eligibility for health services in the following areas:

- access to medical cards

- scope of Maternity and Infant Care Scheme

- introduction of a home subvention scheme for the care of older people

- introduction of a respite care grant for dependent older persons

Having considered these proposals in the context of all of the actions outlined in the Strategy, the Government has committed itself to introducing these changes over a number of years.

The timing of their ntroduction will be determined by Government in the context of the prevailing budgetary situation.

38 Income guidelines for the medical card will be increased

The allocation of medical cards will be on the basis of prioritising groups most in need. In addition to the recent extension of eligibility to all persons over 70, significant improvements will be made in the income guidelines in order to increase the number of persons on low incomes who are eligible for a medical card and to give priority to families with children and particularly children with a disability. In line with the PPF review of the medical card scheme, it is proposed that the income threshold will be increased substantially and reviewed annually on an agreed basis. This would include taking account of changes in the cost of living and movement in relevant social welfare payments and allowances. The review also suggests that the basis for assessment should be net income.

39 The number and nature of GP visits for an infant under the Maternity and Infant Care Scheme will be extended

The number of free GP visits under the existing scheme will be increased from two to six for the first year of life and the additional visits will cover general childhood illnesses.

40 The Nursing Home Subvention Scheme will be amended to take account of the expenditure review of the scheme

A large number of older people would like the option of receiving care in the home rather than in a nursing home. The recent expenditure review of the nursing home subvention scheme has shown that current funding arrangements do not effectively support home care. The Government intends reforming the operation of existing schemes, including the Carers' Allowance, in order to introduce an integrated care subvention scheme which maximises support for home care. In addition, subvention rates payable in private nursing homes will be reviewed.

The Department of Health and Children will begin work immediately with the Department of Social, Community and Family Affairs to develop detailed proposals for the new scheme with a view to introduction as soon as possible.

41 A grant will be introduced to cover two weeks' respite care per annum for dependent older persons

The detailed arrangements for the operation of this scheme will be worked out with the Department of Social, Community and Family Affairs.

42 Proposals on the financing of long-term care for older people will be brought forward

Health care is just one aspect of the overall debate surrounding the funding of long-term care for older people. A major study on this topic, led by the Department of Social Community and Family Affairs, is nearing completion. Policy proposals will be prepared following publication of the consultancy report commissioned by the Department of Social Community and Family Affairs. Funding options to meet the cost of care will be outlined for public debate prior to preparation of legislation.

Objective 3: Equitable access for all categories of patients in the health system is assured

43 Improved access to hospital services for public patients will be addressed through a series of integrated measures

These measures, discussed in Chapter 5, are designed to reduce substantially the waiting times for public patients for elective treatments. Specific targets are set so that, by the end of 2004, no public patient will have to wait for more than three months to commence treatment, following referral from an out-patient department.

44 Availability of information on entitlements including use of information technology will be improved

Health boards will promote the uptake and utilisation of services by improving the availability of information on entitlements. Particular attention will be given to disadvantaged groups, older people and people with disabilities in order to help them to overcome existing barriers. Such barriers may include communication difficulties e.g. literacy or language deficits, or lack of knowledge of entitlements and services.

- A one-stop-shop approach to providing information on health and personal social services will be developed by the health boards in conjunction with Comhairle (the information, advice and advocacy agency). All available opportunities will be taken to raise awareness among at-risk groups by the wide dissemination of information leaflets at community level in health service and other appropriate facilities. In addition to ensuring good coverage, a range of appropriate information materials will be developed for disadvantaged groups including those with disabilities and ethnic minority groups.

- A variety of media, including information technology, will be used by all service providers to provide comprehensive information on services.

- Particular attention will be paid to the provision of translation and sign-language services for staff and patients where these are required.

45 All reasonable steps to make health facilities accessible will be taken

This action includes assessing and planning for transport needs where services cannot be provided locally. It also means taking all reasonable steps to make health facilities accessible to older people and people with disabilities, in line with the PPF commitment regarding access for people with disabilities.

46 Appointment planning arrangements will be reviewed to provide greater flexibility and specific appointment times

The 9am to 5pm nature of many health services and the absence of individual appointment times, particularly at out-patient clinics, have been strongly criticised. Specific initiatives will be taken on both issues as part of the wider programme to improve customer care under the Health Strategy.

47 Waiting areas in health facilities will be upgraded

Waiting areas will be upgraded to ensure that individuals waiting for treatment have easy access to basic facilities. This should take account of the needs of persons accompanying children or older people attending for treatment; as well as adults attending for treatment, who have young children with them. Upgrading should provide ample waiting space, play areas for children, baby-changing facilities and the availability of refreshments.

National Goal No. 3: Responsive and appropriate care delivery

The third goal aims to gear the health system to respond appropriately and adequately to the needs of individuals and families. It is also concerned with ensuring that the various parts of the system are being utilised to their maximum effectiveness and efficiency.

Objective 1: The patient is at the centre in the delivery of care:

One of the guiding principles of the Strategy is that of a people-centred health system. A responsive system must develop ways to engage with individuals and the wider community receiving services. At an individual level, there are now greater expectations about openness and shared decision-making in relation to individual care. Health care workers will be encouraged and facilitated to listen to and accommodate, as appropriate, the wishes of individual patients/clients. At community level, this means allowing the wider community to participate in decisions about services at national, regional and local level.

The health system must become more people-centred with the interests of the public, patients and clients being given greater prominence and influence in decision-making at all levels.

Objective 2: Appropriate care is delivered in the appropriate setting:

Some examples of people receiving services in an inappropriate setting are:

- children being treated in adult wards

- people with intellectual disability being cared for in psychiatric hospitals

- older people being cared for in acute hospitals due to unavailability of more appropriate extended care facilities or community supports

- mentally-ill patients being treated in large psychiatric hospitals unsuited to modern quality care.

Providing improved assessment, community support and rehabilitation services is essential to ensuring care is delivered in the most appropriate setting.

Action will be taken to ensure that the care required is delivered in the appropriate setting. This objective is also concerned with empowering and encouraging communities to become more involved in the provision of informal care in the community.

Objective 3: The system has the capacity to deliver timely and appropriate services:

There is increasing evidence that the system does not have the capacity to meet the current demands being placed on it. Additional investment across the system will be necessary. Also, a reorientation of existing services to meet needs more appropriately and responsively will help to gain better value from available capacity in some areas.

The concerns about capacity and the configuration of services underline the need for ongoing capital investment, expansion of acute hospital services and substantial strengthening of primary care and community services.

Objective 1: The patient is at the centre in the delivery of care

48 A national standardised approach to measurement of patient satisfaction will be introduced

The need to capture customer feedback in a more structured way has been identified as an essential input to policy planning. Routine patient satisfaction surveys and systematic collection and analysis of complaints will be undertaken. The results of this feedback will be made available to the public and will inform local decision-making processes.

49 Best practice models of customer care including a statutory system of complaint handling will be introduced

The vision adopted for the future health system places a high value on treating people with dignity and respect. The Ombudsman already investigates complaints of maladministration against the Department of Health and Children and the health boards. The Government believes that the existing Ombudsman is the appropriate person to deal with complaints relating to the health system. The Government's aim is to extend the role of the Ombudsman to voluntary hospitals and other voluntary agencies in the health area and the legal implications of this step are currently being examined. Complaints against professionals may be made to relevant professional bodies and this area also needs to be strengthened. Complaints procedures at local level also need to be formalised. Action will be taken to strengthen the customer focus of service providers. This will include:

- development of standardised customer services strategies by health boards to ensure a national standard. These plans should have particular regard to the diversity of service users, the particular needs of certain groups and the need for a culturally sensitive approach

- implementation of standardised customer care plans by all service providers

- development of a statutory framework for complaints. Legislation will be prepared by the Department of Health and Children to provide for a statutory complaints procedure. This framework will provide for greater clarity and uniformity of approach in dealing with complaints, structured local resolution processes as well as the opportunity for independent review.

One of the areas which attracts particular criticism in this context is the perceived inability to question the actions or decisions taken by individual practitioners in regard to clinical matters. While acknowledging the need for freedom in exercising clinical judgement, the Government also accepts the need for a stronger framework for questioning and investigating clinical decisions in particular circumstances. Accordingly, the forthcoming legislation on statutory registration of health professionals (discussed in Chapter 5) will contain adequate machinery for the investigation of complaints against individual professionals.

50 Individuals and families will be supported and encouraged to be involved in the management of their own health care

The vision of the future health system is one that 'encourages you to have your say, listens to you, and ensures your views are taken into account.' Health and social care personnel must encourage shared decision-making and, where possible, accommodate patient preferences. This will involve improved communication between health care professionals and patients and clients. For example, doctors should discuss fully the risks and benefits of a treatment and ensure the patient understands any alternative options available.

Communication skills and an appreciation of the need to strike an appropriate balance between the responsibilities of the practitioner, and the views and preferences of patients, will be strengthened in the training programmes for health care professionals. Professional bodies will be asked to devise codes of practice for shared decision-making for clinical care areas. In addition, the Health Information and Quality Authority will examine the introduction of computer 'decision aids' to provide an interactive approach to transmitting information to patients.

51   An integrated approach to care planning for individuals will become a consistent feature of the system

Lack of integration of care between and even within some services is identified as a problem in the existing services. Individual patients or clients may have to access the system several times to have all their needs addressed. This may apply within the hospital system where individuals have needs involving a number of specialties. If the system is to be responsive to the needs of individuals, it is important that a holistic approach is taken to planning and delivering care. This will include:

- greater communication and liaison between individual clinicians within services and across services

- development of care management approaches involving packages of care for groups with multiple needs

- appointment of key workers in the context of care planning, in particular dependent older people such as those on the margins of home and residential care; and children with disabilities.

52   Provision will be made for the participation of the community in decisions about the delivery of health and personal social services

While there are some community participation initiatives already operating in discrete areas of activity at national and regional level, a more structured approach to community participation is required. Such participation has a number of important advantages. The following actions will be taken:

- Initiatives will be taken to inform and educate the public about the health system including greater communication about the choices and competing priorities which feature in the decision-making process.

- Regional Advisory Panels/Co-ordinating Committees (including service providers and consumers) will be established in all health board areas (i) for older consumers and their carers to provide them with a voice and (ii) for people with mental illness to advise on the planning and prioritisation of services, quality of services and promotion of positive mental health initiatives. These committees will be modelled on similar developments in the area of disability services and include representation of statutory and voluntary service providers as well as consumers.

- Randomly selected consumer panels will be convened at regular intervals in each health board area to allow the public to have their say in health matters that concern them locally.

- A National Consultative Forum will be established to meet on an annual basis to monitor the implementation of the Health Strategy.

Objective 2: Appropriate care is delivered in the appropriate setting

53   Initiatives will be developed and implemented to ensure that care is delivered in the most appropriate setting

The underlying principle will be concerned with 'the right care in the right place at the right time'. At present eligibility arrangements and availability of community-based services may encourage people to seek care in a setting that is not appropriate to their needs, e.g. persons who attend at Accident and Emergency (A&E) departments where there is an option to visit their GP.

- Developing the capacity of primary care to deliver a range of care will be a key element in progressing this objective. The implementation of a new model of primary care and the structured programme of investment to support it is outlined in Chapter 5 and also in an accompanying document entitled *Primary Care: A New Direction*.

- Systems in hospitals will be reviewed to enhance clinical pathways. This will be aimed at improving the flow of patients through A&E departments, diagnostic services and the hospital generally.

- Charges can influence the way people use services. An examination of the levels of, and collection arrangements for, charges for service use will be undertaken.

54 Community and voluntary activity in maintaining health will be supported

The Government White Paper on Supporting Voluntary Activity makes a number of recommendations. As a priority:

- programmes to support informal caregivers through the development of informal networks, the provision of basic training and the greater availability of short-term respite care will be developed and implemented

- programmes to foster voluntarism and community responsiveness to local needs will be undertaken.

The 'first responder' service will be developed in the area of pre-hospital emergency care to enhance existing emergency care services. First responders are generally members of the public who have been trained in basic life support and who are available, usually in a rural environment, to respond in emergency medical situations.

In addition, arrangements will be made by health boards to streamline funding for voluntary groups with a national remit.

Objective 3: The system has the capacity to deliver timely and appropriate services

55 A programme of investment to provide the necessary capacity in primary care, acute hospital and other services will begin

Details of the build-up of primary care and acute hospital capacity and system reforms which underpin the achievement of this objective are set out in Chapter 5 – The Frameworks for Change. Key areas for development which have been identified include the following:

Programme of investment to increase capacity

Primary care (details in Chapter 5)

- New model of primary care involving teams and associated networks to be put in place

- Extension of GP co-operatives on a national basis.

Acute hospital capacity (details in Chapter 5)

- An additional 3,000 beds to be provided, of which 650 will come on stream in 2002

Older people

Community services

- Recruitment of a multi-disciplinary range of staff to support the development of primary care services such as domiciliary care, day and respite services

- The provision of 7,000 additional day centre places

- Increased funding for aids and appliances in people's homes.

Hospital services

- 1,370 additional assessment and rehabilitation beds; associated development of acute geriatric medical services and appointment of additional geriatricians

- 600 additional day places with facilities encompassing specialist areas such as falls, osteoporosis treatment, fracture prevention, Parkinson's Disease, stroke prevention, heart failure and continence promotion clinics.

Residential care

- 800 additional extended care/community nursing unit places per annum over the next 7 years including provision for people with dementia

- Improved staffing levels in extended care units.

Mental health

- Community care services, i.e. community nursing; day centres, hostels and day hospitals, training and work programmes; family support

- Acute psychiatric units.

Intellectual disability and autism services

- Expansion of day places, training, residential and respite care and other support services (e.g. in settings such as schools)

- Complete programme to transfer people with an intellectual disability currently in psychiatric hospitals to appropriate accommodation as soon as possible and not later than end 2006

- Investment to provide appropriate support services for people with autism; an information system to provide accurate data on the numbers of persons with autism and their service needs to be established as soon as possible.

Physical and sensory disability services

- Home support services, respite care, day care places, residential care including additional places for people with chronic conditions

- Training

- Other multi-disciplinary support services

- Aids and appliances.

In addition to physical resources of buildings, beds and equipment, the necessary number of skilled people will also be required to enable beds and facilities to be fully and safely utilised. A developmental approach to human resources aimed at rapid expansion in the numbers of people trained is central to the effective implementation of this Strategy. This is dealt with in detail in Chapter 5 – The Frameworks for Change.

56 The Cancer Forum and the Advisory Forum on Cardiovascular Health will work with the National Hospitals Agency and the Health Information and Quality Authority to ensure service quality, accessibility and responsiveness

Building on work which is already under way, services and facilities which should be available in treatment centres at national, regional and local level for people with cancer and cardiovascular disease will be identified. Furthermore, the requirements at these levels to develop, implement and evaluate evidence-based practice guidelines and protocols will be outlined. These guidelines and protocols will cover prevention, treatment, rehabilitation and palliative care in both community and institutional settings. Appropriate outcome and performance indicators will also be developed.

57 Measures to provide the highest standard of pre-hospital emergency care/ambulance services will be advanced

The findings of the review of the ambulance services currently being undertaken by the health boards and the Eastern Regional Health Authority, together with the recommendations of the Report of the Review Group on the Ambulance Services (1993), the Comptroller and Auditor General's Report on the Emergency Ambulance Services (1997) and the Report of the Joint HSEA/SIPTU Working Group on Ambulance Services (2001) will inform further investment in the ambulance and emergency service.

Areas to be targeted will include:

- ongoing upgrading of the ambulance fleet

- 24 hour on-duty staffing for all ambulance stations

- crewing of all ambulances with emergency medical technicians

- strengthening of IT links between ambulances and A and E departments

- augmentation of current response capability

- introduction of first responder schemes, involving general practitioners and voluntary personnel

- development of a dedicated emergency ambulance service through the separation, where appropriate, of emergency and routine work

- strengthening of the performance management function, with an emphasis on audit and monitoring of response times

- ongoing training in the use of defribillators.

The Pre-Hospital Emergency Care Council will build on existing strengths by further developing professional and performance standards and training in the area of pre-hospital care. This will include advice on the introduction of advanced Emergency Medical Technician training, training for GPs and other health-care professionals in life support, and development of, and training in the use of, clinical protocols for the treatment of acutely ill or injured patients.

A study will be commissioned, under the auspices of the Working Group on Pre-Hospital Emergency Care established under the Good Friday Agreement, into the feasibility of an all-island Helicopter Emergency Medical Service (HEMS).

The health boards will undertake a review of the existing major emergency function with a view to ensuring that a comprehensive and common response is provided across the health service in the event of a major emergency.

58 A plan to provide responsive, high-quality maternity care will be drawn up

Four out of five women utilise the maternity services during their reproductive years. Models of maternity care are changing, with increasing demands for choice with regard to type of care and location of birth. In recognition of the changing needs and pressures on existing services, a working party will be established to prepare a plan for the future development of the maternity services. The objective will be to ensure that maternity care in Ireland is:

- woman-centred

- equitable across different parts of the country

- accessible to all

- safe

- accountable.

59 A review of paediatric services will be undertaken

The review will focus on the future organisation and delivery of hospital services for children. The aim will be to enhance the range and level of services available at regional level and to determine the most effective configuration of tertiary services. The scope for developing certain highly specialised services on an all-Ireland basis will also be explored.

60 A national review of renal services will be undertaken

The purpose of the review will be to develop a framework to meet anticipated growth in demand for renal services including the following objectives:

- to ensure that regional dialysis centres are adequately resourced to give patients access to services close to their own home

- to ensure the availability of consultant-led nephrology services in all regions

- to widen the availability of alternative dialysis treatment programmes to allow patients to manage their dialysis care at home.

61 Organ transplantation services will be further developed

Arrangements will be put in place to facilitate the further development of organ transplantational services. The aim will be to strengthen organ procurement and retrieval practices and to increase organ donation awareness and organ utilisation rates. Stronger links will be forged between Irish and UK transplantation services.

62 Specialist dental services will be expanded

The overall objectives of dental health policy as set out in the Dental Action Plan of 1994 were:

- to reduce the level of dental disease in children

- to improve the level of oral health in the population overall

- to provide adequate treatment services to children, medical card holders and persons over 70.

These objectives have largely been met. The available evidence demonstrates significant improvements in the oral health of the general population in recent years. Preventive programmes, including oral health promotion programmes, are being developed and, following review of the Dental Health Action Plan, new goals for oral health will be formulated. The objective of the orthodontic service is to provide timely treatment to patients most in need. Patients with less severe needs will be treated as quickly as the availability of trained specialists allows. A new grade of Specialist in Orthodontics has been created and training programmes have been put in place so that dentists can reach specialist level. A special needs-based approach will be taken to developing dental services over the next five to seven years, as follows:

- A plan for the delivery of specialist dental services on a prioritised basis will be prepared and implemented

- Areas of specialisation in dentistry will be approved and publicly funded specialist training programmes will be established in these areas

- The services of orthodontists in the private sector will be used on a more widespread basis. This, together with additional sessions by health board specialist staff, will enable the treatment of a further 3,500 patients annually.

National Goal No. 4: High performance

The fourth goal relates to quality of care, planning and decision-making, the efficiency and effectiveness of the system, commitment to continuous improvement and full accountability. The principles of quality and accountability are embraced by the objectives identified under this goal.

Objective 1: Standardised quality systems support best patient care and safety:

This objective is concerned with ensuring that the quality and safety of care in the Irish health system meet agreed standards and are regularly evaluated/benchmarked. This does not imply that the current quality of care in the health system is poor. However, the systems necessary to agree standards and establish whether those standards are being met do not generally exist. Regular review of quality standards supports and encourages a culture of continuous improvement – an essential component in a sector where new technology and social and demographic trends require the system to be flexible and responsive to changing needs and priorities.

Improving system performance requires:

- *development of standardised quality systems to support best patient care*

- *development of an evidence-based, strategic approach at all levels in the system.*

A quality outlook must underpin the planning, management and delivery of services within the health system. Quality can then be measured and demonstrated in an objective way.

Objective 2: Evidence and strategic objectives underpin all planning/decision making:

The health system is very complex and requires managerial and operational decisions to be made in many different organisations at many different levels. This objective is concerned with ensuring that the Strategy's high-level goals are put into effect. In addition, evidence of effectiveness must inform the policy and decision-making process across the health system. An evidence-based approach will ensure clearer accountability and support improved outcomes generally.

Quality and continuous improvement must be embedded in daily practice to ensure consistently high standards.

Objective 1: Standardised quality systems support best patient care and safety

63   Quality systems will be integrated and expanded throughout the health system

- National standards and protocols for quality care, patient safety and risk management will be drawn up for all health and personal social services. While driven centrally, these standards will be developed on a partnership basis with relevant stakeholders and will be updated regularly.

Priority areas for quality/safety standards

- National standards for community and long-term residential care of older people

- National standards for residential care of people with disabilities

- Protocols and standards in relation to the care of children in hospital

- Chronic disease management protocols

- Record protocols to improve vaccine traceability.

- Quality assurance mechanisms will be introduced as a means of improving performance and preventing problems using a structured set of planned and systematic activities such as documentation, training and review. This approach will allow the quality of services to be benchmarked as well as improving consistency, increasing accountability and ensuring that good practices are spread throughout the system.

- A Hospital Accreditation Programme has already been introduced in a number of the major acute teaching hospitals and this will be extended. Before the end of 2001, a statutory agency will be established to operate a scheme of hospital accreditation, initially in the major academic teaching hospitals. The scheme will be patient-focused and will promote continuous quality improvement and safety. The aim will be that all hospitals (public and private) will participate. Similar accreditation programmes will be introduced for other care settings. Performance will be assessed against agreed written standards, using a system of external peer review. Accreditation processes will include facilities and standards of both clinical and management practice.

- The Social Services Inspectorate (SSI) will be established on a statutory basis. The remit of the SSI will be extended to include residential care for people with disabilities and older people.

- Risk management is a vital tool in reducing the incidence of avoidable medical error. Government proposals to establish new arrangements for handling clinical negligence claims will allow for better control of the costs but more importantly, facilitate the introduction of improved risk management strategies.

- The development of a framework in which quality is a central tenet will require considerable investment in information systems as well as a comprehensive, centrally driven, integrated approach. These issues are dealt with in detail in Chapter 5.

64   A review of medicines legislation will be undertaken

A complete review of medicines legislation is required so as to provide more effectively for the implementation of EU directives and regulations on medicinal products including appropriate provisions relating to unlicensed medicines.

65   Licensing of alternative medicines will be examined

The European Union is developing a traditional herbal medicines directive that will be transcribed into Irish law. As this is expected to be a slow process, Ireland is developing an interim national licensing scheme for 'traditional and alternative' medicinal products including herbal medicinal products. It is important to establish such a licensing process to ensure the safety of herbal/traditional medicinal products. The Irish Medicines Board is working closely with the Department in formulating an appropriate scheme of regulation for alternative medicines.

66 The highest international standards of safety in transfusion medicine will be set and adhered to

Substantial investment has been made in recent years to ensure that blood safety in Ireland is comparable to the highest standards internationally. The Irish Blood Transfusion Service will continue to be supported in maintaining international standards of safety and quality.

There will be a major drive to develop alternatives to the use of donated blood. Clinical protocols will be developed and hospitals will be resourced to develop pre-deposit autologous transfusion, cell salvage, anaesthetic and pharmacological strategies to reduce the need for blood transfusion.

There will be a significant increase in the number of consultant haematologists to provide clinical leadership and to promote these developments.

67 Legislation on assisted human reproduction will be prepared

Following completion of the Report of the Commission on Assisted Human Reproduction and its presentation to Government, legislation will be prepared to give effect to the recommendations of the Commission as approved by Government.

Objective 2: Evidence and strategic objectives underpin all planning/ decision-making

68 Decisions across the health system will be based on best available evidence

An evidence-based approach forms an essential element of the quality agenda outlined in this Strategy. This action provides that all decisions will be based on some form of evidence. Decisions will be based on

• research findings

• statistical qualitative or quantitative data

• other documented trends and behaviours.

Decisions in all areas must be supported by reference to this kind of evidence or to agreed standards, protocols or models of best practice. This action will apply across the health system in both clinical and non-clinical areas. A Health Information and Quality Authority will be established to drive the quality agenda at national level. The functions of the new authority are set out in detail in Chapter 5.

69 An information/education campaign will be undertaken for all decision-makers in the health system on the Strategy's goals and objectives

The Department of Health and Children and the health boards have a broad range of responsibilities. This leads to potential conflict and competition for resources between different services. It is important that decision-makers within the system, and those interacting with decision-makers, understand the objectives outlined in this Strategy and recognise that all providers in receipt of Exchequer funding will be working towards these priorities for the next 7-10 years.

A detailed information campaign will be carried out to ensure that all stakeholders are familiar with the goals and objectives of the Strategy and the priority developments contained in it.

70 Accountability will be strengthened through further development of the service planning process

Service planning has been introduced in all health board areas. This involves the preparation each year of a service plan which is formally adopted by the board, setting out the service goals to be achieved within budget. This process is underpinned by the Health Amendment Act (No 3), 1996, which places statutory accountability and responsibilities on the chief executive officer of each board. In line with Government policy, the Department of Health and Children will formally set out a statement of national priorities for health, which will then be addressed by the health boards in preparing their individual service plans. This approach together with the use of clear performance indicators will provide a stronger framework for assessment by the Department of the performance of health boards on an annual basis.

Overall, there will be a stronger focus by the Department on monitoring the achievement of deliverables outlined in the service plans. This action will make the service development and planning process a more sophisticated tool for planning based on strategic objectives shared by all health boards. Ultimately, it will provide for greater consistency between health boards, and in the context of the development of the Health Boards Executive Agency, the opportunity for maximum cross-fertilisation of best practice initiatives, expertise and knowledge. Standard formats and performance indicators for service plans will be agreed as part of this process.

71 Each health board will develop implementation plans

This action will ensure that the appropriate links are developed between the annual service plans referred to above, longer-term policy goals and the objectives outlined in the Strategy. The implementation plans will match the Strategy and policy objectives set by the Department with individual health boards' targets and objectives. The implementation plans, which will cover a three to five year time scale, will enable health boards to communicate to the Department, the public and their staff how they intend to implement national policies. In addition, performance indicators will be set nationally by which the implementation of the Strategy's objectives at health board level can be assessed.

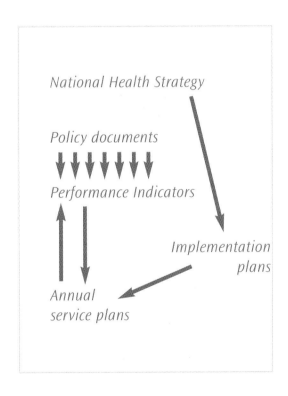

National Health Strategy

Policy documents

Performance Indicators

Implementation plans

Annual service plans

Annual service plans, when identifying service delivery for that year, will take account of the resources available to meet the board's implementation plan.

The involvement of staff in service planning will be advanced in this context, ensuring that this is an inclusive process.

A holistic view will be taken in the development of performance indicators to ensure that policy implementation in one area does not have a negative impact on policies in other areas.

72 Service agreements between the health boards and the voluntary sector will be extended to all service providers and associated performance indicators will be introduced

The development of specific service agreements with providers will bring greater clarity and accountability to the delivery of services. These are developed in some areas but need to be made more specific and extended to all arrangements between voluntary providers and health boards. Performance indicators will also be introduced to measure outcomes against funding provided to voluntary providers.

73 Health research will continue to be developed to support information and quality initiatives

The development of an evidence-based approach is relevant to all of the national goals. The implementation of the Strategy must include support for health research, with particular reference to supporting health professionals who wish to carry out research on identified needs and the speedy application of findings where appropriate to improve service delivery. In addition, access to and the dissemination of findings to assist the relevant health service workers must be improved. The recently published Health Research Strategy (2001) provides the framework within which investment in health research will be made.

An active research environment also plays an important part in attracting graduates to the Irish health workforce. Better post-graduate research opportunities abroad and the opportunity to work with the most advanced technologies has led many Irish graduates to emigrate in the past. Providing the same opportunities in the Irish health system is important in retaining the best of Irish skills and talent at home. Ensuring existing professional staff benefit from and contribute to the development of the latest technologies and research is also an important factor in making the health system an employer of choice.

National Health Research Strategy – key elements

The Strategy proposes a thriving research culture supported by two complementary but distinct pillars:

- Establishment of a research and development function within the health services

- Enhanced support for science for health.

The proposed research and development function in the health services will involve new structures including:

- the appointment of a Research and Development Officer in the Department of Health and Children to provide central leadership to health research policy

- the appointment of Research and Development Officers in health boards and in specialist health agencies

- the establishment of a Forum for Health and Social Care Research to advise on agreed research agendas addressing the main objectives of the health services.

Enhanced support for science for health will require increased resources through the Health Research Board for competitive, peer-reviewed research of high scientific value in the biological and health sciences. This would involve more support for research units, project grants, fellowships and career awards, clinical research centres, equipment, information technology and biological banks.

The framework proposed is built on the foundation of partnership and provides a structure for much greater co-operation between the interests involved. It also recognises the added-value to be gained from co-operation in research for the island of Ireland as a whole.

CHAPTER 5

The frameworks for change

The frameworks

Chapter 4 identifies four national goals and sets out a series of actions to help achieve them. In addition, the health system needs to be reformed and developed so that the national goals can be achieved. This chapter details a series of essential actions under six frameworks for change. The six areas are as follows:

Strengthening primary care

The framework for primary care is concerned with developing a properly integrated system, capable of delivering the full range of health and personal social services appropriate to this setting. Primary care must become the central focus of the health system so that it can help achieve better outcomes and better health status.

Reform of acute hospital system

The overall policy objective for the reform of acute hospitals is improved access for public patients. The reforms involve increasing capacity through further investment, strengthening efficiency and quality of services, and working in closer partnership with the private hospital sector.

Funding

The framework for funding is aimed at improving access and responsiveness in the system by increasing capacity, and at improving performance through evidence-based funding methods such as casemix budgeting, improved accountability and stronger incentives for efficiency.

Developing human resources

The framework for human resources is aimed at harnessing fully the vital contribution made by all staff working in the health system, through further development of all aspects of the human resource function throughout the health services.

Organisational reform

The framework for organisational reform is aimed at providing a responsive, adaptable health system which meets the needs of the population effectively and at affordable cost.

Information

The framework for information is aimed at improving performance by supporting quality, planning and evidence-based decision-making in the health system. Good information systems will also support equity of access.

Framework	Key elements
Strengthening primary care	• A new comprehensive model of primary care to meet the needs of patients and clients in an integrated way, based on close teamwork between health professionals and direct access to services • Close coordination and integration between primary and hospital services • Immediate investment in GP co-operatives • A task force to oversee the phased implementation of the model over the lifetime of the Health Strategy
Reform of acute hospital system	• Additional acute bed capacity to reflect growing needs • A National Hospitals Agency to advise on the configuration and location of acute hospital services • Initiatives to make access for public patients fairer by addressing unacceptably long waiting times, clarifying hospital entitlements and streamlining management of services • Closer strategic links with private hospital sector
Funding	• Continued targeted investment in the health system using an evidence-based approach and prioritised programmes • Transparent systems for funding services, including further development of casemix budget model • Funding linked to service plans, outcomes and incentives for efficiency • Multi-annual budgeting for selected long-term programmes • Annual statements to be published on funding process and criteria
Developing human resources	• Competent, qualified workforce in order to meet growing demands through more active workforce planning and maximising recruitment and retention • The health services to become an employer of choice by developing the HR function, investing in education and training and implementing best practice employment policies • An Action Plan for People Management to develop these initiatives further
Organisational reform	• Department of Health and Children restructured • Health boards focused on a programme of change management • An independent Health Information and Quality Authority set up • A comprehensive independent audit of the structures and functions of the health system to determine the scope for rationalisation of bodies and to improve governance
Information	• Appropriate, comprehensive, high-quality, accessible and timely information on which to plan and organise the health system • Investment in national health information systems as set out in the forthcoming National Health Information Strategy • Development of electronic health record to enhance the quality and safety of care

Strengthening primary care

Introduction

Primary care is the first point of contact people have with the health and personal social services. This Strategy sets out a new direction for primary care as the central focus of the delivery of health and personal social services. It promotes a team-based approach to service provision which will help to provide a fully integrated primary care service. Full details of the new model are contained in an accompanying document, *Primary Care: A New Direction*.

- **Primary care** is an approach to care that includes a range of services designed to keep people well, from promotion of health and screening for disease to assessment, diagnosis, treatment and rehabilitation as well as personal social services. The services provide first-level contact that is fully accessible by self-referral and have a strong emphasis on working with communities and individuals to improve their health and social well-being.

- Primary care includes the range of services that are currently provided by general practitioners (GPs), public health nurses, social workers, practice nurses, midwives, community mental health nurses, dieticians, dentists, community welfare officers, physiotherapists, occupational therapists, home helps, health care assistants, speech and language therapists, chiropodists, community pharmacists, psychologists and others.

Discussion

There are many positive aspects to the current system of primary care. There is same-day access to many primary care professionals, and there have been valuable recent developments such as co-operative working for general practitioners on an out-of-hours basis. In addition, the commitment of individual professionals and their professional organisations has ensured that the public has been able to obtain a good service.

However, the current system has significant weaknesses. Primary care infrastructure is poorly developed; services are fragmented with little teamwork; there are insufficient numbers of trained staff in key areas; liaison between primary and secondary care is often poor; and many services provided in hospitals could be provided more appropriately in primary care. General practitioners can be isolated from many other community services. Communication and work sharing with other primary care professionals is not always readily facilitated or supported. There is also an under-development of primary care services out-of-hours.

Conclusions

Primary care must become the central focus of the health system. It is the appropriate setting to meet 90-95 per cent of all health and personal social services needs. A properly integrated primary care service can lead to better outcomes, better health status and better cost effectiveness. Properly developed primary care services can help prevent or reduce the impact of conditions that might later require hospitalisation and can also facilitate earlier hospital discharge. Overall the strengthened primary care system will have a major impact in reducing demand for specialist services and the hospital system, particularly accident and emergency and out-patient services.

The policy aim is to develop the capacity of primary care to meet the full range of health and personal social service needs appropriate to that setting. This will involve significantly enhanced funding for the development of primary care, in terms of staff, physical infrastructure, information and communication systems and diagnostic support.

Primary care model: a summary

The new model of primary care will have the following main features:

Primary care team

An inter-disciplinary team-based approach to primary care will be introduced. Members of the primary care team will include GPs, nurses, midwives, health care assistants, home helps, physiotherapists, occupational therapists, social workers and administrative personnel. Teams will serve small population groups of approximately 3,000 to 7,000 people depending on whether a region is rural or urban.

Primary care network

A wider primary care network of other primary care professionals such as speech and language therapists, community pharmacists, dieticians, community welfare officers, dentists, chiropodists and psychologists will also provide services for the enrolled population of each primary care team. Clear communication links will be set up between the primary care team and named professionals within the wider network.

Inter-disciplinary approach

An inter-disciplinary team approach will help to develop the capacity of primary care to ensure that a higher percentage of patients can be cared for in the community. The wide skill mix within the team will allow a more appropriate distribution of workload, allowing each team member to work to their maximum professional capacity. It will also facilitate communication between team members, reducing time spent trying to contact other primary care providers.

Information and communications technology

There will be considerable investment in information and communications technology infrastructure to support the new model of primary care. This will include an electronic patient record, based on a unique personal client number. It will also include electronic health-related information and services for professionals and the public.

Enrolment with primary care team

All individuals will be encouraged but not required to enrol with one primary care team, and with a particular GP within the team. Enrolment will be voluntary. The benefits of enrolling with a team will include better continuity of care, improved co-ordination of services, and more attention to preventive services. Enrolment will not reduce people's choice of provider and patients will be free to seek care wherever they wish. Different members of a family will be able to enrol with different teams or with different doctors within the team. The system will also allow people to change their nominated team or doctor. Where appropriate for a patient or client, a key worker will be identified. The team will provide care to a defined group of people.

Access to the primary care team

Individuals will be entitled to self-refer to a given member of the primary care team. For those wishing to use it, triage and referral at the point of access to the system will ensure that people can be linked with the most appropriate professional. Building on the strengths of the co-operative model for general practitioners will improve access to primary care services, particularly out of hours.

Primary care co-operatives

Further development of current GP co-operative models will take place on a national basis over the next two years as a key support to the enhanced availability of a defined range of primary care services on a 24-hour basis. Along with medical cover, it is planned to extend this to 24-hour cover encompassing nursing services, health care assistants and home helps, leading to the development of primary care co-operatives.

Integration of primary care team with specialist services

Improved integration between primary care teams and specialist services will be developed. Local arrangements will cover referral protocols, direct access to diagnostic facilities, discharge plans, individual care plans, integrated care pathways and shared care arrangements. Primary care teams can then more appropriately provide much of the care currently provided by specialist services.

Community-based diagnostic centres

Community-based diagnostic centres will be piloted to support primary care and community-based care. These will be evaluated on the basis of their ability to provide more accessible services and their cost-effectiveness in terms of reducing the pressure on hospital-based diagnostic facilities. In this regard, the potential of public-private partnerships will be actively explored.

Location of primary care team

A 'one-stop-shop' is the ultimate goal, although buildings and infrastructural implications mean that team members may not be housed together initially. Effective electronic communications and electronic record systems mean that a single location will not be required for communication between team members.

Actions

The new model of primary care will be implemented on a phased basis through implementation projects located around the country. The model will be refined and developed by agreement in partnership with all stakeholders. The model will depend on adequate information and communications technology infrastructure and on the ability and willingness of all parties to utilise available technologies. Availability of relevant personnel will also be a crucial factor. In the short term, reliance will be on existing human resources to get implementation projects up and running. Immediately, there will be a concentration on full development of GP co-operatives, the identification of the first set of implementation sites and an increased number of training places in the relevant disciplines.

The key actions in primary care will be as follows:

74 A new model of primary care will be developed

The detailed description of the new model, *Primary Care: A New Direction*, is being published alongside this Strategy, and will be circulated to all key stakeholders. The model described sets out the principles for progress; it does not purport to address all of the detailed issues that will need to be worked through in the implementation phases. This will require consultation on an ongoing basis with all the relevant stakeholders. The model will be implemented on a phased basis over a two to ten-year timeframe.

75 A National Primary Care Task Force will be established

A small full-time task force will be established to take responsibility for driving the implementation of the changes and developments set out in the model. The task force will be inter-disciplinary and will report to a wider representative Steering Group which will be chaired by the Department of Health and Children and include representation from health boards, primary care professional groups, unions, and other relevant stakeholders. The task force will focus on

- driving the implementation of the primary care model as outlined in this Strategy

- identifying representative locations for the implementation projects

- planning human resources, information and communications technology and capital requirements for primary care on a national basis

- putting in place a framework for the extension of GP co-operatives on a national basis with specific reference to payment methods and operational processes.

The Steering Group will give leadership in

- defining a broad set of primary care services which should be provided by primary care teams

- co-ordinating the development of quality initiatives in primary care

- identifying locations for the establishment of academic centres of primary care as a source of policy and practice advice

- developing a national framework for achieving closer integration with the secondary care system

- providing policy advice to the Department of Health and Children, health boards and other bodies as appropriate

- evaluating progress, including an annual report on implementation on the basis of an agreed set of performance indicators.

76 Implementation projects will be put in place

Locations for implementation projects will be chosen in each health board region for the development of primary care teams over the next two to four years (40-60 teams nationally). The concentration in the initial stages will be in locations where there is already evidence of successful partnership and co-operation between general practice and health board services. Evaluation of these implementation projects will inform the further phased development of teams in remaining parts of the country which will lead to the development of 400-600 teams to cover approximately two-thirds of the population by 2011.

77 Investment will be made in extension of GP co-operatives and other specific national initiatives to complement the primary care model

In the short-term, GP co-operatives will be established on a national basis so that effective out-of-hours services are available in all parts of the country. In addition, other specific developments on a national basis will include:

- general increases in personnel needed for primary care teams and wider networks leading to improved out-of-hours services

- new physical infrastructure and equipment

- improvements in information and communications technology.

Reform of acute hospital system

Introduction

The acute hospital system faces ever-increasing demands. In 2001 the acute hospital system will provide treatment for over 550,000 people on an in-patient basis and a further 320,000 people on a day basis. These figures represent a growth in service provision of more than 20 per cent since 1995. In addition, there will be over 2 million out-patient attendances in acute hospitals in 2001, an increase of 8 per cent since 1995, and some 1.2 million visits to casualty departments, an increase of 6 per cent since 1994.

Discussion

Capacity and organisation

The number of acute hospital in-patient beds in Ireland has decreased from 17,665 in 1980 to 11,862 in 2000. This represents just 3.1 beds per 1,000 population, compared to 5.1 beds per 1,000 population in 1980. Despite the reduction in bed numbers, activity levels were increased by steps such as reducing average lengths of stay (from 9.7 days in 1980 to 6.6 in 2000), and increasing the use of day beds and availing of new technology.

International evidence shows that an increasing proportion of certain procedures, both medical and surgical, can be carried out on a day basis. There has been a huge growth of one-day procedures in Ireland. In 1980, approximately 8,000 day case treatments were recorded, constituting only 2 per cent of hospital activity in Ireland. In 2000, day activity accounted for 38 per cent of acute hospital activity (excluding out-patient departments) and 65 per cent of elective activity. These proportions are even higher in some of the larger hospitals. The growth in day-case activity offers considerable advantages: it reduces the time patients have to spend in hospital and frees up beds for other patients, including those on waiting lists. However, there are noticeable variations between Irish hospitals in the proportion of procedures provided on a day basis. In addition, based on international comparisons, there would appear to be scope for further increases in day activity in Irish hospitals.

Numbers of beds

It has become increasingly apparent that it will not be possible to sustain further overall increases in activity without expanding bed numbers. The Department of Health and Children, in conjunction with the Department of Finance and in consultation with the Social Partners, has carried out a detailed study of acute hospital bed requirements for the ten-year period to 2011. The study examined current capacity and activity and developed a framework for estimating future bed requirements, taking account of current pressures, changing demographics, increasing demand and potential changes to clinical practice over the next ten years. The study highlights the need for a significant expansion of hospital beds and associated staff and treatment facilities in the years ahead.

Increases in the total population, including a rise in the number of older people, and overall growth in demand for services, underline the need for additional capacity. In 2000, people over 65 years constituted 11 per cent of the population but consumed 46 per cent of the in-patient bed days. This is of major significance for hospital services in view of the projected increases in the number of older people. By 2011 the population aged 65 and over will have increased to 503,900. By 2026 this group will have almost doubled in number to an estimated 767,300, constituting 16.4 per cent of the population.

Efficiency, equity and the mix between public and private care

Waiting times for public patients for some non-emergency (elective) treatment are unacceptably long. While this is due primarily to the problems of capacity discussed above, the current mix between public and private practice is a contributory factor.

Under the present arrangements, 80 per cent of beds in acute hospitals may be currently designated as public while 20 per cent may be private. In general, this ratio is operating reasonably well in the case of emergency admissions. The position regarding elective (planned or non-emergency) admissions is less than satisfactory. In 2000, 29 per cent of elective admissions were private while 71 per cent were public patients. In summary:

- The position of public patients in public hospitals relative to private patients has deteriorated in recent years.

- What should ideally be an 80/20 division between public and private patients has, in the case of elective treatment, become 71/29.

- This has an impact on the extent to which public patients on waiting lists can be treated within a reasonable period of time.

Both public and private patients have an entitlement to access needed care within a reasonable period of time. Also consultants have a contractual right to carry out private practice in public hospitals. The challenge is to ensure that a fair balance is achieved and that those who depend on the public system are not disadvantaged.

Feedback from the consultation process

The consultation process for the Health Strategy confirmed the many challenges currently facing acute hospitals. These include:

- shortages of beds, staff and other resources

- unacceptably long waiting times for public patients needing elective procedures

- long delays in accident and emergency departments

- frequent cancellation of elective admissions and procedures

- inappropriate occupancy of acute hospital beds by persons requiring follow-up care in a more appropriate setting

- unacceptably high bed occupancy levels in major hospitals.

These problems must be addressed so that acute hospitals can meet the needs of patients fully and appropriately.

Conclusions

The overall policy objective is to improve access for public patients.

- Public patients will be provided with a high-quality, efficient and cost-effective service, whether directly in public hospitals or by arrangements with private hospitals.

- Private practice within public hospitals will not be at the expense of fair access for public patients.

- All additional beds will be designated solely for public patients. (Intensive Care Unit and other specialised beds will continue to be non-designated.)

- Co-operation between public and private hospitals will be developed to ensure a cohesive, integrated hospital system.

- Out-patient and accident and emergency services will be greatly improved so that services are better able to provide an efficient, high-quality service.

  - The Strategy places a new focus on waiting times. The target is that by the end of 2004 all public patients are scheduled to commence treatment within a maximum of three months of referral from an out-patient department. The intermediate targets to achieve this aim will be as follows:

    - By the end of 2002, no adult will wait longer than twelve months and no child will wait longer than six months to commence treatment following referral from an out-patient department

    - By the end of 2003, no adult will wait longer than six months and no child will wait longer than three months to commence treatment following referral from an out-patient department

    - By the end of 2004, no public patients will wait longer than three months for treatment following referral from an out-patient department.

  - A new dedicated Treatment Purchase Fund will be used for the sole purpose of purchasing treatment for public patients who have waited more than three months from their out-patient appointment, until the target of treatment within three months is met by the end of 2004.

  - These targets will apply only where waiting times are currently longer than these periods. Hospitals must continue to ensure that patients are treated without unnecessary delay in all areas, including those in which there are no significant waiting times.

To achieve these objectives a mix of actions is required which will address the capacity, efficiency and equity issues:

- Resolve the present under-supply of beds through a major investment programme in hospital capacity

- Strengthen strategic management of acute hospital services

- Introduce a new ear-marked treatment purchase fund to reduce waiting times

- Reform the management of waiting lists

- Improve integration of hospital and non-hospital services

- Enhance patient referral and discharge functions

- Improve accident and emergency services

- Increase availability of diagnostic facilities

- Ensure a fair balance between the mix of public and private patients

- Seek to conclude contractual agreements which maximise the incentives for greater equity.

Actions

The actions for change and development of the acute hospital system are set out below. Some actions relate to capacity and the mix between public and private patients, while others are concerned with specific organisational and practical steps that will help to promote equity, people-centredness, quality and accountability.

Capacity

78 Additional acute hospital beds will be provided for public patients

- Over the next ten years a total of 3,000 acute beds will be added to the system. This represents the largest ever concentrated expansion of acute hospital capacity in Ireland. The study of acute hospital bed requirements concluded that a figure of between 2,800 and 4,300 beds would be required over the period to 2011. The Government has decided to provide for a total of 3,000 beds, taking account of investment in non-acute facilities and community support services, increased use of day beds and a number of other factors.

- 650 of the extra beds will be provided by the end of 2002, of which 450 will be in the public sector, thus providing extra capacity for the treatment of public patients on waiting lists. The private hospital sector will be contracted to provide 200 beds, all for treatment of public patients on waiting lists.

79 A strategic partnership with private hospital providers will be developed

The Government is committed to exploring fully the scope for the private sector to provide additional capacity. Accordingly, the extra beds in the period to 2011 will be provided by a combination of public and private providers. To achieve this, a strategic partnership will be developed with the private hospital sector to provide more treatment for public patients. This will be progressed by setting up a Forum under the aegis of the new National Hospitals Agency (described below) involving the public and private sectors and insurers. The key objective is to provide the required extra capacity, whether this is in the public or private hospital sector.

80 A National Hospitals Agency will be established

This Strategy commits the Government to a significant increase in the number of hospital beds over the next ten years.

An objective, evidence-based means is required to determine the specialties in which these extra beds will be provided and their location around the country. Key decisions will need to be taken about the future configuration of existing hospitals.

Co-operation between hospitals needs to be reinforced so that a fully integrated hospital system is achieved. In addition, specialist advice is regularly required on the priority that should be attached to the development of individual specialties and services in acute hospitals throughout the country.

An independent agency is required which can provide expert, objective advice on these matters as they arise.

A National Hospitals Agency will be established on a statutory basis under the aegis of the Department of Health and Children. Its staff will have or draw upon appropriate expertise and specialist knowledge to carry out its tasks. Its main functions are outlined in more detail below.

National Hospitals Agency functions

- *To prepare a strategic plan for expanding the capacity of acute hospitals*

- *To advise on the organisation and development of all acute hospital services*

- *To advise on the designation and funding of national specialist services*

- *To facilitate closer linkages with the private hospital sector*

- *To liaise with regulatory and professional bodies on matters affecting acute hospitals*

- *To manage a new national waiting time database*

Functions of the National Hospitals Agency

To prepare a strategic plan for the expansion of capacity in the acute hospital system

This will involve planning the strategic configuration, by specialty and location, of the additional acute bed capacity announced in this Strategy, having regard to issues of quality, efficiency, clinical standards and access to services. It will enable developments to be progressed more rapidly as a result of clear direction and decision-making parameters for those charged with implementing national policy at a local level. In carrying out its functions, the Agency will work in collaboration with the health boards and the Eastern Regional Health Authority (ERHA) to ensure that the planning and delivery of hospital services is fully consistent with the health system as a whole. The Agency will not be involved in the ownership or day-to-day operation of hospitals.

To advise on the organisation and development of all acute hospital services

The Agency will advise the Minister and Department on the organisation, planning and co-ordination of acute hospital services, including the location and configuration of particular services or specialties. The Agency will consult with health boards and the ERHA, health professionals, user groups and others as appropriate in the course of its work. The input of all relevant health professionals, including consultants, will be drawn upon by the Agency in carrying out its tasks. These arrangements will have implications for Comhairle na nOspidéal, many of whose existing functions will be carried out by the National Hospitals Agency on its establishment. These implications will now be examined carefully as part of the independent audit of functions and structures of the health system, discussed later in this chapter, and arrangements will be made for transferring the relevant functions of Comhairle accordingly.

To advise the Minister on the designation of national specialist services and the development of designated services

The Agency, in consultation with health boards and ERHA, will advise the Minister and Department on the designation of acute hospital services as national specialist services and will keep such designations under review as clinical practice evolves. The Agency will also advise on the establishment of appropriate funding mechanisms for national specialist services generally and on the appropriate level of funding for those services.

To develop a strategic relationship with the private hospital sector

The Government recognises the scope for a significantly enhanced role for the private hospital sector. In this regard, the Finance Act, 2001 provides for significant tax allowances for the establishment of private hospital facilities under conditions which will also benefit public patients. The National Hospitals Agency, in collaboration with the health boards and the ERHA, will work to facilitate closer working relationships between the public and private hospital sectors. This will be of particular importance in ensuring that patients, both public and private, derive the maximum benefit from the expected growth in the private hospital sector.

To manage a new national waiting time database and to co-ordinate actions to reduce waiting lists and waiting times

The Agency will develop a national waiting time database to help streamline the system and help avoid any potential duplication of patients on the waiting lists of various hospitals.

To liaise with regulatory and professional bodies with decision-making roles in areas that affect acute hospital service delivery

The policy decisions of regulatory and professional bodies can have a significant impact on hospital services, for example, where a training body makes recommendations on staffing ratios or minimum caseloads for a specialty.
The National Hospitals Agency will liaise with regulatory and professional bodies to ensure that the impact of such decisions for hospital services are fully assessed prior to implementation. It will also liaise with the Health Information and Quality Authority, discussed later in this chapter.

Efficiency

81   A comprehensive set of actions will taken to reduce waiting times for public patients, including the establishment of a new ear-marked Treatment Purchase Fund

A new focus will be placed on waiting times. The target is that by the end of 2004, all public patients will be scheduled to commence treatment within a maximum of three months of referral from an out-patient department. The intermediate targets to achieve this aim will be as follows:

- By the end of 2002, no adult will wait longer than *twelve* months and no child will wait longer than *six* months to commence treatment following referral from an out-patient department

- By the end of 2003, no adult will wait longer than *six* months and no child will wait longer than *three* months to commence treatment following referral from an out-patient department

- By the end of 2004, no public patients will wait longer than *three* months for treatment following referral from an out-patient department.

The target improvements in waiting times will be achieved by:

- a major expansion in acute bed capacity, as described above, together with reform of primary care, strengthening of Accident and Emergency services and provision of additional non-acute places

- an ear-marked Treatment Purchase Fund which will be used to purchase treatment from private hospitals in Ireland, and from international providers. It may also make use of any capacity within public hospitals to arrange treatments for patients.

A National Treatment Purchase Team appointed by the Minister for Health and Children will manage the new Treatment Purchase Fund, working closely with the health boards. The team will commence its work immediately, in parallel with other reforms below. It will work in partnership with the health boards, hospitals and consultants to ensure that waiting times for public patients are reduced as quickly as possible.

The National Treatment Purchase Team will enter into immediate discussions with relevant hospitals and consultants to make streamlined arrangements to ensure that patients are offered the treatment they need. It is essential for the successful operation of the scheme that management procedures are highly efficient and that there is no avoidable delay in sourcing and referral of patients to the treatment needed.

Where it is not possible to treat patients within a reasonable period in Ireland, either in public or private hospitals, health boards will make arrangements under the Treatment Purchase Fund to refer public patients for treatment abroad, having regard to quality, availability and cost. This will always be subject to the patient's prior agreement and will be done in co-operation with the patient's consultant and/or general practitioner.

Alongside this process, a national waiting time database will be developed by the National Hospitals Agency to help channel patients awaiting treatment to an appropriate hospital with sufficient capacity. It will also help to eliminate any duplication of patients on the waiting lists of more than one hospital.

82   Management and organisation of waiting lists will be reformed

In addition to the initiatives above, the management and organisation of waiting lists will be reformed.

- The National Hospitals Agency, working with the health boards and ERHA, will, in consultation with relevant professional bodies, lead the development of guidelines for referral and prioritisation of patients within and between specialties, particularly those where there are lengthy waiting times. The guidelines will assist general practitioners in making referrals in keeping with best clinical practice and consultants in managing waiting lists/times.

- The management and classification of waiting lists will be reorganised in several important ways and used in the operation of the Treatment Purchase Fund:

  - Lists will be categorised by waiting times; broken down to sub-specialty/procedure level; and will include the referring doctor's name.

  - In every case where a patient is placed on a waiting list, a standardised placement record will be completed which will enable waiting lists to be classified and more easily monitored.

  - To aid decisions by GPs regarding referrals, waiting lists will be categorised by consultant and published on a dedicated intranet site. GPs will be able to access the data on the waiting lists of consultants.

  - GPs will be enabled to notify significant changes in the medical status of patients and to propose that the priority of the patient for treatment be reviewed.

  - At hospital level, waiting lists will be managed at specialty level rather than at individual consultant level. This will aid referral of patients to consultants with shorter lists.

  - Waiting times will continue to be audited regularly to assure uniformly high standards of validity. Health boards and hospitals will be required to use validation procedures that ensure accurate and up-to-date information on their caseload.

83   One-day procedures will be used to the maximum consistent with international best practice

The National Hospitals Agency will work with the health boards and the ERHA to achieve increases in one-day procedures in line with international best practice.

84   The organisation and management of services will be enhanced to the greatest benefit of patients

Short-term measures

- The existing contract for hospital consultants will be utilised to the full to ensure agreement between consultants and managers on issues affecting the level of consultant services to public patients and to avoid unnecessary delays in discharging patients. This will include regular monitoring of consultant workloads.

- Health boards and the ERHA will optimise the use of operating theatres by extending their hours of work at evenings and weekends. The details of this initiative will be discussed with staff and unions in the context of partnership and IR structures.

- Health boards and the ERHA will work to integrate more fully the planning and provision of services between acute hospitals and primary care providers.

- The discharge planning function in each acute hospital will be further enhanced to ensure that patients do not have to remain in hospital for any longer than necessary.

Medium to long-term measures

- Despite the development of hospital services around the country, many patients are referred outside their own region, mostly to Dublin, for treatment even though the procedure required is available locally. The National Hospitals Agency will work with the health boards, the ERHA and clinicians to encourage patients to use services within their regions where the necessary treatment is available locally.

- The forthcoming National Health Information Strategy will provide for increased investment in improving information-sharing/technology within and between hospitals and primary care services.

- The National Hospitals Agency and health boards will work with the Economic and Social Research Institute in developing further relevant hospital in-patient enquiry (HIPE) data and casemix data to assist in decisions on managing hospital services.

- The National Hospitals Agency will pursue a co-operative approach with the private hospital sector with a view to extending HIPE to all private hospitals.

85 The operation of out-patient departments will be improved

- Protocols for investigation and referral to hospital out-patient departments will be developed in conjunction with general practitioners.

- Acute hospitals will allocate individual appointments to each out-patient, where this is not already the practice. This will change the current situation where a number of patients who are given the same appointment time may experience a lengthy delay.

- An assessment of out-patient recall rates will be undertaken.

- Nurse-led clinics for selected conditions will be introduced where feasible.

86 A substantial programme of improvements in accident and emergency departments will be introduced

Significant initiatives will be taken to improve the operation of accident and emergency departments by directing patients to the most appropriate form of care and ensuring that those who need treatment are seen as quickly as possible.

- Additional A&E consultants will be appointed to organise and run A&E departments. The increased availability of senior medical staff will facilitate rapid clinical decision making, enhanced management, diagnosis and treatment of patients.

- Triage procedures will be put in place to help channel patients quickly to the most appropriate form of care.

- The establishment of 24-hour GP co-operatives as part of the strengthening of primary care will help to reduce demand from, and treat appropriately, patients who would otherwise have to attend at an A&E department.

- Minor injury units will be established to ensure appropriate treatment and management of non-urgent cases.

- Chest pain clinics, respiratory clinics and in-house specialist teams will be used to fast-track patients as appropriate.

- Diagnostic services will be organised to ensure increased access to and availability of services at busy times in A&E departments.

- Advanced Nurse Practitioners (ANPs) (Emergency) will be appointed in acute hospitals. ANPs diagnose and treat certain groups of patients independently within agreed protocols.

- Admission protocols will ensure that emergency patients will be the only group of patients admitted to hospital through the A&E department.

- Hospitals will ensure that a member of staff will be available to liaise with patients while they await diagnosis and treatment at A&E departments.

- Information systems will be introduced that record comprehensive, comparable and reliable data on activity in A&E departments. Such information will provide staff with a valuable tool in structuring services to meet the needs of patients.

87 Diagnostic services for GPs and hospitals will be enhanced

- The diagnostic facilities available to GPs will be strengthened.

- Arrangements for GPs to have direct access to local hospital diagnostic facilities will be enhanced.

- Diagnostic departments such as radiology and laboratory will have extended service hours, to maximise the use of the facilities and provide services as soon as possible to patients. The details of this initiative will be discussed with unions and staff in the context of partnership and industrial relations structures.

Equity

88 The extra acute beds in public hospitals will be designated for use by public patients

All of the extra acute hospital capacity within the public sector, both in-patient beds and day beds, will be designated for use by public patients. The only exceptions will be Intensive Care Units, Coronary Care Units and other specialised beds which will continue to be non-designated. The provision of additional beds announced in this Strategy will be a significant step forward in ensuring that the needs of public patients are adequately met.

89 Greater equity for public patients will be sought in a revised contract for hospital consultants

The terms of the common contract for hospital consultants are central to the establishment of an appropriate balance between public and private care in public hospitals. The forthcoming negotiations on the contract must be undertaken using a developmental agenda which will involve restructuring of key elements of the current system to promote equity of access, organisational improvements and more clinical involvement in and responsibility for management programmes. In addition, the introduction of more flexible work practices, including teamworking, rostering, cover arrangements, competence assurance and accountability initiatives must be addressed. The aim will be to build on the strengths of the present system while also providing the necessary flexibility to implement the improvements which are required in the provision of health services to public patients.

In particular, it will be proposed that newly-appointed consultants would work exclusively for public patients for a specified number of years. This would mean that consultants would concentrate on treating public patients in the early years of their contract, but would be in a position to develop private practice at a later stage where their contract so permits.

90 The rules governing access to public beds will be clarified.

Current rules require that patients must make a clear choice between fully private and fully public status (i.e. in respect of both consultant and accommodation). These rules are not always adhered to, particularly where patients are admitted as an emergency. In some circumstances, private patients may be accommodated in public beds. Public patients may also occupy private beds on occasions. The Government is determined to ensure admissions are managed so that the designated ratio between public and private patients is maintained and access by public patients is protected.

91 **Action may be taken to suspend admission of private patients for elective treatment if the maximum target waiting time for public patients is exceeded**

- Actions 81-90 are aimed at addressing capacity, greatly improving equity for public patients and streamlining efficiency. The health boards (or in the case of the Eastern region, the ERHA) will monitor hospital performance on waiting times for public patients against agreed targets by specialty.

- If the health boards and the ERHA conclude that targets for reduction in waiting times are not being achieved, despite implementation of these actions, a hospital may be directed to suspend admission of private patients for elective procedures in a specialty until the waiting time for public patients is restored to within the target period of time. This direction can be set aside if hospital management and the consultants can agree on alternative means of restoring the target waiting time.

- This measure offers an important safeguard to the interests of public patients. It provides an incentive for hospitals and consultants to use all available means to address unacceptably long waiting times.

Addressing capacity and organisation

- An extra 3,000 beds will be provided over the period to 2011, of which 650 will be in place by the end of 2002

- A strategic partnership with the private sector will be developed in providing services for public patients

- A National Hospitals Agency will be set up to plan the configuration of hospital services

Addressing efficiency

- A new Treatment Purchase Fund will be established to help reduce waiting times

- The management of waiting lists will be reformed

- The use of day-case treatments will be increased in line with international standards

- The organisation and management of services will be enhanced to the greatest benefit of patients

- The operation of out-patient departments will be improved

- A substantial programme of improvements in accident and emergency departments will be implemented

- Diagnostic services for GPs and hospitals will be enhanced

Addressing equity and mix between public and private care

- Targets will be set to commence treating all public patients within a defined timeframe of referral from an out-patient department

- All extra beds will be designated for public patients

- Greater equity for public patients will be secured in a revised contract for hospital consultants

- The rules relating to access of patients to public beds will be clarified

- Incentives will be introduced to safeguard the interests of public patients

Funding the health services

Introduction

The issue of the funding of the health system has been the subject of much public debate and was discussed in detail during the consultative process for the development of the Strategy. The following key elements have been considered:

- The method of raising health funding

- The level of health funding

- The method of allocating health funding.

  This framework outlines the Government's position on these issues and how funding for the system will be allocated in order to ensure that our health system is developed to deliver a high-quality, accessible and equitable service for all.

Discussion

Health funding methods

Throughout the world, there is a variety of methods used for raising and allocating the funds required by health systems. In many cases, what appear to be simple models can in fact be much more complicated, with items such as co-payments not being immediately obvious. Similarly, systems have generally evolved over a considerable period and reflect distinct administrative, political and economic traditions. This said, there are some common factors which can be seen in all systems, such as the presence of an element of private finance. Similarly, there are some problems, such as waiting lists, which can occur across widely different systems.

During the preparation of the Strategy, considerable analysis was carried out on the most appropriate method of funding the Irish health system. In particular the relative merits of social insurance, private insurance and tax-based systems were carefully examined.

Social insurance

In social insurance systems, the bulk of health care funding is financed separately from general income tax. Contributions are made into a 'sickness fund' or set of competing funds, usually by employers and employees, with the government sometimes topping up contributions.

Those who advocate such systems claim that they give stability through 'ring-fencing' funding and promote both equitable access and responsiveness.

In response, the critique of such systems is that they undermine reasonable cost control, involve significantly higher administrative and transaction costs and prevent integrated service planning. It is also noted that many social-insurance systems require top-up payments from the Exchequer and are not in fact separate from general taxation. Therefore, they do not even achieve the objective of stability through ring-fencing funding.

Private health insurance

A significantly less common approach is that of private health insurance. As a universal system, this would involve completely separating the planning and funding of services, as all services would receive funding on the basis of competitive bidding.

Advocates for this approach suggest the following as benefits:

• Being aware of the needs of subscribers would make insurers more responsive.

• Access would be more equitable.

• Competition between providers would ensure efficiency.

• Insurers would ensure that the supply of services would meet public demand.

In response, various weaknesses have been pointed to:

• International experience indicates that this is the most expensive system to run, with major increases in administrative costs.

• The integrated planning of services, particularly community and regionally important services would not be possible.

• Where they are non-profit, it is difficult to create an effective competitive environment between insurers; and where they are for-profit, insurers have an incentive to deprioritise the most vulnerable groups.

More fundamentally, a central element of the issues identified in the course of the preparation for the Strategy, and in the in-depth reviews which the Government has carried out in recent years, is that many of the key problems in our health system, most particularly those which relate to acute hospital care, stem from a core lack of capacity in the system; not from a lack of competition.

As is outlined elsewhere, the largest ever concentrated expansion in acute hospital facilities is required in order to deliver a system capable of treating all patients to the highest standards within an acceptable period. As such, there could be no real 'competition' between hospitals for public contracts for at least the next decade. More importantly, it is increasingly clear that the system requires more rather than less co-operation between health service providers. The integration of primary, acute and continuing care services is an essential part of achieving the level and quality of care that the public demand.

General taxation

The Irish health system is funded primarily through general taxation. There are certainly challenges which can be made to this funding method. The health sector must argue for its priority with all other areas of public spending and it is easier for the system to be less responsive. Key strengths are as follows:

• It has been demonstrated to be the most progressive of different methods of funding.

• It has the lowest administrative costs and a more focused approach to cost containment.

• It gives the greatest scope for integrating service plans.

The Government believes that each of the alternative funding models has weaknesses. However, it believes that there is no compelling evidence that any alternative approach to the tax-based system would deliver significant improvements while each would undermine the ability of the system to deliver the integrated expansion of capacity required both immediately and across the next decade. In addition, it believes that the reforms to accountability and planning proposed in the Strategy will help address clear deficiencies in the existing system without diverting resources away from the needs of care services.

Private health insurance in Ireland

Private health insurance (PHI) is a long-established feature of the system of acute care provision in Ireland and acts as a strong complement to the publicly funded system. It has grown to the point where nearly 50 per cent of the population now has insurance cover against the cost of private treatment in public hospitals or private hospitals.

Claims expenditure by insurers, on behalf of their customers, is estimated to exceed £450m (€570m) annually. As part of this expenditure, health insurance payments represent a considerable source of revenue to public hospitals, at approximately £100m (€127m) annually. PHI is very much an integral part of the funding and delivery of hospital services to the population.

As a voluntary system, PHI in Ireland is characterised by the availability of extensive benefits with relatively few restrictions on utilisation. These qualities, when combined with a fee-for-service system of reimbursing service providers, increase the pressure on premium costs year-on-year. The need to manage claims costs, as a key determinant of premium levels, in such circumstances is one of the major challenges facing the sector. In line with the proposals set out in the White Paper on Health Insurance (1999), the immediate issues facing PHI include:

- completion of the regulatory framework, on which arrangements are at an advanced stage

- attraction of more competition, on the basis of a revised regulatory structure

- introduction of new products, to satisfy demand identified by insurers, including a focus on primary care.

While the method of financing the services in Ireland is tax-based and centrally-funded, PHI will continue to play a vital part in the overall resourcing of health care in this country.

Levels of funding

As is outlined in Part One, health expenditure has been expanding very significantly in recent years, doubling in the period 1997 to 2001. In terms of per capita spending, Ireland's position has risen from a low base to approximate EU averages. This expanded funding has enabled the considerable expansion in key services and provided for significant increases in remuneration for health service employees.

This said, there remain considerable challenges and pressures for further expansion in funding. These include:

- the need to address currently unmet demand

- population growth

- increased numbers of older people

- continuing advances in technology

- considerable expansion in the scope of health and personal services.

It has been submitted that Ireland should seek to link health spending to a fixed percentage of national income. It is not proposed to adopt this approach. Leaving aside the issue of the lack of certainty which would ensue, such an approach benchmarks financial inputs alone. It is a basic approach of this Strategy that all elements of the health system must be moved to a clear strategic focus on achieving output objectives.

It is service levels, not funding levels, which must be the focus. It is the responsibility of all elements of the health service to ensure that the public's funds are used to the maximum effect in the delivery of high-quality, responsive and efficient services.

In terms of *capital funding*, the National Development Plan offers substantial funding of some £2 billion (€2.54) (1999 prices) for the health system over the period 2000-2006. This will enable continuing significant capital developments in the health sector. The NDP will equalise investment between the acute and non-acute hospital sectors and give greater balance to regional development throughout the country. Serious pressures remain in capital funding: these include a history of previous under-investment in health infrastructure and the impact that inflation in the construction sector is having on the real cost of developments originally envisaged under the NDP. That Government appreciates the urgent need for significant levels of investment in health infrastructure and is determined to progress the NDP for the health service as a matter of priority in future years.

Funding allocation

Decisions on allocation methods are vital to ensure equity as a whole and to create the incentives for the direction in which we want to take our health system. Each year, the Department of Health and Children allocates funding to the health boards, which in turn make decisions on the distribution of available resources to the agencies in their area. The Department takes account of a range of factors to determine what proportion of the funding should be allocated to each board. These include the cost of providing services in the previous year, pay costs, service developments, funding for agreed specific items and, in the case of acute hospitals, the casemix budget model (described below).

There is a clear need to ensure that all funding is allocated on the basis of implementing sound strategic plans and that funding clearly relates to service outcomes. Performance measurement and transparent, evidence-based allocations are essential elements of this. Where appropriate, the allocation of development funding on the basis of competitive procedures should be incorporated. Similarly, the Government should make maximum use of resources outside the public system where their use can deliver quality care to public patients in a timely and cost-effective manner.

Conclusions

In summary:

- The present centrally funded tax-based system of funding, complemented as at present by private health insurance will be retained.

- Capital and revenue funding of the system will be increased.

- A clear evidence-based methodology for funding, linked to strategic objectives, will create positive incentives to improve access and increase levels of service.

Actions

The Government will take a series of actions in relation to funding levels and allocation methods to help achieve the objectives of the Health Strategy. These actions are set out below.

92 Additional investment will be made in the health system

The Government is committed to devoting the resources necessary for the health system, in line with the needs of the people and the availability of funding. The Government will provide the additional investment needed to support the objectives of this Strategy. While the level of investment each year must take account of the overall Exchequer position and the many competing demands for resources, the Government will give priority to investment in the health system over the period of this Strategy, provided that the necessary reforms and improvements in practice called for in the Strategy are seen to be advanced. Decisions on additional investment will be linked to the achievement of specific reforms and outcomes.

93 Capital funding will be allocated for the regular maintenance of facilities and the planned replacement of equipment

The maintenance of buildings and equipment is essential to an efficient, people-centred health system. Failure to maintain assets leads to extra costs later on, which could otherwise have been avoided. Accordingly, specific capital funding for maintenance and planned replacement of assets will be provided.

94 Public-private partnerships will be initiated to help in the development of health infrastructure

A public-private partnership (PPP) is an agreement between a public authority and a private sector business entity for the purpose of designing, building, and possibly financing and operating, a capital asset or its associated service, where it has traditionally been provided by the public sector. The National Economic and Social Council has concluded that PPPs have the potential to

- play a pivotal role in accelerating delivery of national infrastructure

- yield long-term value for money for the Exchequer

- ensure quality public services.

Public-private partnerships (PPPs) will be used in the health sector to speed up the provision of health infrastructure in accordance with general Government policy. As a matter of priority, the Government will commence using PPPs for the development of community nursing units and health centres.

95 Multi-annual budgeting will be introduced for selected programmes

A core theme of this Strategy is that there must be a more effective planning and development of services over a period of years. Specific targets and a framework for development are, as a result, set out for each major programme area. It is intended to move towards greater multi-annual planning and budgeting within the obvious constraints of the prevailing economic situation and the constitutional role of the Oireachtas in relation to Estimates of expenditure. In addition, it is intended to move towards multi-annual service and support agreements with organisations funded by health agencies.

96 The allocation process will be reviewed by the Department of Health and Children

It is important to reduce the dependency on incremental approaches, which are influenced significantly by the allocation given in a previous year. The amounts allocated by the Department to each health board must take full account of all relevant local factors so that the available funding is distributed fairly and to best effect. In particular, account must be taken of the specific needs of the population, which may vary between boards, depending on age profile, morbidity and income levels. The Department of Health and Children will examine the current system for allocating funding to health boards with the aim of taking as much account as possible of specific local factors. The Department will also take account of service outcomes using the strengthened framework which is proposed below for service planning.

97   Financial incentives for greater efficiency in acute hospitals will be significantly strengthened

Funding systems, when properly targeted, can help create incentives for greater efficiency. They can also greatly improve the equity of the system by providing a clear basis for decisions regarding allocation of funding. In turn this improves the transparency of the allocation process. A key focus of the Health Strategy will be to take initiatives which improve equity, efficiency and transparency in the health system.

At present, the most developed system for assessing comparative efficiency and for creating incentives for good performance is the casemix budget model currently used in 32 acute general hospitals. Casemix classifies patients by reference to type of illness and resources used in treating them. The casemix budget model uses details of activity and cost to compare the relative efficiency of hospitals and to influence, in part, the total allocation given to each hospital. Under the Health Strategy, the casemix budget model will be further refined as a tool of financial allocation and a growing emphasis will be placed on the scope for using it as a means of creating positive incentives for efficiency and equity within the health system. The following steps will be taken to develop the casemix budget model:

- The casemix programme will be supported at national and regional level to ensure that it receives the resources needed for its continuing development and refinement.

- A structured broadening of casemix as a financial allocation tool will be implemented, and incorporated into the existing casemix medium-term strategy.

- As part of this broadening, the Department will increase the casemix adjustment rate from 15 per cent to 20 per cent for in-patient cases and from 5 per cent to 7 per cent for day cases[1]. From 2002 these rates will be increased progressively each year. Given that the adjustment rates are cumulative and can have a significant impact on the budgets of individual hospitals, the pace of increase in the rates will be sensitive to the capacity of hospitals to bring about the efficiency improvements which the casemix budget model entails.

98   Annual statements of funding processes and allocations will be published

In their submissions regarding the Strategy, a number of organisations argued for greater clarity about the basis for determining funding allocations and other aspects of the funding process. This was a particular concern of the community and voluntary sectors. Under the Health Strategy, the Department of Health and Children and the health boards will prepare and publish annual public statements on funding which set out:

- the specific objectives of funding being allocated under different programmes and service headings

- the criteria for allocating funding at national and regional level, (This would ensure that funding of the voluntary and community sector is consistent with the overall objectives of the Health Strategy and individual service plans).

- a clear explanation of individual funding mechanisms, such as the casemix budget model.

Each board will prepare individual regional statements. The Department will be responsible for a statement in the national context.

99   The management of capital projects will be enhanced

The management of capital projects from initial stages to completion will be streamlined in order to speed up the process. To achieve this the Department of Health and Children, in consultation with the health boards, will urgently review all elements of the management of capital developments such as planning, design, construction, equipping and commissioning. This will ensure the optimum use of capital investment; the speedy provision of a quality infrastructure which meets the needs of service users; and compliance with Government and EU requirements, including those relating to procurement.

---

1   The adjustment or 'blend' rate refers to the proportion of average costs used for a group of comparator hospitals. At present, 15 per cent of the in-patient costs of a group of hospitals is 'blended' with 85 per cent of an individual hospital's own costs to produce a casemix-adjusted allocation for that hospital.

Developing human resources

Introduction

The health services are among the largest employer in the public service. In wholetime equivalent terms there are some 81,500 employed, which equates to almost 90,000 individuals, taking account of those who work part-time.

The personal commitment of health service staff and the quality of the service they provide are extremely high. They work hard, often in difficult circumstances, to provide the best possible services to patients, clients and their families.

A key objective of the human resources framework is to develop and explicitly value staff at all levels of the health system. This in turn benefits service users.

The focus in this Strategy will be to develop the human resources function further, moving it on from what is sometimes perceived as a traditional personnel administration model to a modern human resource management model. The framework will build on the many strengths of the existing human resource system and of the workforce itself.

Discussion

Since 1994 many initiatives have been taken in the area of human resources including the publication of *A Management Development Strategy for Health and Personal Social Services in Ireland* (1996) and the establishment of the Health Services Employers Agency in 1996 and of the Office for Health Management in 1997. Important reports affecting key personnel were published also, including the *Report of the Commission on Nursing* (1998), the *Report of the Expert Group on Various Health Professionals* (2000), the Report of the Medical Manpower Forum (2001) and the Report of the Working Group on the *Effective Use of the Professional Skills of Nurses and Midwives* (2001).

Nevertheless there are serious challenges facing staff and managers in the health system at the moment including skills shortages, difficulties in recruiting and retaining qualified staff, stressful working conditions, high turnover rates, poor morale, and complex industrial relations. The constraints caused by staff shortages place an extra burden on existing staff. Despite these constraints, people working in the health and personal social services have demonstrated enormous commitment and resilience in the face of the growing pressures on the services.

The Health Strategy is being published at a time when the country's prosperity, competitiveness, public services and the future role of partnership are all in a critical phase of transition. The difficult issues faced by the health system reflect conditions in the economy more generally. The Government is committed to continuing to work through partnership, during a period of slower economic growth, to consolidate recent achievements and improve the quality of life, while maintaining competitiveness in the economy.

In line with the advice received from the National Centre for Partnership and Performance (NCPP), the Government believe that across the economy generally, it will be necessary to embrace radical organisational change to cope successfully with the new challenges presenting. Improving performance through organisational change and capacity building, including new forms of management and more flexibility of work organisation will be put at the heart of the partnership process.

Conclusions

Two key strands are addressed in the framework for human resources:

- **Ensuring a qualified, competent workforce to meet the changing demands of the people:** It is vital to plan effectively at national and local level so as to recruit, retain and develop a workforce with the capacity and skills to meet service needs. Recent studies of workforce requirements for nurses, doctors and certain grades of health and social care professionals have assisted in this process.

- **Becoming an employer of choice:** Many factors, other than financial rewards, draw workers to join and remain with a particular employer. These include:

  - best practice employment policies and procedures

  - positive strategies for improving the work environment and the quality of working life

  - a positive and participative style of management which makes for a stimulating work environment

  - a culture that emphasises the value of continuous learning and improvement in the skills and experience of everyone working in the system.

These issues are interlinked. The first is concerned with ensuring the availability of an appropriately trained workforce. The second is concerned with attracting new staff, retaining existing staff and ensuring that health-care workers who have shown their commitment to working in the health system find it a challenging but rewarding and safe place to work.

The Government has asked the NCPP to work closely with Government departments, state agencies, employees, unions and staff to promote organisational change in a way that will improve the delivery of services and develop the workplace of the future. In this context, the partnership model must be central to meeting the challenges ahead.

Actions

Ensuring a qualified, competent workforce to meet the changing demands of the health system

100   Integrated workforce planning will be introduced on a national basis

The Department of Health and Children will lead the development of an integrated system of workforce planning aimed at anticipating the number and type of staff required to provide a quality health service. This process will:

- align workforce planning with strategic objectives and the service planning processes being undertaken in health boards

- promote the use of skill mix, facilitating those in support roles to upgrade their skills and enabling specialists to focus on core functions. This may mean extending the role of existing grades–for example, health care assistants, who have the scope to take on additional duties supporting nursing, following appropriate training – or new grades created for this purpose

- involve integration with education, training and professional bodies in order to ensure that numbers of training places match the demand for skills within the health sector. For example, it is estimated that the new primary care model will require an additional 500 general practitioners over the next ten years. The implications for the number of doctors to be trained each year will be assessed in this context.

Workforce planning, led by the Department of Health and Children, will build on existing initiatives and available data regarding workforce needs. The Department will work closely with the Health Services Skills Group set up under the Programme for Prosperity and Fairness to help identify ways of meeting the workforce requirements of the health system.

101 The required number of extra health staff will be recruited

Eight thousand extra staff were recruited to the health services during 2000 through a range of proactive recruitment programmes. A comparable number is being recruited during 2001. Substantial further numbers of staff will be employed over the next five to seven years, including consultants, nurses, allied and paramedical and support grades.

In order to achieve the additional numbers required, a number of initiatives are being or will be undertaken.

Initiatives to achieve the additional numbers required

Medical personnel: There will be substantial increases in the number of consultants. The number and location of these will be determined taking account of the advice of the National Task Force on Medical Manpower.

Further initiatives

- Increase significantly the number of postgraduate places in medical colleges and, if required, the number of undergraduate places; and provide additional places on training schemes for specialist registrars to the level required to ensure that a fully trained doctor is available to all hospital patients when necessary

- Continue and expand international recruitment initiatives and exchange programmes

- Pursue closer links with FÁS and its equivalent agencies in other EU states and with medical and training colleges overseas. The aim is to increase the level of senior clinical decision makers and, where appropriate, to attract more doctors to the Irish health service

- Encourage Irish graduates abroad to return to Ireland

- Review requirements for permanent registration

- Build on recent improvements in employment conditions of non-consultant hospital doctors

- Provide extra resources for medical research programmes and placements

- The Government has approved the establishment of a National Task Force on Medical Manpower, which will prepare and oversee the implementation of detailed strategies for:

  - The phased reduction of the working hours of non-consultant hospital doctors (as required under the EU Working Time Directive)

  - Address the medical staffing needs of the Irish hospital system and the associated medical training requirements

- A key issue for the Task Force will be to quantify the resource requirements and costs that would arise if a consultant-delivered hospital service were developed in place of the existing consultant-led system, with a reduction in the number of non-consultant hospital doctors. The Medical Manpower Forum and the Report on the Working Hours of Non-Consultant Hospital Doctors saw considerable advantages in such a move.

Nurses/Midwives: 10,000 nurses will be trained over the lifetime of the Strategy

Further Initiatives

- Implement the final report on the Study of the Nursing and Midwifery Resource

- Introduce degree-level education for nursing in 2002

- Build on existing steps including recent introduction of flexible working arrangements; payment of fees to registered nurses and midwives undertaking part-time post-registration degrees and courses in specialised areas of clinical practice

- Provide flexible return to nursing and midwifery courses for nurses wishing to rejoin the workforce and continue drives to recruit from overseas. (Some 2,000 work authorisations /visas have been issued to nurses and midwives from abroad in the year up to June 2001.)

- Develop further clinical specialist and advanced practitioner posts in nursing and midwifery within the framework of the new National Council for the Professional Development of Nursing and Midwifery.

Health and social care professionals: An extra 1,330 physiotherapists, 985 speech and language therapists and 875 occupational therapists will be trained, to meet the requirements up to 2015 identified by the recent report (Bacon, 2001) on these grades

Further Initiatives

- Recruit/train extra staff in a range of other grades, including social workers, psychologists, radiographers, dieticians and chiropodists, on the basis of workforce planning studies in these areas

- Provide additional training places to increase the number of therapists

- Pursue scope for conversion courses and for introduction of support/assistant grades

- Continue overseas recruitment drives

- Provide information campaigns for potential employees

- Continue implementation of the Expert Group on Various Health Professionals to promote both recruitment and retention by enhancing the attractiveness of posts.

Health care assistants: 340 Health care assistants will be trained by April 2000

Further Initiatives

- Introduce grade of health care assistant (HCA) as a member of health care teams to assist and support nurses and midwives. A national 6-month training programme for health care assistants is commencing in November 2001. Seventeen pilot programmes to be delivered by the Health Services in conjunction with the Further Education Training Awards Council (FETAC).

It will also be necessary to expand existing educational and training facilities to meet the substantial extra numbers of health professionals provided for in the Health Strategy.

- The Government will provide the necessary additional resources, both capital and non-capital, to enable the education sector to respond to the skills needs of the health sector.

- The Department of Health and Children and the Department of Education and Science will develop closer links between the health and education sectors in order to promote integrated training and education at all levels.

102 The approach to regulating the number and type of consultant posts will be streamlined

The way in which consultant posts are regulated in future will be streamlined. Where it is decided to establish a new hospital service or to expand an existing service (on the recommendation of the National Hospitals Agency), approval to the provision of any consultant post(s) involved will be dealt with through the relevant health board's service plan, taking account of the recommendations of the National Task Force on Medical Manpower. In the case of a replacement post (as arises following a retirement or resignation) the relevant health board will again deal with it in the context of its service plan.

103 Best practice in recruitment and retention will be promoted

The Office for Health Management will prepare guidelines on best practice in advertising policies and recruitment for staff of the health system. These will be circulated to all health employers. The guidelines will include guidance on induction arrangements for all staff. The Health Services Employers Agency will work with the Office for Health Management to advise employers on implementation of the guidelines.

Retention rates for the system and individual employers will be measured in order to benchmark minimum standards and set targets for reducing turnover rates. Health service employers will be encouraged to adopt innovative approaches to job design. Initiatives such as flexible working and training, arrangements for atypical working hours and specific family-friendly approaches will be aimed at meeting the needs of health service workers and their families as well as the efficiency of the service.

The Chief Nursing Officer has convened a group to prepare *Guidance for Best Practice on Recruitment of Overseas Nurses and Midwives*. The document will be published shortly.

104 Greater inter-disciplinary working between professions will be promoted

Current practices in some professions can greatly hinder the development of inter-disciplinary work. To provide integrated, continuous, high-quality services, professionals need to work closely with each other, in a structured way, through formal or informal teams. An inter-disciplinary approach extends the range of skills available to patients, improves the deployment of scarce professional skills and provides greater continuity in the care of patients and clients.

The Department of Health and Children will work with the relevant professional bodies and teaching institutions to adapt training programmes so that the professions are brought more closely together from an early part of their training. The professional bodies will also need to work much more intensely and collaboratively to break down barriers between professions and to develop a culture of inter-disciplinary work. Progress should be planned on the basis of key milestones to be reached within agreed timeframes.

The development of inter-disciplinary working could be assisted by the development of joint programmes at the initial stages of undergraduate training. This might include, for example, a common medical sciences degree before specialised training for individual professions commences. This issue will be explored further within the health and education sectors.

105 Provisions for the statutory registration of health professionals will be strengthened and expanded

At present, five professions are subject to statutory registration: doctors, nurses, pharmacists, opticians and dentists. New legislation will provide for the statutory registration of a number of other health professional groups. The Government is committed to strengthening existing legislation regarding registration of certain professions, such as doctors, nurses and pharmacists. In addition, new legislation will be introduced for the registration of health and social care professionals including physiotherapists, occupational therapists, social workers, child care workers and others.

The primary purpose of statutory registration is to protect and guide members of the public, so that they can be confident that the professional treating them is fully qualified and competent. Registration also provides the facility for legal action against the very small number of professionals who may harm patients or clients and bring their profession into disrepute through professional misconduct or serious illness.

All legislation on statutory registration of health professionals will be formally reviewed within five years of its introduction. The review will pay particular attention to the accountability of regulatory bodies to the Oireachtas and to the importance of reflecting the public interest on these bodies.

The legislation for professionals already registered, and for health and social care professionals being registered for the first time, will provide for consumer representation on the relevant statutory registration bodies, to ensure that the views of service users are represented. The legislation will also enable registration boards to provide for a system requiring re-accreditation of professionals at regular intervals, based on a structured system of continuing education and training.

106   Registration of alternative/complementary therapists will be introduced

A number of the submissions on the Health Strategy called for a scheme of registration of alternative and complementary therapists who work in the area of health and personal services.

The Minister for Health and Children has established a forum involving representatives of alternative therapies to explore how best to provide for a system of registration. Any registration scheme will take account of:

* the categories of therapists to be covered

* the evidence base for each therapy

* the educational qualifications, training and experience of therapists

* the scope of practice involved

* the protection of the public and promotion of a quality service, including the efficacy of the therapies offered

* regulations governing alternative therapists in other countries

* the current proposals for statutory registration of health and social care professionals in Ireland.

Becoming an employer of choice

107 The HR function in the health system will be developed

The human resources function in the health system is relatively under-developed. Too often the emphasis is almost solely on industrial relations, to the detriment of many other aspects, including personal development, education and training and a range of HR issues affecting quality of working life and job satisfaction. Some progress has been made in the health boards, with the appointment of Directors of Human Resources who are responsible for the wider HR agenda. However, these individual initiatives need to be developed into a composite framework for human resources throughout the system.

- Where not already in place, a formal human resource function will be established in all health boards and health agencies, combining existing personnel planning, recruitment and training functions. Flexible models of HR will be implemented, based as appropriate on individual agencies or on specific care groups.

- In line with these flexible models, a manager of human resources will be appointed to head up the HR function, where such a post or its equivalent is not already in place.

- In developing the HR function, full account will be taken of benchmarks for HR investment in other sectors. Comparisons with industry indicate a need to increase considerably the number of HR professionals per thousand staff employed. Priority areas for HR development will include such areas as recruitment, workforce planning and employee relations.

- The human resource function of health agencies will be further strengthened by:

  - ensuring new staff have human resource expertise and/or experience

  - establishing a clear career path within the HR function

  - introducing a development plan for staff working in HR.

The human resource function will have responsibility for:

- devising and promoting best employment procedures and practices

- recruitment and retention policies, including contributing to workforce planning as an integral part of strategic planning within the organisation

- organisation of training and education programmes to include skills development, management development, personal development of staff, and dealing with diversity in culture and ethnicity of staff, clients, patients and their families

- leading the development and implementation of performance management systems

- ensuring a healthy workplace through initiatives to develop teamworking and mentoring programmes, promote anti-discrimination and anti-bullying policies and assist health and safety.

108 A detailed Action Plan for People Management will be developed

This Action Plan will provide a clear road map for action over the next five to seven years. It will be developed in consultation with the Health Services National Partnership Forum and implemented jointly through management, unions and partnership structures.

> The **Action Plan for People Management** will seek to ensure that the health service has the right people, with the right competencies, in the right numbers, organised and managed in the right way, to deliver the goals and objectives of the Health Strategy.

In particular, the action plan will elaborate on how the following actions will be developed and implemented:

- Invest in training and education

- Devise and implement best practice employment policies and procedures

- Improve the quality of working life

- Manage people effectively

- Develop performance management

- Promote improved industrial relations in the health sector

- Develop the partnership approach further.

Action Plan for People Management

Invest in training and education

Central to the Health Strategy is the need to provide the financial and practical supports necessary for training and developing people in the health system. In addition to the commitments to training and development of new staff, health service employers will demonstrate a commitment to continuous learning by facilitating existing staff to undertake programmes that enhance the quality of patient care and contribute to their own career development. Continuing professional education, personal development planning and management development training will also be emphasised.

Devise and implement best practice employment policies and procedures

To establish the health service as an employer of choice, health employers will be asked to:

- review current employment practices and modernise them in line with research on international best practice

- survey staff on current employment practices and desired changes

- improve the system of staff communications

- achieve greater involvement by staff in planning and delivering services, and developing policy on staff participation which builds on the partnership model

- implement best practice guidelines for staff retention

- initiate new approaches to job design and broaden flexible working arrangements to achieve better work-life balance

- design and promote skill development programmes for HR staff

- pursue a gender equality policy in the health system in line with the approach recently approved by the Government for the civil service. Specific targets will be set in this regard

- establish a policy for managing diversity in the workplace. In line with the Employment Equality Act, 1998 and the Equal Status Act, 2000, this policy should challenge prejudice at all levels and provide practical support to enable everybody, regardless of gender, marital or family status, race, religion, age, disability, sexual orientation or membership of the Travelling community to work in the health system. Such a policy will incorporate:

  - policy, procedures, audit and training programmes

  - awareness-raising training programmes in relation to diversity, equality, bullying and harassment

  - a mechanism for monitoring equality in relation to recruitment, selection and career development.

Manage people effectively

Building and enhancing management capacity, including frontline managers, will be central to the health system's ability to deliver real change. Poor people management leads to higher turnover rates, lower morale and higher levels of stress.

A management style based on participation rather the exercise of authority, and which encourages and promotes transformation change, must prevail in the health system.

This participative approach implies major cultural change. The initial focus will be on managers, underlining the importance of securing their commitment to and involvement in developing the change agenda. In addition:

- People management and communication skills will be considered core competencies in recruiting and assessing managers. Training in these skills will be a priority.

- HR skills development programmes for line managers will be developed.

- Line managers will be trained in personal development planning techniques, particularly skills in giving and receiving feedback.

- There will be renewed emphasis on the clinicians in management initiative, taking account of the discussion papers published by the Office for Health Management

- Staff at all levels will be empowered by devolving decision-making responsibility to the lowest feasible level.

- A proactive approach to change in response to the developing needs of the health system will be encouraged as in initiatives such as the work currently being carried out by the Empowerment of Nurses and Midwives Steering Group – an agenda for change.

Improve the quality of working life

A working environment where people feel valued, recognised and safe is important to the improvement of morale and the retention of staff. The following key actions will be taken to improve the quality of working life:

- Active engagement by employers in promoting physical, mental and social well-being in the workplace, through further improvements in the management of health, safety and welfare at work. The emphasis will be on providing comfortable and appropriate work environments, free from danger and mistreatment.

- Occupational health services will be made available for everybody working in the health system.

- Health promotion initiatives in the workplace will be encouraged.

- Provision of crèches in the workplace will be encouraged.

- With the advice of the Health and Safety Authority, a standardised system will be introduced to monitor workplace accidents and incidents of violence against staff, as one aspect of risk management and prevention.

- Staff surveys will be undertaken to measure and benchmark improvements to the quality of working life over time.

- Standardised systems for monitoring sick leave absence rates by reference to good practice 'benchmark levels' will be introduced by employers, in consultation with the health unions.

Develop performance management

Performance management programmes are aimed at providing clear feedback to individuals in order to make best use of available skills and help advance the strategic objectives of the organisation. They also offer a useful means of setting work and personal development goals and give people an opportunity to contribute ideas for improving delivery of services. Performance programmes must be fair and transparent. Performance management systems are already being introduced in the public sector generally. They will now be extended more comprehensively to the health system, in consultation with staff and unions.

Promote improved industrial relations in the health sector

The Action Plan for People Management will include measures to implement the recommendations of the recent report of the Advisory Development and Research Service of the Labour Relations Commission (2001) with particular regard to:

- the operation of procedures for dealing with negotiations, disputes and grievances

- the interaction between management, workers and their respective representatives.

Develop the partnership approach further

The partnership approach can play a key role in driving the changes proposed in the Health Strategy and it will be strongly supported by the Government. The Action Plan for People Management will reflect the Government's commitment to assisting partnership in the health system to reach its potential and will deal with how best to develop further the role of the Health Services Partnership Forum and its local partnership structures. In line with the national strategy for improving performance through organisational change being developed by the NCPP, the action plan will place particular emphasis on the development of organisation-based projects on which all staff can work together to be part of the change process.

Organisational reform

Introduction

The way in which health and personal social services are planned, organised and delivered has a significant impact on the health and well-being of the population. Organisational structures must be geared to providing a responsive, adaptable health system which meets the needs of the population effectively and at affordable cost.

It cannot be assumed that any particular organisational structure for the health system will, of itself, ensure the provision of an effective, people-centred service. It must be combined with the right policies and practices in a range of other areas, including an effective human resource function and a clear sense of direction. The framework for organisational reform in this Strategy aims to support effective decision-making, based on the best available evidence and to promote high-quality services.

Health care organisations that systematically emphasise quality are the best places to work. They respect and maximise the contributions of all staff, they reduce the amount of unnecessary and ineffective work, they reduce error rates and they produce better outcomes and job satisfaction.

Saskatchewan Commission on Medicare, April 2001

Discussion

The present structures in the health system have largely been in place for some thirty years, although there have been changes to the internal structures of many health boards. The structure of the system is set out in broad outline in Chapter 3.

The overall structure of the Department of Health and Children has altered relatively little in recent years, but changes have been made to reflect growing developments in areas such as services for children, older people and people with a disability. A shift in emphasis is occurring under the Strategic Management Initiative (SMI), which involves moving from detailed executive involvement to a stronger role for strategic policy-making.

Recent changes to the system have included the establishment of the Eastern Regional Health Authority in 2000 and the provision for a Health Boards Executive (HeBE) which will carry out agreed joint functions on behalf of all or a number of health boards. A number of additional advisory and executive agencies has also been established over the years.

The strengths and weakness of the present system are discussed in Chapter 3. The main conclusion is that while the system has served well in many respects, some significant issues remain. These relate to the co-ordination and integration of services, better needs assessment and planning on foot of these needs, and consistent standards of access and quality throughout the health system.

Conclusions

It is important to develop a single integrated system, rather than one which varies between the approaches taken in individual health board areas. This requires more co-ordination between health boards in the way they work, particularly in areas of planning and service delivery. Structures are required to support the central development of national quality standards and to ensure consistent

The Irish health service ought to be one organisation made up of a constellation of many organisations

Quote from the consultation process

national application of those standards. Continuing close co-ordination with the non-statutory sector will also be required.

> The aim is to have a consistent, national approach to the planning and delivery of services based on clear and agreed national objectives. Improving co-ordination and integration also means reviewing the roles of existing executive and advisory agencies to maximise efficiency and reduce overlaps.

Actions

109   The Department of Health and Children will be restructured

The Department will be restructured to focus on the priorities set out for the health system of the future. To progress this, an independent review of the structure and resources of the Department of Health and Children, with proposals for change, will be completed within six months. The Department is assigned a lead role in implementing the very challenging programme of development and reform outlined in this Strategy. It is already visibly under pressure and will require strengthening if it is to provide credible and authoritative leadership during the period of major transformation ahead.

The devolution of executive work under the Strategic Management Initiative will continue to be progressed. The Department needs to be positioned to focus on the strategic aspects of health policy, such as national service planning and overall governance of the health system. The review of structure and resources will be carried out with these requirements in mind.

110   Health boards will be responsible for driving change, including a stronger focus on accountability linked to service plans, outputs and quality standards

The health boards have important responsibilities under the Accountability Legislation (1996) regarding the level and type of services to be provided under their service plan. This accountability framework will be further strengthened to underline the boards' role in providing the best possible value for money and pursuing quality standards. The health boards will continue to play a major role in the planning and delivery of health and personal social services and will be crucial to delivering on the reform agenda set out in this Strategy. In particular, they will:

* have explicit responsibilities for driving change at regional level, in partnership with relevant bodies such as the Health Boards Executive (HeBE) and the Office for Health Management

* focus on the actual outcomes of the services for which they are responsible, in line with service plans, performance measures and casemix measurement

* publish a user-friendly summary of their annual service plan and distribute it widely within their area. This will promote the local accountability of boards and help explain the level and type of services which they propose to provide

* continue to be responsible for delivering (or arranging the delivery of) the full range of health and personal social services at local level, taking account of the work of relevant bodies such as the new National Hospitals Agency and the Health Information and Quality Authority.

In discussing the role of the health boards, it is important to distinguish between the board itself (which comprises elected members of local authorities, representatives of health professions and nominees of the Minister) and the management and staff of the boards. Under the Accountability Legislation, the decision-making functions of the board were clarified to emphasise their role in overall strategic direction and policy, and formal authority and accountability was assigned to management regarding the planning, management and delivery of services.

The Government has carefully considered whether the current number of health boards best meets the requirements of the health system. It is satisfied that changing the number of boards would not of itself lead to improvements in services. Instead, the focus will be on improving delivery of services and developing a stronger framework of accountability, linked to service plans, outputs and standards of quality as set out in this Strategy. The establishment of a National Hospitals Agency will free the boards to concentrate on other important aspects of their work.

111   An independent Health Information and Quality Authority will be established

A key policy aim is to deliver high-quality services that are based on evidence-supported best practice. To promote this aim a Health Information and Quality Authority will be established. The Authority will:

- ensure the services provided in the health system meet nationally agreed standards, both at clinical and managerial level

- assess whether the health and personal social services are managed and delivered to ensure the best possible outcomes within the resources available.

The Authority will have responsibility for:

- developing health information systems

- promoting and implementing structured programmes of quality assurance

- reviewing and reporting on a selected set of services each year

- overseeing accreditation and developing health technology assessment.

The Health Information and Quality Authority will be established on an independent statutory basis enabling it to set and monitor standards in an objective manner. Its structure will be designed to allow for considerable operational flexibility. This may involve drawing upon panels of short-term expert staff, both national and international, who work for a limited period on a specified project. The Authority's work will lend itself to an all-Ireland remit; this will be explored in the context of discussions on North-South co-operation in the area of health.

Health information is fundamental to assessing and implementing quality programmes. It is also vital to the wider areas of value for money, information for management, information for the public, knowledge management systems and knowledge bases. The Health Information and Quality Authority will lead the development of health information to support these requirements.

Quality assurance means improving performance and preventing problems through a structured set of programmes and systematic activities such as documentation, training and review.

Functions of the Health Information and Quality Authority

Develop health information which best meets the needs of the health system

The Health Information and Quality Authority will:

- provide the lead on information development, in line with the forthcoming National Health Information Strategy

- develop information standards, definitions and data dictionaries

- develop and agree minimum datasets

- quality-assure data and information

- assess proposed information developments relating to data and technical standards

- promote education, training and skills development for information staff

- promote and co-ordinate national research and development on eHealth

- develop a national e-library to guide decision-making

- promote a common approach to security, privacy and confidentiality

- develop and agree guidelines governing access to information from health agencies

- assist efficient and effective procurement of health information technology for the health system.

Promote quality nationally

Quality is one of the guiding principles of the Health Strategy. It must infuse activity at all levels of the health system. The Health Information and Quality Authority will:

- develop and disseminate agreed standards and guidelines/models of best practice as templates for the development of local care protocols

- introduce and oversee accreditation processes across the health system. This will include, in relation to the acute hospitals area, working closely with the Hospitals Accreditation Body which will soon be established

- promote formal health impact assessment programmes

- promote and advise national initiatives on patient safety

- liaise with the proposed new Irish Clinical Negligence Claims Agency on risk management.

Develop an annual programme of service reviews

The Authority will develop an annual programme of service reviews, in consultation with the Minister for Health and Children, those working in the health system and the public. The reviews may be by care groups, such as people with a mental illness; by type of disease or condition, such as cancer or renal services; or by sector such as primary care. Reviews will normally be at a national level, but regional reviews may also be undertaken. Reviews will be linked to the development of quality standards for different services and may cover any aspect of performance, including clinical or managerial aspects.

Publish a report assessing national performance in relation to each service area examined, against specified national standards

The Authority's report on each selected area will detail clearly whether the required standards have been met, not met, or exceeded. Reviews will examine health outcomes, to determine whether services are leading to real improvements for patients and clients. It will be a critical task of the Authority to report on outcomes for care groups and specific services so that guidance can be provided regarding future investment decisions. The Authority's focus will be on encouraging and promoting the development of quality standards, rather than simply attaching blame where standards or outcomes fall short. The reports will make suggestions for specific improvements and will be widely distributed.

While the Authority will develop standards in agreement with agencies, and report on selected services regularly, the relevant health boards, hospitals and other bodies will have responsibility and accountability for taking action in response to the Authority's reports.

While responsibility for this range of functions will be vested in the Authority, it may commission work from a number of established sources, such as the Social Services Inspectorate and the Inspector of Mental Hospitals, to support it in its role. It will work closely with the health boards and other relevant agencies and will have a national rather than local focus. The health boards' responsibilities in these areas at local level will remain, but will be supported by the national perspective brought by the Authority.

Oversee health technology assessment

There is a growing need to analyse all forms of new developments in health care to establish if they are effective, and if their use is justified.

Health technology assessment (HTA) involves analysing the research findings about the medical, organisational, social, ethical and economic implications of the development, diffusion and use of health technologies. HTA can play a key role in ensuring that the most modern appropriate care and treatments are used, in a way that maximises health gain and achieves value for money. HTA is a key component of evidence-based health care.

As highlighted recently by the Value for Money Audit (2001), there is currently no coherent structure for carrying out evidence-based HTA in Ireland. This results in a slower response to changes in health technology than would be desirable. A structured system of HTA will enable the system to:

- introduce technologies speedily with proven, significant health benefits

- prevent the introduction of technologies which fail to meet the requirements of evidence-based analysis

- continuously monitor the effectiveness of technologies after introduction.

Under the Strategy, the Health Information and Quality Authority will oversee the development of HTA and promote its use to inform vital policy decisions, from initial evaluation, to implementation, monitoring and review of outcomes. It will draw upon HTA work carried out in other countries, and the scope for North-South co-operation will be explored.

112   The Health Boards Executive (HeBE) will be developed as a key instrument in the change agenda

The Health (Eastern Regional Health Authority) Act, 1999 provides for the establishment of a Health Boards Executive (HeBE). Its purpose is to carry out certain executive functions on behalf of the health boards, and other executive functions as may be directed by the Minister, aimed at improving the efficiency and effectiveness of services.

HeBE will provide an important avenue for ensuring that the health boards can operate jointly on issues where a national approach to implementing a programme or service is the best way of achieving the objectives of the Strategy. The functions given to the HeBE will be regularly reviewed by the health boards and the Department of Health and Children to ensure it is efficient and effective.

The HeBE will rely on management and personal development work undertaken throughout the system by the Office for Health Management.

113 The role of the Office for Health Management will be expanded

The change and modernisation programme will also require an enhanced role for the Office for Health Management. Developing current and future managers to support the modernisation agenda and meet the objectives for improvement set out in the Strategy will be vital in implementing change. In addition, the need for organisation development must also be addressed, to ensure that all health agencies are fit for the challenges facing them. There is well-documented inter-dependency between the structure of an organisation, its processes, strategy, culture and people. Encouraging, promoting and rewarding a culture of continuous learning and improvement will be important in adapting to new ways of working.

* The brief of the Office for Health Management will be expanded to include *organisation development* as well as management development i.e. to drive and support the organisation development and the management and personal development agendas being pursued by health service employers.

* The OHM will work closely with the Department of Health and Children and health agencies to initiate organisation development programmes aimed at co-ordinating structures, strategy, culture, processes and people.

* Health agencies will be required to include in their annual service plans specific provision for advancing staff, management and organisation development.

114 An independent audit of functions and structures in the health system will be carried out

The framework for organisational development will help clarify roles and co-ordinate the work of different organisations. It will also place a stronger emphasis on high-quality outcomes, and on ensuring that major policy decisions are taken in an objective way, based on the best available evidence.

As part of the process of implementing these changes, the Department of Health and Children will commission an audit of organisational structures and functions in the health system, to ensure clear lines of accountability and communication between each part of the system, no overlap or duplication between organisations, and a proper alignment of the structure as a whole to the vision and objectives outlined in the Health Strategy. The audit will consider the number and configuration of existing health boards and other agencies and the scope for rationalisation. The audit, which will start immediately, will ensure that structures in the health system:

* are the most appropriate and responsive to meet current and future service needs

* constitute an adequate framework for overall governance of the health system

* achieve an effective integration of services across all parts of the system

* adequately represent the views of consumers in the planning and delivery of services

* focus upon the principles of equity, accountability, quality and people-centredness and the national goals of the Health Strategy.

A list of the organisations to be encompassed by the audit is at Appendix 3.

Developing health information

Introduction

To meet the objectives of the Health Strategy and to deliver the quality of health services that people require, information is needed which is appropriate, comprehensive, high-quality, available, accessible and timely. Good information systems based on fast, efficient flows of shared information are, therefore, essential to the success of the Strategy.

Discussion

The recent Value for Money Review of the Irish health system (Deloitte and Touche, 2001) identified inadequate information as a critical weakness which limits the capacity for prioritisation, planning, evidence-based decision-making, efficient service delivery, and monitoring and evaluation at all levels. A clear basis is needed for identifying priorities in health care and for demonstrating performance and value for money. Improvements in health information are central to establishing the evidence for any such decisions.

Improvements in health information can be facilitated greatly by worldwide developments in information and communications technology (ICT). This technology has the power to improve radically the provision of health information and to streamline and improve health service provision. Full co-operation among health agencies is essential to ensure that the benefits of ICT can be exploited.

There is now a considerable public policy commitment to eGovernment with the intention of promoting Ireland as a centre of eCommerce excellence. The widespread availability of low-cost, high-speed, internet access will be a critical enabler of eHealth developments. The health system is working with the eGovernment programme, including REACH,[2] which will ensure that the benefits from these developments are fully realised.

In recognition of the importance and value of improving public access to health information, there is a need to develop a national health internet site for the public that provides standardised information on health and health care (e.g. the management of health problems and the safety and effectiveness of interventions), the availability of local health services, and entitlements. The processing of health entitlements should be available on-line as far as is practicable.

Mobile communication technologies are evolving rapidly and could enable the development of new eHealth service delivery models, especially for staff working in the field such as public health nursing, and out-of-hours and emergency services, by providing access to medical and administrative records. Telemedicine and telecare systems can bring images and other clinical data (rather than the patient) to the care provider, thus providing remote consultation. By limiting the need to travel, this technology has the potential to increase the accessibility of some services.

Conclusions

The Department of Health and Children is currently preparing a National Health Information Strategy (NHIS). Its implementation has been identified as key in supporting the attainment of the Health Strategy's national goal of high performance. Information has been included in the Health Strategy as a specific framework for change because it plays an integral role in the development of the health system. It is vital that the development of a health information system is integrated into the agenda for change identified in the Health Strategy.

---

2 REACH is an independent agency established by the Government to develop a strategy for the integration of public services and to develop and implement a framework for electronic government.

Information plays a central role in supporting strategic goals and in underpinning the principles of the Health Strategy. It must not be seen merely as an add-on.

The actions set out below should be seen as supporting and prioritising key areas for attention which are developed in greater detail in the forthcoming National Health Information Strategy.

Actions

As described earlier in this chapter, the Health Information and Quality Authority will exercise a pivotal role in relation to a number of key information functions. In addition, the following actions will be taken to meet the information requirements of the Health Strategy:

115   The National Health Information Strategy will be published and implemented

The Information Strategy will be designed to promote:

- ready access to good-quality information about health and personal social services and health matters for the public, patients, health professionals, administrators, managers, and policy makers

- best use of information and communication technology to improve operational service delivery and the responsiveness of services

- evidence-based decision-making and planning processes

- evaluation of the real service impact of investment decisions

- a greatly enhanced appreciation of the role of information in improving health, including the importance of healthy lifestyles

- education and training to ensure knowledge is exploited efficiently to the benefit of all

- faster and more effective communication across all sectors concerned with health.

116   There will be a sustained programme of investment in the development of national health information systems as set out in the National Health Information Strategy

Considerable development of the information infrastructure will be required to support improvements in the availability and quality of health information. Operational systems which support the delivery of health services are fundamental to success and will be the only viable source of the bulk of evidence for management. Investment levels currently fall short of best practice in industry despite the complexity of the health system. Addressing these shortfalls is a fundamental objective.

117   Information and communications technology will be fully exploited in service delivery

Modern ICT has the potential to improve radically the range and type of services, as well as the method of delivery, for professionals and the public. ICT can provide rapid access to clinical and administrative records as well as a range of knowledge to assist with decision-making. Data collected at this stage will be a key source of information for planning and performance measurement.

Telecare and telemedicine has the potential to bring specialised diagnostic and clinical expertise closer to people, especially those in remote locations, making the health service more accessible and responsive.

118 Information-sharing systems and the use of electronic patient records will be introduced on a phased basis

The electronic patient record (EPR) is a developing technology. Its phased introduction will support the clinical process and offer great potential to enhance the quality and safety of care. In particular, the linkage of EPRs to create an electronic health record (EHR) will provide new opportunities for supporting shared care. A method of uniquely identifying individuals and service providers is essential for realising the full potential of the electronic record. The planned extension of the use of the personal public services number (PPSN) to cover the delivery of all public services, within the Government's overall strategy for integration of public services, may provide this method of identification in the future. In any event, the use of unique identifiers in the health field is of major importance in achieving the highest quality of care and in the delivery of patient-centred services.

119 A national secure communications infrastructure will be developed for the health services

A robust communications network and services infrastructure is a necessity for the effective and efficient collection, sharing and use of health information. Individual agencies and organisations have already developed communications networks to a varied extent on a local or regional basis. National initiatives, including the development of a government network for state services and the REACH initiative, may offer ways of providing this network. It is essential to consider current and future capacity, including the potential to utilise the network for newer and heavier demands. These include video, image transfer, and telephony in support of telemedicine, conferencing and eLearning. Security will be a crucial consideration.

120 Information system development will be promoted as central to the planning process

Service planning must be evidence-based. All service developments must be based on a good business case which, in turn, requires good supporting information. Appropriate information systems are central to the collection and analysis of the information required to underpin this planning process.

121 Health information legislation will be introduced

The legislation required for developing information systems to support the objectives of the National Health Information Strategy will be introduced. The legislation will address concerns about privacy and confidentiality, while ensuring that health information can be utilised for the benefit of all.

CHAPTER 6

Responding to people's needs

Introduction

Chapter 4 sets out the goals and objectives of the Health Strategy. In Chapter 5 the structural changes required to deliver these objectives are set out. Some system-wide changes are outlined which are relevant to everyone and will improve delivery and quality of services. They include the following:

Quality assurance

- National standards, protocols, guidelines/models of best practice will be developed and disseminated across the system.

- A system of quality, evaluation, assurance and accreditation will be developed and introduced.

- An evidence-based approach will be taken to decision-making in both clinical and non-clinical areas.

Information systems

- There will be an immediate investment in the development of national health information systems as set out in the National Health Information Strategy.

- Use of information technology in service delivery will be improved.

- Information system development will be promoted as central to the planning process.

Human Resources

- Integrated work-force planning will be introduced on a national basis.

- The required number of extra staff will be recruited.

Research

- Research will be advanced in the context of the National Health Research Strategy.

- Research projects relating to the needs of specific care groups will be expanded in line with research agendas agreed by the Forum for Health and Social Care Research.

In this chapter, the implications of the Strategy for specific groups of the population are described.

Children's health and well-being

Policy context and recent developments

It is well recognised that social, economic and environmental conditions all have an impact on child health and management and that an integrated approach is required. The recently published National Children's Strategy provides an integrated framework as well as the broader policy context for all new initiatives for children, including this Health Strategy. The National Children's Strategy sets out three goals and an action plan to address these dimensions in an integrated way. While it identifies the main actions to be taken, it requires more detailed measures to be developed in the different sectors. This section of the Health Strategy provides for more detailed action in relation to two of the dimensions, 'physical and mental' and 'emotional and behavioural well-being', although it is relevant in some degree to all aspects of child care.

This Strategy's approach to children's health and well-being

- recognises children as active participants in shaping their own health and well-being

- supports families and their central role in protecting and promoting children's health and well-being

- seeks to strengthen the effectiveness of the supports and services provided by the health services to children.

Figure 6.1 shows how children interact with the different parts of the health system and shows the nature of their needs, ranging from basic to more complex.

All children have basic needs. These needs can be met by the child's family and social networks or by themselves. Some basic needs must also be supported by the health system.

Some children have additional needs. Small numbers of children will need to access different parts of the system to support their physical, mental, emotional and behavioural well-being. The system must be flexible enough to be able to respond to more complex needs. The system also must be better integrated to allow for continuity of care and for the development of individualised care planning for children.

Fig 6.1 Children and the Health System

Levels of care

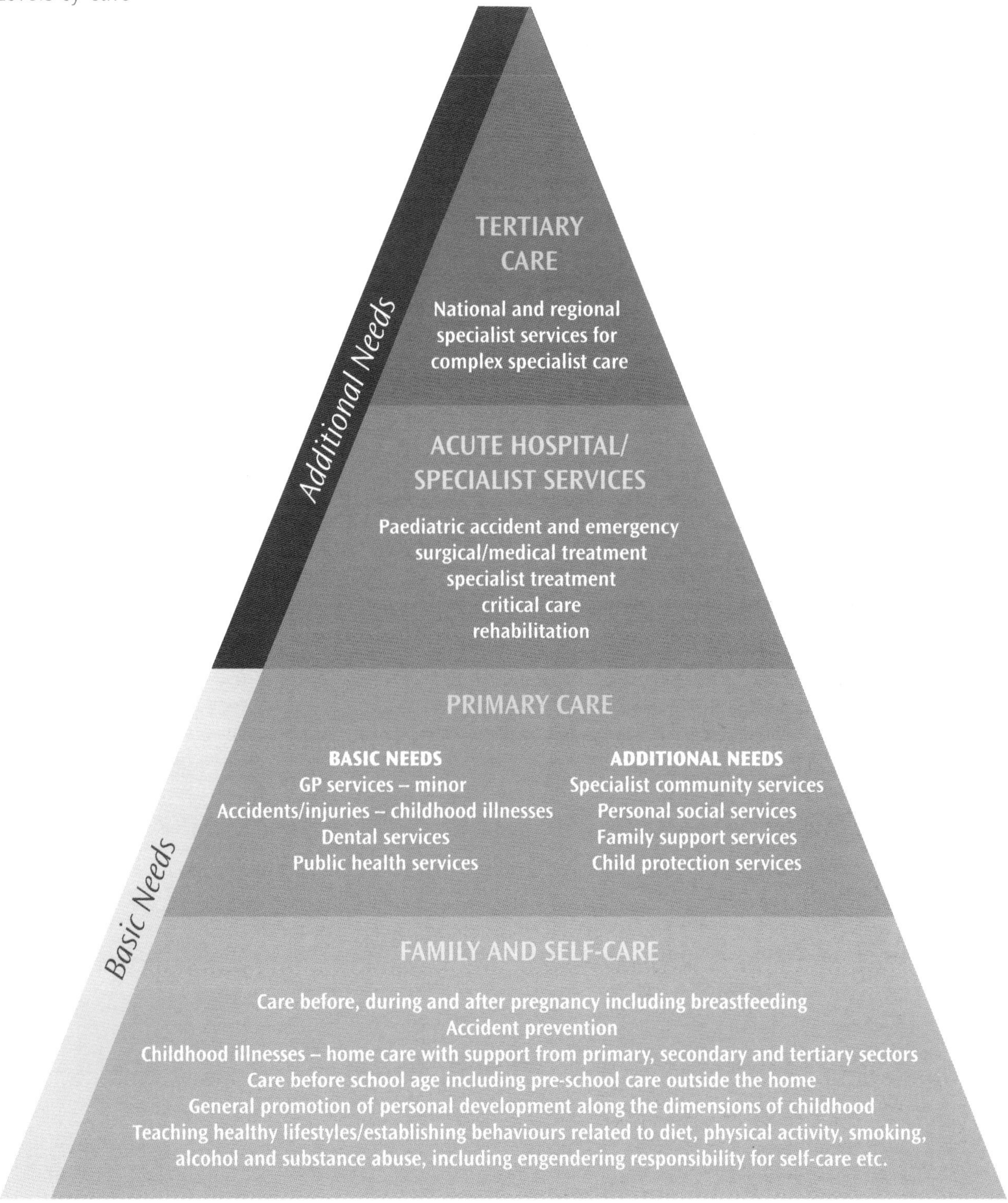

Additional Needs

Basic Needs

TERTIARY CARE

National and regional
specialist services for
complex specialist care

**ACUTE HOSPITAL/
SPECIALIST SERVICES**

Paediatric accident and emergency
surgical/medical treatment
specialist treatment
critical care
rehabilitation

PRIMARY CARE

BASIC NEEDS
GP services – minor
Accidents/injuries – childhood illnesses
Dental services
Public health services

ADDITIONAL NEEDS
Specialist community services
Personal social services
Family support services
Child protection services

FAMILY AND SELF-CARE

Care before, during and after pregnancy including breastfeeding
Accident prevention
Childhood illnesses – home care with support from primary, secondary and tertiary sectors
Care before school age including pre-school care outside the home
General promotion of personal development along the dimensions of childhood
Teaching healthy lifestyles/establishing behaviours related to diet, physical activity, smoking,
alcohol and substance abuse, including engendering responsibility for self-care etc.

Issues in child health

Health status

Despite improvements in the health status of children in recent years, certain areas of our health services for children still show shortcomings. For example, many of the causes of morbidity and mortality in children are preventable such as injuries and poisonings, infectious diseases and certain congenital anomalies such as neural tube defects. Waiting times for certain services are unacceptable. Of particular concern is the evidence of a lower health status in disadvantaged groups, including Traveller children. Best Health for Children (1999) represents a co-ordinated approach to protect and promote children's health in partnership with parents and health professionals and this approach is fully endorsed in the Health strategy.

> **Child health – legislation, strategic policy documents and expert reports**
>
> - Best Health for Children – Developing a Partnership with Families (National Conjoint Child Health Committee, 1999)
>
> - The National Children's Strategy, 2000
>
> - The National Health Promotion Strategy, 2000-2005
>
> - The Health of Our Children, Annual Report of the CMO, 2000
>
> - Adolescent Health Strategy (National Conjoint Child Health Committee, 2001)
>
> - First Report of the Review Group on Child and Adolescent Psychiatric Services , 2001

Preventive actions

The measles epidemic of 2000 highlights the dangers involved in low vaccine uptake rates. Vaccine-preventable diseases represent one area of communicable diseases for which highly effective and cost beneficial measures exist for prevention and control. The success of these programmes depends on achieving high levels of vaccine uptake which at present fall short of the target figures.

Breastfeeding of infants and young children provides one of the best opportunities to give children a good start in life. Since Ireland currently has the lowest breastfeeding rates in Europe, there is a need to promote, support and protect breastfeeding in homes, schools, workplaces and in society generally.

Actions to improve children's health and child health services

Better health for everyone

- An integrated national programme for child health will be developed.

- National minimum standards/targets for surveillance and screening will be drawn up.

- Measures to promote and support breastfeeding will be strengthened.

- Initiatives to promote healthy lifestyles for children will be extended.

- A National Injury Prevention Strategy to co-ordinate action on injury prevention will be prepared.

Health inequalities

- A programme of actions will be implemented to achieve National Anti-Poverty Strategy and Health targets for the reduction of health inequalities. By 2007, the gap in low birth weight rates between children from the lowest and highest socio-economic groups should be reduced by 10 per cent from the current level.

Fair access

- Income guidelines for the medical card scheme will be extended to cover more people on low incomes and targeted increases will be implemented to ensure that more children are covered.

- The number and nature of GP visits for an infant under the Maternity and Infant Care Scheme will be extended.

Responsive and appropriate care

- An integrated approach to care planning for individuals will become a consistent feature of the system. This will include the appointment of key workers in the context of care planning for children with disabilities.

- Mental health services for children and adolescents will be expanded:

  - implementation of the recommendations of the First Report of the Review Group on Child and Adolescent Psychiatric Services

  - development of mental health services to meet the needs of children aged between 16 and 18 (currently being reviewed by the Review Group on Child and Adolescent Psychiatric Services).

- A review of paediatric services will be undertaken.

- Protocols and standards in relation to the care of children in hospitals will be prepared.

Issues in child welfare and protection

A specialised infrastructure was put in place from the early 1990s where the dominant focus was on child protection and on fulfiling statutory responsibilities to identify children at risk. While these services were both necessary and important, awareness has grown in recent years of the need to target preventive approaches and in particular to develop and expand family support services. This involves a cross-sectoral approach as emphasised in the National Children's Strategy and led by the National Children's Office. The approach also emphasises greater co-ordination between child welfare and protection and primary care services such as general practice and public health nursing. Effective co-ordination is also essential between these services and therapeutic services such as child and adolescent psychiatric teams. Better integration and inter-sectoral working has particular relevance in relation to the effective implementation of the Children Act, 2001.

Child welfare – legislation, strategic policy documents and expert reports

- Child Care Act, 1991

- The United Nations Convention on the Rights of the Child (ratified by Ireland in 1992)

- The Protection for Persons Reporting Child Abuse Act, 1998

- Children First – National Guidelines for the Protection and Welfare of Children, 1999

- Standardised Framework for Inter-Country Adoption Assessment, 2000

- National Children's Strategy, 2000

- Children Act, 2001

- Report of the Working Group on Foster Care. Foster Care – A Child-Centred Partnership, 2001

- Youth Homelessness Strategy, 2001

An underlying issue contributing to problems in service provision is the lack of good-quality information about the needs of children and the existing capacity of the system to deliver good outcomes. A major project is underway to create an integrated management information system for child welfare and protection services.

The Children Act, 2001, the establishment of the Social Services Inspectorate and Children First–National Guidelines for the Protection and Welfare of Children, represent major developments in strengthening arrangements for the protection and care of children. In the area of adoption, new legislation is being prepared on information rights and inter-country adoption.

Considerable investment has been made in human resources in child welfare and protection services over the last number of years. However, due to the stressful nature of this work, it is critical that issues such as training, caseload management and working practices for child care professionals are further strengthened and developed. These will be addressed in the context of the Action Plan for People Management which will set out specific actions to support staff and strengthen management support. In addition, career structures, skills mix and multidisciplinary working will be examined as part of the initiative on workforce planning.

Actions to strengthen child welfare and protection services

Better health for everyone

- Family support services will be expanded:

  - Child welfare budgets will be refocused over the next seven years to provide a more even balance between safeguarding activities and supportive programmes.

  - Springboard Projects and other family support initiatives will be further developed.

  - Positive parenting supports and programmes will be expanded.

  - Effective out-of-hours services will be developed in all health board areas as a priority.

  - Family welfare conferences and other services required to support the Children Act, 2001 will be introduced.

  - Priority will be given to early intervention for children with behavioural difficulties.

- The Youth Homelessness Strategy will be implemented.

People with disabilities

Policy context and recent developments

Current Government policy on the provision of services to people with disabilities places emphasis on the importance of mainstreaming. In essence this policy requires that specific services for people with disabilities should be the responsibility of those government departments and state agencies which provide the services for the general public.

The Department of Health and Children in consultation with other government departments will concentrate on the enhancement of the health and personal social service needs of people with disabilities. Health services have an impact on people with disabilities through:

- the use of primary, secondary and tertiary health-care services which are used by everyone in the community

- the use of disability support services developed specifically to meet the needs of people with different types of disability.

The principle which underpins policy is to enable each individual with a disability to achieve his or her full potential and maximum independence, including living within the community as independently as possible. A major proportion of the services for people with disabilities is provided by agencies in the voluntary sector.

> **Disability services – legislation, strategic policy documents and expert reports**
>
> - *Needs and Abilities – Report of the Review Group on Mental Handicap Services (1990)*
>
> - *Services for People with Autism, Department of Health (1994)*
>
> - *Towards an Independent Future – Report of the Review Group on Health and Personal Social Services for People with Physical and Sensory Disabilities (1996)*
>
> - *A Strategy for Equality – Report of the Commission on the Status of People with Disabilities (1996)*
>
> - *Employment Challenges for the Millennium – Report of the National Advisory Committee on Training and Employment (1997)*

Issues in disability

Since the publication of *Shaping a Healthier Future* in 1994, there has been considerable investment and expansion in a range of services for people with disabilities. Additional funding of £256m has been provided for services for people with intellectual disability and those with autism and £119m has been provided for services for people with physical and sensory disabilities.

Despite a significant expansion of services, there are still unmet needs in the overall range of support services required by people with disabilities. There are concerns about access to services including the adequacy of provision in some geographical areas and the varying criteria for access to day, residential and respite care.

Access to information on services and entitlements for people with disabilities was also raised in the consultation process.

Intellectual disability and autism

Since 1997 the programme of investment in services has been based on the needs identified in the National Intellectual Disability Database, which came into operation in 1996.

Intellectual disability – some facts

There were 26,760 people registered on the National Intellectual Disability Database in 2000, 460 more than in 1996.

Currently, 24,035 people with intellectual disability are in receipt of services, representing 89.8 per cent of the total population. Of these 1.8 per cent are without services at present and are wait-listed for appropriate services. The remaining 8.4 per cent, most of whom have a mild degree of intellectual disability or have not had their level of disability verified, have no identified requirement for services in the next five years.

An additional 1,291 people are in receipt of services since the first data were reported in 1996; 238 of this group are in full-time residential services and 1,052 are attending services on a daily basis.

Provision of respite services has increased by 70% since 1996. Particularly significant increases are observed in the number of people availing of planned or emergency respite care (up 135%), respite breaks with host families (up 88%) and regular part-time care (up 19%).

A number of factors contributing to the increased demand for services in this area include:

•   improved medical technology and treatments

•   changing family structures

•   greater longevity of this client group

•   increased identified incidence of autism.

Concerns have also been expressed that a number of people with intellectual disability are still receiving services in a psychiatric hospital setting.

Physical and sensory disability

It is important to note that people with physical and sensory disabilities are a very heterogeneous group. The term covers a wide variety of conditions and levels of disability. A person with a visual or hearing impairment has very different needs to a person with a physical disability. This has implications for the levels of support required from the health services. A multifaceted approach involving other government departments and agencies is required to meet the needs of this client group.

A major obstacle to the planning and development of appropriate services for people with physical and sensory disability has been the lack of statistical information on numbers and needs. The National Physical and Sensory Disability Database Development Committee was established in December 1998 to address this issue. The establishment on a national basis of the Physical and Sensory Disability Database is a priority so that the extent of unmet need can be measured.

Despite increased development funding, there are considerable unmet needs in regard to people with physical and sensory disabilities. Further investment is required to expand family support and day and residential facilities for people with physical and sensory disabilities. Other gaps which were highlighted in submissions on the Health Strategy were: respite care, personal assistance services, funding of aids and appliances and the development of appropriate rehabilitation services.

Training and work

Training

In June 2000 the Government assigned responsibility for vocational training to the Department of Enterprise, Trade and Employment and for rehabilitative training to the Department of Health and Children. Since the dissolution of the National Rehabilitation Board responsibility for the management of rehabilitative training has been assigned to the health boards. A standard for delivery of rehabilitative training has been recently agreed and is in place.

Sheltered work

Over the years the provision of day activity services for people with disabilities has evolved in many instances into the provision of a range of sheltered work activities. *Employment Challenges for the Millennium,* the Report of the National Advisory Committee on Training and Employment (1997), estimated that there are 7,900 people with disabilities working in 215 sheltered workshops. A more structured policy framework covering all aspects of the provision of sheltered work for people with disabilities is required.

Actions for disability services - general

Fair access

- The forthcoming Disabilities Bill will outline a statutory framework for the assessment of need and provision of services for people with disabilities.

- The Inter-Departmental Working Group examining the feasibility of introducing a cost of disability payment will report during 2002. This will include a review of the wide range of existing allowances and concessions for people with disabilities.

Responsive and appropriate care delivery

- An integrated approach to care planning for individuals will become a consistent feature of the system. This will include the appointment of key workers in the context of care planning for children with disabilities.

- Community and voluntary activity in maintaining health will be supported.

  - Programmes to support informal caregivers through the development of informal networks, the provision of basic training and the greater availability of short-term respite care will be developed and implemented.

  - Programmes to foster voluntarism and community responsiveness to local needs will be undertaken.

High performance

- The remit of the Social Services Inspectorate will be extended to include residential care for people with disabilities.

- National standards for residential care for people with disabilities will be prepared.

- Service agreements between the health boards and the voluntary sector will be extended to all service providers and associated performance indicators will be introduced.

Actions for intellectual disability and autism

Responsive and appropriate care delivery

- A programme of investment will take place in the following services:

  - Expansion of day places, training, residential and respite care and other support services (e.g. in settings such as schools).

  - Complete programme to transfer people with an intellectual disability currently in psychiatric hospitals to appropriate accommodation as soon as possible and not later than end 2006.

  - Investment to provide appropriate support services for people with autism; an information system to provide accurate data on the numbers of persons with autism and their service needs will be established as soon as possible.

Actions for physical and sensory disability

Responsive and appropriate care delivery

- A programme of investment will take place in the following services:

  - Home support services, respite care, day care places, residential care including additional places for people with chronic conditions

  - Training

  - Other multi-disciplinary support services

  - Aids and appliances

- An action plan for rehabilitation services will be prepared

- All reasonable steps to make health facilities accessible will be taken

Mental health

Policy context and recent developments

Policy on mental health is based on *Planning for the Future*, published in 1984. This report recommended the establishment of a comprehensive community-oriented mental health service as an alternative to institutional care. The main legislative provision relating to mental health services is the Mental Health Treatment Act, 1945.

Structural developments

Planning for the Future (1984) recommended the closure of the old psychiatric hospitals and their replacement with acute psychiatric units in general hospitals and a range of community-based residential accommodation. While considerable progress has been made in many health board areas in implementing the change from institutional to community-based care, few have as yet completed the process. Pressures on acute psychiatric units, particularly in the Eastern Region, will be significantly eased by the provision of additional community residences in these catchment areas where the rate of community places per head of population is lower than average.

> **Mental health services – legislation, strategic policy documents and expert reports guiding activity**
>
> - *Mental Treatment Act, 1945*
> - *Planning for the Future (Report of a Study Group on the Development of Psychiatric Services) 1984*
> - *National Task Force on Suicide Report, 1998*
> - *Annual Reports of the Inspector of Mental Hospitals*
> - *Good Practice Guidelines, 1998*
> - *Mental Health Act, 2001*
> - *First Report of the Review Group on Child and Adolescent Psychiatric Services (2001)*

Eighteen acute psychiatric units are at various stages of development. These will be accelerated with a view to ensuring that, by 2008, there will be no further acute admissions to psychiatric hospitals.

Among those with mental illness, a small but significant minority of patients are disturbed. In a modern mental health service, the needs of the disturbed mentally ill are best met by the development of psychiatric intensive care units (PICUs). Following a lengthy consultation process, the Department of Health and Children issued a policy document in 1999 proposing the development of such a unit in each health board area and setting out the staffing and protocols which would be required. All health boards will be developing these units over the next few years as part of the modernisation of the mental health services.

Legislation

The Mental Health Act, 2001 is the most significant legislative provision in the field of mental health for over fifty years. It significantly reforms existing legislation concerning the involuntary detention of people for psychiatric treatment. The legislation brings Irish mental health law into conformity with the European Convention for the Protection of Human Rights and Fundamental Freedoms. It provides for the establishment of an independent agency to be known as the Mental Health Commission. The Commission's primary function will be to promote and foster high standards and good practices in the delivery of mental health services and to ensure that the interests of persons detained under the terms of the Act are protected. The Commission will be responsible for overseeing the process of review of detention by mental health tribunals and will also employ the new inspector of mental health services, who will have wide-ranging powers. The Commission will be appointed before the end of 2001, to enable it to commence the implementation of the new Act as quickly as possible.

Suicide prevention

The Report of the National Task Force on Suicide, published in 1998, outlined a comprehensive strategy to reduce the incidence of suicide and attempted suicide in Ireland.

Since its publication, over £3m has been invested in suicide prevention measures in the health boards. Each board now has a suicide resource officer in place and regional suicide prevention plans are being drawn up. Additional resources will be allocated to suicide prevention in the coming years.

The National Suicide Review Group was established by the chief executive officers of the health boards in response to the Task Force Report. Its main responsibilities are to review ongoing trends in suicide and parasuicide (attempted suicide), to co-ordinate research into suicide and to make appropriate recommendations to health boards. The Health (Miscellaneous Provisions) Act, 2001 requires the Minister for Health and Children to report to the Oireachtas each year on the measures taken to address the problem of suicide. The work of the National Suicide Review Group will inform the preparation of this report.

Issues in mental health

Policy

There is now a need to update mental health policy, to take account of recent legislative reform, developments in the care and treatment of mental illness and current best practice. The role of the new Mental Health Commission, to be established under the Mental Health Act, 2001, in ensuring quality and high standards in the delivery of services will also need to be considered.

Structures

Policy and objectives for mental health services also need to be updated to take account of legislative reform, developments in the care and treatment of mental illness and delivery of services in modern society. This is required in order to deal with issues such as:

* the need to integrate mental health care into primary care

* concerns about using only the traditional 'medical' model of care for mental illness rather than considering alternative therapies such as psychotherapy or psychological treatments

* the development of a more holistic approach to mental health treatment and care in order to deal with the need of mental health service users for support in other aspects of their lives, such as housing, finance, employment, education and physical health.

Service levels

Despite some progress in recent years, the existing level of services is inadequate. In particular, community services such as home nursing, day centres, family support, hostels and day hospitals will continue to be developed. There are also gaps in services for specific groups with mental health problems including:

* children and adolescents

- people with eating disorders

- homeless people

- older people.

Advocacy

There is a need to generate greater public awareness and understanding of mental illness and to change attitudes to mental illness among the general public and health professionals. In addition, the development of advocacy services for people with mental health problems has emerged as an issue. In terms of the principle of people-centred health services, the strengthening of advocacy services is a priority.

An advocate is someone who represents and defends the views, needs and rights of an individual who does not feel able to do this for him or herself. Within the mental health services, an advocate helps the patient to explore and understand his or her concerns and then represents these concerns to service providers and others in positions of authority. The advocate thereby facilitates the service user's participation in decision-making about his or her own care and treatment. Advocacy encourages recovery by enabling the patient to take control and it can act as a mechanism for changing attitudes towards mental illness.

The development of advocacy services will help to address the civil and human rights of the mentally ill. The Mental Health Act, 2001 makes statutory provision for legal advocacy for people with a mental disorder, by requiring the Mental Health Commission to provide an independent legal representative to each person who is detained involuntarily under the terms of the Act. The development within the voluntary sector of other forms of independent advocacy for mental health services users, e.g. peer advocacy and self-advocacy, needs to be encouraged and supported.

There is also a need for increased input from patients of the mental health services into the planning of services and the promotion of mental health.

Actions for mental health

Policy development

- The Mental Health Commission will be established by end of 2001 to begin the implementation of the Mental Health Act, 2001.

- A national policy framework for the further modernisation of the mental health services, updating Planning for the Future, will be prepared.

Better health for everyone

- Services aimed at specific groups will be further developed including:

  - older people

  - those who would benefit from community-based alcohol treatment programmes.

- A report on services for people with eating disorders will be prepared by the Review Group on Child and Adolescent Psychiatric Services .

- Programmes to promote positive attitudes to mental health will be introduced.

- Independent patient advocacy services will be encouraged and resourced.

- Mental health services for children and adolescents will be expanded through:

  – Implementation of the recommendations of the First Report of the Review Group on Child and Adolescent Psychiatric Services

  – Development of mental health services to meet the needs of children aged between 16 and 18 (currently being reviewed by the Review Group on Child and Adolescent Psychiatric Services).

- Suicide prevention programmes will be intensified.

Responsive and appropriate care delivery

- A programme of investment will take place in:

  – community care services, i.e. community nursing, day centres, hostels and day hospitals, training and work programmes; family support

  – acute psychiatric units.

- Regional advisory panels/co-ordinating committees (including service providers and consumers) will be established in all health board areas for people with mental illness to advise on the planning and prioritisation of services, the quality of services and the promotion of positive mental health initiatives. These committees will be modelled on similar developments in the area of disability services and will include representation of statutory and voluntary service providers as well as consumers.

Services for older people

Policy context and recent developments in services

The level of investment in services for the elderly was low during the 1980s and into the mid-1990s. In 1997 an additional £10m was provided, increasing to £36m in 2000 and £57.42m in 2001. Between 1997 and 2000 an additional 800 posts were approved, 400 additional beds were provided in 10 new community nursing units and over 1,000 day places per week were provided in 10 new day care centres.

> **Services for older people – legislation, strategic policy documents and expert reports**
> - The Years Ahead: A Policy for the Elderly (Report of the Working Party on Services for the Elderly), 1988
> - The Health (Nursing Homes) Act, 1990
> - The Years Ahead – A review of the Implementation of its Recommendations, 1997
> - Adding years to life and life to years – A Health Promotion Strategy for Older People, 1998
> - An Action Plan for Dementia, 1999

Issues for older people

Older people often experience a poor level of health accompanied by pain, discomfort, anxiety and depression. There is a need to develop a comprehensive approach to meeting the needs of ageing and older people if the problems in the care and quality of life of older people are to be addressed and the increased demands over the next 20-30 years are to be met. This must include both acute health care provisions for the sick elderly and active health maintenance programmes for continuance of health in the elderly.

The continued growth in the population of those aged 65 years and over will give rise to additional demands for services. Significant development of these services will be required as a priority to meet such demands. Currently, the main gaps in service provision relate to:

- community-support services (e.g. paramedic services, community nursing services, health promotion, home help service, day care)

- acute hospitals (e.g. shortages in assessment and rehabilitation beds and day hospital facilities)

- long-stay places (e.g. need for additional community nursing units).

The Ombudsman's Report on the Nursing Home Subvention Scheme published in 2001 has raised issues regarding service eligibility and charging for long-stay care. There is a need for a clear policy on eligibility and on the balance in planning both public and private services in relation to this issue. This is particularly important given the demographic trends in relation to older people as a percentage of the overall population, the increased expenditure on the scheme and the risk that current provisions create incentives to enter residential care when community care would be more appropriate and preferable to older people and their families.

The problem of inadequate co-ordination of services for older people, applies both within services for older people and to the interface between those services and acute hospital and other specialised services such as mental health.

The National Council for Older People has produced a number of reports in recent years relating to specific areas of need. A clear framework for implementing the recommendations contained in reports on health promotion and dementia is required.

Actions for older people

Better health for everyone

- A co-ordinated action plan to meet the needs of ageing and older people will be developed by the Department of Health and Children in conjunction with the Departments of the Environment and Local Government; Social Community and Family Affairs; and Public Enterprise.

- Community groups will be funded to facilitate volunteers in providing support services such as shopping, visiting and transport for older people.

- Health boards will continue to take the lead role in implementing the Health Promotion Strategy for Older People, Adding Years to Life and Life to Years (1998).

- An action plan for dementia based on the recommendations of the National Council for Ageing and Older People will be implemented.

Fair access

- Eligibility arrangements will be simplified and clarified. The Ombudsman has drawn attention to the uncertainty surrounding the eligibility of older people for long-term residential care. Clarification of entitlement in this regard will be given particular attention in the general review of legislation on entitlement. Emphasis will also be placed on implementing a standard approach to dependency assessment and the payment of subventions in each area of the country.

- The Nursing Home Subvention Scheme will be amended to take account of the expenditure review of the scheme. A large number of older people would like the option of receiving care in the home rather than in a nursing home. The recent expenditure review of the Nursing Home Subvention Scheme has shown that current funding arrangements do not effectively support home care. The Government intends reforming the operation of existing schemes, including the Carers' Allowance, in order to introduce an integrated care subvention scheme which maximises support for home care. In addition, subvention rates payable in private nursing homes will be reviewed. The Department of Health and Children will begin work immediately with the Department of Social, Community and Family Affairs to develop detailed proposals for the new scheme with a view to introduction as soon as possible.

- A grant will be introduced to cover two weeks' respite care per annum for dependent older persons.

- Proposals on the financing of long-term care for older people will be brought forward.

Responsiveness and appropriate care delivery

- An integrated approach to care planning for individuals will become a consistent feature of the system. This will include the appointment of key workers for dependent older people such as those on the margins of home and residential care.

- Regional advisory panels/co-ordinating committees (including service providers and consumers) will be established in all health board areas for older consumers and their carers, to provide them with a voice.

- Community and voluntary activity will be supported:

  - Programmes to support informal caregivers through the development of informal networks, provision of basic training and the greater availability of short-term respite care will be developed and implemented

  - Programmes to foster voluntarism and community responsiveness to local needs will be undertaken.

- A programme of investment to increase capacity as follows:

Community services :

- Recruitment of a multi-disciplinary range of staff to support the development of primary care services such as domiciliary care, and day and respite services

- The provision of 7,000 day centre places

- Increased funding for aids and appliances in people's homes

Hospital Services:

- 1,370 additional assessment and rehabilitation beds; associated development of acute geriatric medical services and appointment of additional geriatricians

- 600 additional day hospital beds with facilities encompassing specialist areas such as falls, osteoporosis treatment, fracture prevention, Parkinson's Disease, stroke prevention, heart failure and continence promotion clinics

Residential care

- 800 additional extended care/community nursing unit places per annum over the next 7 years including provision for people with dementia

- Improved staffing levels in extended care units.

High performance

- The remit of the Social Services Inspectorate will be extended to include residential care for older people

- National standards for community and long-term residential care of older people will be prepared.

Women's health

Policy context and recent developments

Policy initiatives

A *Plan for Women's Health* 1997-1999 set out four key objectives for the health services in relation to women. These were:

- to maximise the health and social gain of Irish women

- to create a woman-friendly health service

- to increase consultation and representation of women in the health services

- to enhance the contribution of the health services to promoting women's health in the developing world.

All health boards have produced women's health plans in accordance with the national *Plan for Women's Health*. They concentrate on issues of particular concern to the health board region and were developed by women's health advisory committees in the various health boards.

Women's Health – legislation, strategic policy documents and expert reports

- *National Breastfeeding Policy for Ireland, 1994*

- *Developing a policy for women's health – A discussion document, 1995*

- *Report of the Department of Health Cervical Screening Committee, 1996*

- *National Cancer Strategy 1996*

- *A Plan for Women's Health, 1997-1999*

- *Building Healthier Hearts, 1999*

- *National Health Promotion Strategy, 2000*

- *Services for Patients with Symptomatic Breast Disease, 2000*

- *Towards a Tobacco-Free Society, 2000*

The Women's Health Council was established on a statutory basis in 1997. Its functions include evaluating progress towards meeting the objectives of the *Plan for Women's Health* and advising the Minister for Health and Children on women's health issues generally. The Women's Health Council involves a partnership between consumers, health-care professionals, policy makers and other representative groups including the National Women's Council of Ireland.

Preventive actions

Phase 1 of Breastcheck, the National Breast Screening Programme, commenced in February 2000 and covers the Eastern Regional Health Authority, Midland Health Board and North-Eastern Health Board areas. Screening in these areas is available to all women aged between 50-64 years. This service is being delivered in two central units with outreach to the community by means of three mobile units.

Phase 1 of the Irish Cervical Screening Programme commenced in the Mid-Western Health Board region in October 2000. All women in the health board area aged between 25 and 60 years (72,000 approx) have been encouraged to register with the programme. Those registered will have a cervical smear taken free of charge at five-yearly intervals. As stated in Chapter 4 breast and cervical cancer screening programmes will be extended nationally, having regard to the experience gained in implementing the programmes to date.

Issues in women's health

Health status

Using a number of indicators the health of Irish women can be compared to that of our EU neighbours. Irish women have a relatively lower life expectancy, particularly in middle age, than their EU counterparts. Death rates from heart disease in Irish women are amongst the highest of any country in the EU. In 1997 the incidence of lung cancer in females in Ireland was the sixth highest out of 23 European countries.

The prevalence of smoking amongst young women has increased in recent years and rates among young women are now similar to those among young men. This is of particular concern where, for example, diseases such as cardiovascular disease and lung cancer are concerned.

Other important issues for women include maternity services and support for victims of domestic violence.

Actions for women's health

Better health for everyone

- Targeting a reduction in smoking for young women will be one of the actions to achieve targets set out in the National Health Promotion Strategy.

- The programmes of screening for breast and cervical cancer will be extended nationally.

- A comprehensive strategy to address crisis pregnancy will be prepared.

- Measures to prevent domestic violence and to support victims will continue.

Responsive and appropriate care delivery

- A plan to provide responsive, high-quality maternity care will be drawn up.

Men's health

Policy context and recent developments

Men's health – legislation, strategic policy documents and expert reports

- National Alcohol Policy, 1996
- Report of the National Task Force on Suicides, 1998
- Report on the Men's Health Conference, North Western Health Board, 1999
- Building Healthier Hearts, The Report of the Cardiovascular Health Strategy Group, 1999
- Us Men, Our Health, Western Health Board, 2000
- The National Health Promotion Strategy, 2000-2005
- Towards a Tobacco-Free Society, 2000.
- Inequalities in Mortality, A Report on All-Ireland Mortality Data, Institute of Public Health, 2001
- Men talking, North Eastern Health Board, 2001

Issues in men's health

Health status

Gender differences in mortality are emerging as a fundamental inequality in health. In 1950, the male/female difference in life expectancy at birth was 2.5 years. It is now over 5.5 years. The difference in life expectancy at age 65 was 1 year and now approaches 4 years. The Institute of Public Health report on mortality demonstrated that death rates were more than 50 per cent higher for males than for females. These differences applied across the major causes of premature mortality including cancer, circulatory disease, respiratory disease, and especially for injuries and poisonings where the rate was 169 per cent higher in males.

Much of this premature mortality is preventable and lifestyle behaviours are particularly important. Men experience more accidents than women during sporting activities and in the workplace; they are more likely to engage in risk behaviours such as speeding, drink driving and not wearing seatbelts. Males aged 20-24 years have the highest death rate from unintentional injury of all age groups up to age 70 years. Over 30 per cent of road traffic accident deaths occur in the 15-24 year age group; the highest rate of deaths from road traffic accidents is in males aged 20-24 years. Falls and being struck or cut are also a very high proportion of unintentional injury hospital admissions for males as compared to females (Scallan et al, 2001).

Males have less healthy diets than females, are more likely to be overweight or obese, drink more alcohol and are more likely to become involved with substance abuse. Men also experience considerable mental health problems; the most common causes of male admissions to psychiatric hospitals are depressive disorders, schizophrenia and alcohol dependency. Of particular concern in recent years has been the increase in the number of young males committing suicide.

Research suggests that men take few preventive health measures and are less willing than women to seek medical help. Developing awareness of men's health issues and encouraging men to present earlier for treatment and support is an important element in developing a plan for men's health.The North-Eastern Health Board has been to the forefront in researching men's health and will shortly appoint a men's health co-ordinator. This initiative will be evaluated carefully with a view to extending the model to other health board areas.

Actions for men's health

Better health for everyone

- A National Injury Prevention Strategy to co-ordinate action on injury prevention will be prepared.

- A policy for men's health and health promotion will be developed.

- Measures to prevent domestic violence and to support victims will continue.

Population health

Policy context and recent developments

Population health aims to improve the health of entire populations or subgroups of the population and to reduce health inequalities among population groups.

A wide range of policy documents and legislation governs activity in this area. The implementation of key strategy documents such as the National Health Promotion Strategy, the Cancer Strategy and the Cardiovascular Strategy has been central to developments in this area in recent years. These areas have already been addressed in some detail in Chapter 4.

Issues in population health

Health and health status

Chapter 2 described the health status of the Irish people. It highlighted the unfavourable life expectancy and death rates in Ireland when compared to those of our EU neighbours and provided evidence of health inequalities in Ireland relating to social class.

> **Population health – legislation, strategic policy documents and expert reports**
>
> - Irish Medicines Board Act, 1995
> - National Cancer Strategy, 1996
> - National Alcohol Policy, 1996
> - Medicinal Products (Prescriptions and Control of Supply) Regulations, 1996–2000
> - The Food Hygiene Act, 1998
> - National Cardiovascular Health Strategy, 1999
> - Draft Environmental Health Action Plan, 1999
> - Towards a Tobacco-Free Society, 2000
> - National Health Promotion Strategy, 2000-2005
> - European food law
> - EU Standing Committees on foodstuffs and medicinal products
> - Reports and Guidelines issued by the FSAI, WHO, CJD Advisory Group, Food Safety Promotion Board

Some of the principal population health issues in Ireland today, therefore, include tackling inequalities in health as well as reducing deaths from the principal causes of premature mortality, namely cardiovascular disease, cancer and accidents. Health promotion and prevention of disease through initiatives such as immunisation are also crucial elements of a population health approach. Other issues include ensuring the safety of food, medicines and the environment.

A population health approach reflects the evidence that many factors outside the health care system significantly affect people's health. These include social, economic and environmental factors that are often beyond the control of the individual. Addressing these areas requires concerted inter-sectoral action.

The actions proposed in this section recognise the need for an organised response to improve the health status of the Irish population. Central to this is the need for the introduction of dedicated population health sections at both Department of Health and Children and health board levels. Another important action will be the health-proofing of all decisions related to public policy by all government departments. Other specific actions relate to tackling health inequalities and promoting healthy lifestyles for all.

Environmental health, food and medicines

In the area of environmental health, the Institute of Public Health in Ireland is supporting co-operation across boundaries to sustain and develop public health work. The role of the Institute is vital in providing public health leadership which can cut across sectors and contribute to the reduction/elimination of health inequalities. There is a need to provide a comprehensive plan to support the Institute in enjoining the partners in environmental action and health planning.

This country has a reputation for producing food products of a very high quality. The Food Safety Authority of Ireland Act, 1998 placed primary responsibility for food safety with the Department of Health and Children and created a new, independent organisation, the Food Safety Authority of Ireland (FSAI), to implement this policy. Also, funding for the development of the health boards' food control services, including sampling, inspections, micro-biological laboratories and public analyst laboratories, has been relatively generous over the past few years. The establishment of the Food Safety Authority of Ireland and the Food Safety Promotion Board (FSPB) has made a significant contribution to the development of an effective and comprehensive policy on food safety and hygiene for the entire island of Ireland. The constant developments in this area, particularly with regard to EU legislation, require sustained momentum in drawing up new legislation.

The capacity of the FSAI and the FSPB will continue to be developed to ensure the protection of the health and well-being of the public in relation to food safety. This will include strengthening and further developing inspectorate and laboratory services for food safety and supporting the delivery of public awareness campaigns on an all-island basis by the FSPB. Food safety will continue to be addressed through awareness/education campaigns for the food industry.

The Irish Medicines Board Act, 1995 created a new executive agency, the Irish Medicines Board (IMB), with responsibility for implementing policy. The role of the Irish Medicines Board is to ensure the safety, quality and efficacy of all medicines placed on the Irish market. The ability of the board to police enforcement and compliance, while greatly improved, still needs further strengthening.

Complementary and alternative medicine is a range of healing resources that encompasses treatments and practices not availed of in the politically dominant health system. The popularity of complementary and alternative medicine (CAM) was evident from the range of submissions received for this strategy. CAM is perceived to deliver health care from a holistic point of view, which is welcomed by consumers. Many submissions viewed CAM as complementary to primary health care and called for greater integration with conventional health care. However, concerns were raised about the lack of regulation in relation to the medicinal products that are involved.

Actions for population health/better health for everyone – general

- Health impact assessment will be introduced as part of the public policy development process.

- Statements of strategy and business plans of all relevant Government departments will incorporate an explicit commitment to sustaining and improving health status.

- A population health division will be established in the Department of Health and Children and in each health board.

Actions for population health/better health for everyone: health promotion

- Actions on major lifestyle factors targeted in the National Cancer, Cardiovascular and Health Promotion Strategies will be enhanced.

- The Public Health (Tobacco) Bill will be enacted and implemented as a matter of urgency.

- A reduction in smoking will continue to be targeted through Government fiscal policies.

- Initiatives to promote healthy lifestyles in children will be extended.

- Measures to promote and support breastfeeding will be strengthened.

- A National Injury Prevention Strategy to co-ordinate action on injury prevention will be prepared.

- The programmes for screening for breast and cervical cancer will be extended nationally.

- A revised implementation plan for the National Cancer Strategy will be published.

- The Heart Health Task Force will monitor and evaluate the implementation of the prioritised cardiovascular health action plan.

- Initiatives will be taken to improve children's health.

- A policy for men's health and health promotion will be developed.

- Measures will be taken to promote sexual health and safer sexual practices.

Actions for population health/better health for everyone: health inequalities

- A programme of actions will be implemented to achieve specific targets in the reduction of health inequalities.

- Initiatives to eliminate barriers for disadvantaged groups to improve lifestyles will be developed and expanded.

- The health of Travellers will be improved.

- Initiatives to improve the health and well-being of homeless people and drug misusers will be advanced.

- The health needs of asylum seekers/refugees will be addressed.

- Initiatives to improve the health of prisoners will be advanced.

- Income guidelines for the medical card will be increased.

- Improved access to hospital services for public patients will be addressed through a series of integrated measures.

- Availability of information on entitlements including use of information technology will be improved.

Actions for population health/better health for everyone: environmental health, food and medicines

- The National Environmental Health Action Plan will be prepared.

- Legislation in the area of food safety will be prepared to take account of developments in food safety regulation at national and EU level.

- A review of medicines legislation will be undertaken.

- Licensing of alternative medicine will be examined.

- The highest international standards of safety in transfusion medicine will be set and adhered to.

CHAPTER 7

Action Plan

Introduction

Government non-capital funding of health services has doubled since 1996, and has meant greatly enhanced services throughout the health sector. However, this investment was made against a background of historically low levels of funding by international comparisons. Also, some two-thirds of the new investment over recent years have been committed to pay and technical costs, with just one-third available for new developments.

The costings of the Strategy are estimated at just over £10 billion (€12.7 billion) as expressed in 2001 prices. The breakdown of the figures are £6.1 billion (€7.7 billion) capital and £4 billion (€5 billion) non-capital.

The capital figure provides for all costs in regard to projects from planning, through construction and equipping. It is additional to the £2 billion (€2.54 billion) already committed by the Government to the health services as part of the National Development Plan (NDP) 2000-2006. The inclusion of the health services in the NDP was the first time that this sector had been funded by the NDP and it represented a significant increase over previous funding levels. However, this must be measured against historically low investment in the Health Capital Programme, leading to a situation where many of the buildings in use are now old, poorly maintained and overall in bad repair. The provision currently made for ongoing maintenance and replacement of major items of equipment also needs to be increased.

The capital cost of £6.1 billion (€7.7 billion) is the estimate for putting in place across all service programmes a modern and quality infrastructure which meets the needs of providers and users of services. This investment will benefit acute hospitals, the development of a range of facilities in the community and the provision of much-needed facilities for client groups such as older people, children and people with an intellectual, physical or sensory disability. The investment will also support necessary improvements in research and information systems.

The non-capital estimated cost of £4 billion (€5 billion) will fund major initiatives such as extensions of eligibility for medical cards, additional bed capacity in acute hospitals, significant enhancement of services for older people, together with resourcing ongoing developments such as services for people with a disability and child care.

The Action Plan

National Goal No. 1: Better health for everyone

Objective 1: The health of the population is at the centre of public policy

	Action	Deliverable	Target date	Responsibility
1	Health impact assessment will be introduced as part of the public policy development process.	• Health impact assessment to be carried out on all new Government policies	June 2002	Relevant Government departments
2	Statements of strategy and business plans of all relevant Government departments will incorporate an explicit commitment to sustaining and improving health status.	• Departmental statements of strategy to include commitments to sustaining and improving health status	With immediate effect	Relevant Government departments
3	The National Environment and Health Action Plan will be prepared.	• Plan submitted to Government	June 2002	Relevant Government departments and agencies
4	A population health division will be established in the Department of Health and Children.	• New division to be established and begin	March 2002	Department of Health and Children (DoHC)
	A population health function will be established in each health board.	• Reorganisation and expansion of existing function	June 2002	Health boards

Objective 2: The promotion of health and well-being is intensified

	Action	Deliverable	Target date	Responsibility
5	Actions on major lifestyle factors targeted in the National Cancer, Cardiovascular and Health Promotion Strategies will be enhanced.	To achieve targets set out in the National Health Promotion Strategy (2000-2005) through:	Ongoing	DoHC and health boards
		Smoking		
		• Enhanced health promotion initiatives aimed at addressing the risk factors associated with cancers such as smoking	Ongoing	
		• Targeting a reduction in smoking for young women	Ongoing	
		Alcohol		
		• Introducing further actions to promote sensible alcohol consumption on the basis of a review of the National Alcohol Policy	Mid 2003	
		• Examining possible further restrictions on the advertising of alcohol		
		Diet and exercise		
		• Continuing action to improve Irish diet so that essential nutrients and energy levels are maintained and fat consumption is controlled	Ongoing	
		• Continuing measures to promote physical exercise	Ongoing	
6	The Public Health (Tobacco) Bill will be enacted and implemented as a matter of urgency.	• Enactment of Bill	Passed by Easter 2002	DoHC
		• Implementation of Act		
		– Policing of bans on advertising and sponsorship	Ongoing	Tobacco Control Agency
		– Establishment of register of retailers	End 2002	Tobacco Control Agency

7	A reduction in smoking will continue to be targeted through Government fiscal policies.	Decisions on tax and excise duties on tobacco products	Ongoing	Department of Finance
8	Initiatives to promote healthy lifestyles in children will be extended.	Extension of substance abuse prevention programme and social, personal and health education programmes	On an ongoing basis – full extension to all schools by December 2005	Department of Education/ DoHC/health boards
9	Measures to promote and support breastfeeding will be strengthened.	• Appoint national breastfeeding committee • Review the national breastfeeding policy and make recommendations to the Minister	December 2001 End 2003	DoHC/service providers
10	A National Injury Prevention Strategy to co-ordinate action on injury prevention will be prepared.	• Action plan drawn up	End 2002	Department of the Environment (lead) DoHC/National Safety Council/ Health and Safety Authority
11	The programmes of screening for breast and cervical cancer will be extended nationally.	• Full extension of breast screening programme • Full extension of cervical screening programme	Ongoing Ongoing	Health boards in conjunction with Breastcheck
12	A revised implementation plan for the National Cancer Strategy will be published.	• Revised implementation plan published	End 2002	National Cancer Forum
13	The Heart Health Task Force will monitor and evaluate the implementation of the prioritised cardiovascular health action plan.	• Monitoring and implementation processes agreed and in place	End 2002	Heart Health Task Force/ Health Information and Quality Authority

14	Initiatives will be taken to improve children's health.	• Integrated programme for child health developed
		• National minimum standards and targets for surveillance and screening drawn up
		• Mental health services for children & adolescents will be expanded:
		  – Implementation of the recommendations of the First Report of the Working Group on Child & Adolescent Psychiatry
		  – development of mental health services to meet the needs of children aged between 16 and 18
			December 2002
			
			2002
			
			Ongoing
			
			Ongoing
			
			Ongoing
				DoHC
				
				DoHC
				
				DoHC/Health boards in conjunction with Review Group on Child and Adolescent Psychiatric Services
				
				Health Information and Quality Authority

15	A policy for men's health and health promotion will be developed.	• Working group established • Consultation commenced • Working group report finalised	Early 2002 Mid 2002 Mid 2003	DoHC/Health boards
16	Measures will be taken to promote sexual health and safer sexual practices.	• Action plan prepared	End 2003	DoHC
17	Legislation in the area of food safety will be prepared to take account of developments in food safety regulation at national and EU level.	• Legislation prepared	Ongoing to meet EU target of 2003	DoHC

Objective 3: Health inequalities are reduced

Action	Deliverable	Target date	Responsibility
18 A programme of actions will be implemented to achieve National Anti-Poverty Strategy and Health targets for the reduction of health inequalities.	• Target for premature mortality achieved • Target for life expectancy for the Travelling community achieved • Targets for health of Travellers, asylum seekers and refugees developed • Targets for birth weight rates achieved	2007 2007 Immediate commencement of monitoring targets developed by 2003 2007	DoHC (lead)/ Service providers/ Relevant Government departments/ Inter-Departmental Group on the National Anti-Poverty Strategy
19 Initiatives to eliminate barriers for disadvantaged groups to achieve healthier lifestyles will be developed and expanded.	• Implement fully existing policy in the National Health Promotion Strategy • Community-level programmes introduced	Ongoing Ongoing	Health boards
20 The health of Travellers will be improved.	• Travellers Health Strategy published • Implementation commenced	Published 2001 Immediately	DoHC/health boards
21 Initiatives to improve the health and well-being of homeless people will be advanced.	• Implementation of 'Homelessness – an Integrated Strategy' • Implementation of Youth Homelessness Strategy	Ongoing Implemented by End 2003	Department of Environment (lead) DoHC/health boards/National Children's Office
22 Initiatives to improve the health and well-being of drug misusers will be advanced.	• Implementation of National Drugs Strategy	All actions by 2008	Department of Tourism, Sport and Recreation/DoHC/health boards
23 The health needs of asylum seekers/refugees will be addressed.	• Statement prepared and published • Implementation commenced	 5 year implementation	DoHC/Department of Justice, Equality and Law Reform/health boards/service providers
24 Initiatives to improve the health of prisoners will be advanced.	• Implementation commenced	Ongoing	Irish Prisons Service

Objective 4: Specific quality of life issues are targeted

Action	Deliverable	Target date	Responsibility
25 A new action programme for mental health will be developed.	• A national policy framework prepared • A programme of ongoing investment in the development of specialist services • Report on services for people with eating disorders prepared • Patient advocacy services introduced • Programmes to promote positive attitudes introduced • Suicide prevention programme will be intensified	Mid 2003 Ongoing Following completion of second (current) report Ongoing Ongoing	DoHC Review Group on Child and Adolescent Psychiatric Services Health boards DoHC/health boards DoHC/National Suicide Review Group/health boards

26	An integrated approach to meeting the needs of ageing and older people will be taken.	•	A programme of investment	Ongoing	DoHC
		•	A co-ordinated action plan to meet the needs of ageing and older people	Mid 2002	DoHC in conjunction with relevant Government departments
		•	Funding of community groups	Ongoing	Health boards
		•	Health Promotion Strategy implemented	Ongoing	Health boards
		•	Action plan for dementia will be implemented	7 year programme	DoHC/health boards
27	Family support services will be expanded.	•	Percentage of child welfare budget spent on supportive measures increased	From 2002	Health boards
		•	Marked increase in number of family support projects		
		•	Wider availability of parenting programmes		
		•	Out-of-hours service available		
		•	Children Act, 2001 fully implemented		
28	A comprehensive strategy to address crisis pregnancy will be prepared.	•	Crisis Pregnancy Agency established	Immediate	Crisis Pregnancy Agency
		•	Strategy prepared	To be agreed	
29	Chronic disease management protocols to promote integrated care planning and support self-management of chronic disease will be developed.	•	Protocols published	2003	Health Information and Quality Authority
30	An action plan for rehabilitation services will be prepared.	•	Working group established	End 2001	DoHC
		•	Action plan prepared	End 2002	
31	A national palliative care service will be developed.	•	Report of Expert Group to examine design guides for specialist palliative care completed	2002	Expert Group
		•	Research on the specialist palliative care service requirements of non-cancer patients commissioned	2002	DoHC
		•	Needs assessment studies for specialist palliative care needs completed for each health board area	2002	DoHC/health boards
32	Entitlement to high-quality treatment services for people with Hepatitis C, infected by blood and blood products, will be assured.	•	Services kept under review	Ongoing	DoHC
33	Resources will be provided to support the full implementation of AIDS Strategy 2000.	•	Liaison nurse identified in all health boards to act as liaison person between patients and medical service providers	Mid 2002	DoHC
		•	Uptake of routine antenatal testing of HIV to reach 90 per cent or more	End 2003	Service providers
34	Measures to prevent domestic violence and to support victims will continue.	•	Initiatives will be included in health board service plans	From 2002	Health boards
35	A national policy for the provision of sheltered work for people with disabilities will be developed.	•	Policy prepared	End 2002	DoHC/Department of Enterprise, Trade and Employment

National Goal No. 2: Fair Access

Objective 1: Eligibility for health and personal social services is clearly defined

Action	Deliverable	Target date	Responsibility
36 New legislation to provide for clear statutory provisions on entitlement will be introduced.	• Publish Bill	2002	DoHC
37 Eligibility arrangements will be simplified and clarified.	• Guide to schemes updated and published incorporating guidelines proposed by PPF Medical Card Review Group	Ongoing in line with changes Actions 38-41 below	DoHC

Objective 2: Scope of eligibility framework is broadened

Action	Deliverable	Target date	Responsibility
38 Income guidelines for the medical card will be increased.	• Revised income Guidelines	*	DoHC
39 The number and nature of GP visits for an infant under the Maternity and Infant Care Scheme will be extended.	• 4 extra free GP visits under the Maternity and Infant Care Scheme to cover general childhood illnesses	*	DoHC
40 The Nursing Home Subvention Scheme will be amended to take account of the expenditure review of the scheme.	• Introduction of a Pilot Home Subvention Scheme • Increased subvention rates.	* *	DoHC/Health boards
41 A grant will be introduced to cover two weeks' respite care per annum for dependent older persons.	• Scheme finalised	*	DoHC/Department of Social, Community and Family Affairs
42 Proposals on the financing of long-term care for older people will be brought forward.	• Proposals submitted to Government	2002	Department of Social, Community and Family Affairs (lead)/Department of Health and Children/Department of Finance

* The timing of the introduction of actions 38-41 will be decided by Government in the context of the prevailing budgetary situation.

Objective 3: Equitable access for all categories of patients in the health system is assured

Action	Deliverable	Target date	Responsibility
43 Improved access to hospital services for public patients will be addressed through a series of integrated measures.	• Reduction in waiting times for hospital services	See Action 81	DoHC/service providers/ National Hospitals Agency
44 Availability of information on entitlements including use of information technology will be improved.	• Updated 'Guide to Services' prepared • Ensure easy local access in a variety of settings • Maximise use of alternative media and communication channels targeting hard-to-reach groups	March 2002 Ongoing Ongoing	DoHC Service providers in conjunction with Comhairle and community representative groups DoHC/health boards

Action	Deliverable	Target date	Responsibility
45 All reasonable steps to make health facilities accessible will be taken.	• Transport needs of users considered when planning services that cannot be provided locally • All health facilities designed and adapted to provide access for all users	Ongoing Ongoing	Service providers Service providers
46 Appointment planning arrangements will be reviewed to provide greater flexibility and specific appointment times.	• Specific appointment times introduced • Extended/more user-friendly clinic and out-patient opening times	2002 End 2003	Service providers Service providers
47 Waiting areas in health facilities will be upgraded.	• Improvement/adaptation of waiting facilities	End 2006	Service providers

National Goal No 3: Responsive and appropriate care delivery

Objective 1: The patient is at the centre in the delivery of care

Action	Deliverable	Target date	Responsibility
48 A national standardised approach to measurement of patient satisfaction will be introduced.	• Agreed system published and implemented	End 2002	Health boards/Health Boards Executive Agency (HeBE)
49 Best practice models of customer care including a statutory system of complaint handling will be introduced.	• Customer care programme prepared and implemented in all boards • Legislation on statutory complaints procedure published	June 2003 End 2002	DoHC/service providers DoHC
50 Individuals and families will be supported and encouraged to be involved in the management of their own health care.	• Codes of practice for shared decision-making developed • Codes incorporated into professional training programmes • Training of existing staff	2002 2003 2003	Professional bodies Training bodies Service providers/professional bodies
51 An integrated approach to care planning for individuals will become a consistent feature of the system.	• Training initiatives to promote inter-disciplinary working for existing staff delivered • Inter-disciplinary working incorporated into professional training programmes • Extension of key workers for older people and children with disabilities.	Programmes to commence 2002 Ongoing Commence early 2002	Professional bodies/service providers Training bodies Service providers
52 Provision will be made for the participation of the community in decisions about the delivery of health and personal social services.	• Public information/education campaign devised • Regional advisory panels/co-ordinating committees established. • Establishment of consumer panels • Establishment of National Strategy Forum	2002 Mid 2002 Mid 2002 Mid 2002 First meeting Oct. 2002	DoHC/HeBE DoHC/ health boards DoHC/Health boards DoHC

Objective 2: Appropriate care is delivered in the appropriate setting

Action	Deliverable	Target date	Responsibility
53 Initiatives will be developed and implemented to ensure that care is delivered in the most appropriate setting.	• Primary care development	Ongoing	DoHC/Primary Care Task Force
	• Review of clinical pathway systems • Review of charges	Ongoing Completed 2002	Service providers Health boards/HeBE
54 Community and voluntary activity in maintaining health will be supported.	• Programmes to support informal carers expanded and extended	Commencing 2002 in all health boards	Health boards
	• Programmes to support voluntarism developed	December 2002	Steering Committee for the White Paper on Supporting Voluntary Activity
	• First responder service developed	Ongoing	DoHC/health boards
	• Funding arrangements for national bodies streamlined	From 2002 onwards	HeBE

Objective 3: The system has the capacity to deliver timely and appropriate services

Action	Deliverable	Target date	Responsibility
55 A programme of investment to provide the necessary capacity in primary care, acute hospital and other services will begin.	• Enhanced services across a range of programmes	2002-onwards	DoHC
56 The Cancer Forum and the Advisory Forum on Cardiovascular Health will work with the National Hospitals Agency and the Health Information and Quality Authority to ensure service quality, accessibility and responsiveness.	• Services at local, regional and national levels agreed	End 2003	National Cancer Forum/Advisory Forum on Cardiovascular Health, Health Information and Quality Authority
	• Structures and requirements for evidence-based practice agreed	End 2003	
	• Appropriate outcome and performance indicators agreed	End 2003	
57 Measures to provide the highest standard of pre-hospital emergency care/ambulance services will be advanced.	• Development of standards • Community training of GPs and other health care professionals • Training in clinical protocols • Resuscitation training for all staff in acute hospitals	All ongoing	DoHC/Pre-Hospital Emergency Care Council/ service providers
58 A plan to provide responsive, high-quality maternity care will be drawn up.	• Working Party established • Working Party report submitted to Minister	2002 2003	DoHC
59 A review of paediatric services will be undertaken.	• Working Party established • Working Party report submitted to Minister	2002 2003	DoHC
60 A national review of renal services will be undertaken.	• Patients to have access to adequately resourced centres close to home • Consultant-led nephrology services to be available in all regions • Alternative dialysis services will be available • The IKA supported to develop targeted programmes to address the health and social needs of the renal population	Ongoing	DoHC
61 Organ transplantation services will be further developed.	• Increase in organ donation and utilisation rates	Ongoing	DoHC/health boards
62 Specialist dental services will be expanded.	• New goals for oral health formulated • Action plan prepared	Immediate Mid 2002	DoHC
	• Recognition of additional areas of specialisation	Ongoing – 2003	
	• Establishment of training programmes • More widespread use of private sector orthodontic services	From 2002 onwards	DoHC/Dental Council Health boards

National Goal No. 4: High performance

Objective 1: Standardised quality systems support best patient care and safety

Action	Deliverable	Target date	Responsibility
63 Quality systems will be integrated and expanded throughout the health system.	• National standards and protocols for quality care, patient safety and risk management drawn up for all health and personal social services	Commencing on establishment of Health Information and Quality Authority	Health Information and Quality Authority
	• Quality assurance systems introduced • The Hospital Accreditation Programme extended • The Social Services Inspectorate (SSI) to be established on a statutory basis	Ongoing Ongoing 2003	DoHC Service providers/DoHC
64 A review of medicines legislation will be undertaken.	• Review to commence	End 2001	DoHC
65 Licensing of alternative medicines will be examined.	• Submission of recommendations to Minister	End 2001	DoHC/Irish Medicines Board
66 The highest international standards of safety in transfusion medicine will be set and adhered to.	• Standards achieved	Ongoing	DoHC /Irish Blood Transfusion Service/Irish Medicines Board
67 Legislation on assisted human reproduction will be prepared.	• Bill published	On completion of the work of Commission on Assisted Human Reproduction	DoHC

Objective 2: Evidence and strategic objectives underpin all planning/decision-making

Action	Deliverable	Target date	Responsibility
68 Decisions across the health system will be based on best available evidence.	• Part of quality programme – to include staff training	Ongoing	Health Information and Quality Authority Service providers
69 An information/education campaign will be undertaken for all decision-makers in the health system on the Strategy's goals and objectives.	• National, regional and local communications programme	Commencing immediately	DoHC/health boards/service providers
70 Accountability will be strengthened through further development of the service planning process.	• Standard formats for service plans agreed • Standardised performance indicators agreed • Reporting mechanisms agreed	End 2002 End 2002 End 2002	DoHC/health boards
71 Each health board will develop implementation plans.	• Format for implementation plans agreed • Framework for linkages between service plans, national policy and implementation plans established	Early 2002 End 2002	DoHC/health boards
72 Service agreements between the health boards and the voluntary sector will be extended to all service providers and associated performance indicators will be introduced.	• Service agreements for all voluntary providers	2002-2003	Health boards/voluntary providers
73 Health research will continue to be developed to support information and quality initiatives.	• Implementation of the Health Research Strategy	2002 onwards	DoHC/Health Research Board/service providers

Frameworks for change

Primary care

Action	Deliverable	Target date	Responsibility
74 A new model of primary care will be developed.	• Primary Care: A New Direction published	Immediate	Primary Care Task Force/health boards
75 A National Primary Care Task Force will be established.	• National Primary Care Task Force established	January 2002	DoHC
76 Implementation projects will be put in place.	• 40-60 primary care teams and networks in place • 400-600 primary care teams and networks in place	End 2006 End 2011	Primary Care Task Force/health boards
77 Investment will be made in extension of GP co-operatives and other specific national initiatives to complement the primary care model.	• GP co-operatives nationally • Increase in personnel needed in both teams and networks • New physical infrastructure and equipment • Improved information and communications technology	End-2003 Ongoing Ongoing End 2011	Primary Care Task Force/health boards Primary Care Task Force/health boards/Health Service Employers Agency Primary Care Task Force/health boards Primary Care Task Force/health boards/Health Information and Quality Authority

Acute hospital services

Action	Deliverable	Target date	Responsibility
78 Additional acute hospital beds will be provided for public patients.	• 650 extra beds • Rising to 3,000 extra beds	End 2002 2011	Health boards National Hospitals Agency/health boards
79 A strategic partnership with private hospital providers will be developed.	• Forum established under National Hospitals Agency	2002	DoHC/National Hospitals Agency
80 A National Hospitals Agency will be established.	• Agency established	End 2002	DoHC
81 A comprehensive set of actions will be taken to reduce waiting times for public patients, including the establishment of a new ear-marked Treatment Purchase Fund.	• Targets to ensure that no public patient will wait longer than three months for treatment following referral from an out-patient department	End 2004 Intermediate targets in end 2002 and end 2003	DoHC/National Treatment Purchase Team/Health boards
82 Management and organisation of waiting lists will be reformed.	• Set of measures implemented	Ongoing	Health boards/service providers
83 One-day procedures will be used to the maximum consistent with international best practice.	• Increase in proportion of one-day procedures	Ongoing	Health boards/service providers
84 The organisation and management of services will be enhanced to the greatest benefit of patients.	• Set of short-term measures • Long-term measures	June 2002 Ongoing	Health boards/service providers
85 The operation of out-patient departments will be improved.	• Provision of individual appointment times • Referral protocols development	Immediate Ongoing	Health boards/service providers

	Action	Deliverable	Target date	Responsibility
86	A substantial programme of improvements in accident and emergency departments will be introduced.	• Additional A & E consultants appointed • Assessment unit to channel patients quickly • Advanced nurse practitioners (emergency) appointed	Ongoing	Health Boards/service providers
87	Diagnostic services for GPs and hospitals will be enhanced.	• Improve facilities	Ongoing	Health boards
88	The extra acute beds in public hospitals will be designated for use by public patients.	• Formal designation order	Immediately as beds are provided	DoHC
89	Greater equity for public patients will be sought in a revised contract for hospital consultants.	• Agreement on revised contract	End 2002	DoHC
90	The rules governing access to public beds will be clarified.	• Implementation of rules	End 2001	DoHC/health boards/hospitals
91	Action may be taken to suspend admission of private patients for elective treatment if the maximum target waiting time for public patients is exceeded.	• Monitoring of public/private mix	Ongoing	Health boards/service providers

Funding

	Action	Deliverable	Target date	Responsibility
92	Additional Investment will be made in the health system.	• Continued increases for specified purposes	2002 onwards	Department of Finance/DoHC
93	Capital funding will be allocated for the regular maintenance of facilities and the planned replacement of equipment.	• Facilities and equipment properly maintained	Ongoing	DoHC/health boards
94	Public-private partnerships will be initiated to help in the development of health infrastructure.	• Selected projects	Ongoing	DoHC/health boards
95	Multi-annual budgeting will be introduced for selected programmes.	• Movement towards multi-annual budgeting and planning	Ongoing	Department of Finance/DoHC
96	The allocation process will be reviewed by the Department of Health and Children.	• Document on allocation system	2002	DoHC
97	Financial incentives for grater efficiency in acute hospitals will be significantly strengthened.	• Refinement of casemix budget model and extension in coverage	October 2002	DoHC
98	Annual statements of funding processes and allocations will be published.	• Annual statements by Department and health boards	2002 onwards	DoHC/health boards
99	The management of capital projects will be enhanced.	• Review of process completed/proposals for change	December 2002	DoHC/health boards

Human resources

Action	Deliverable	Target date	Responsibility
100 Integrated workforce planning will be introduced on a national basis.	• Integrated set of plans for health staff	Ongoing	DoHC/health boards
101 The required number of extra staff will be recruited.	• Increases in each targeted area	Specified increases in number trained in 2002; subsequent increases over lifetime of Strategy	Health boards/other relevant health agencies
102 The approach to regulating the number and type of consultant posts will be streamlined.	• New procedure in line with the service planning process	2002	DoHC/health boards
103 Best practice in recruitment and retention will be promoted.	• Guidelines on best practice	September 2002	Office for Health Management/Health Services Employers Agency
104 Greater inter-disciplinary working between professions will be promoted.	• Adaption of training programmes	Ongoing	DoHC/professional bodies
105 Provisions for the statutory registration of health professionals will be strengthened and expanded.	• Revise legislation on doctors • Revise legislation on nurses • New legislation on other health professionals	2003 2003 2003	DoHC
106 Registration of alternative/complementary therapists will be introduced.	• Independent study of the practical steps required to be published	March 2002	DoHC
107 The HR function in the health system will be developed.	• Flexible human resource models established	December 2002	Relevant health agencies
108 A detailed Action Plan for People Management will be developed.	• Publication of Action Plan	October 2002	DoHC/Health Services Employers Agency

Organisational reform

Action	Deliverable	Target date	Responsibility
109 The Department of Health and Children will be restructured.	• Independent review completed • New organisational structure in place	June 2002 December 2002	DoHC/independent consultants
110 Health boards will be responsible for driving change, including a stronger focus on accountability linked to service plans, outputs and quality standards.	• Increased link between service planning and service provision	Ongoing	Health boards
111 An independent Health Information and Quality Authority will be established.	• Authority established	2002	DoHC
112 The Health Boards Executive (HeBE) will be developed as a key instrument in the change agenda.	• HeBE established and operational	March 2002	DoHC/health boards
113 The role of the Office for Health Management will be expanded.	• Expanded role agreed with Office for Health Management	2002	DoHC/Office for Health Management
114 An independent audit of functions and structures in the health system will be carried out.	• Audit completed	June 2002	DoHC/independent consultants

Information

Action	Deliverable	Target date	Responsibility
115 The National Health Information Strategy will be published and implemented.	• Publication of National Health Information Strategy	December 2001	DoHC
116 There will be a sustained programme of investment in the development of national health information systems as set out in the National Health Information Strategy.	• Specific developments in the information infrastructure	Ongoing	DoHC/health boards/Health Information and Quality Authority
117 Information and communications technology will be fully exploited in service delivery.	• Implementation of the National Health Information Strategy	Ongoing	DoHC/Health boards/Health Information and Quality Authority
118 Information-sharing systems and the use of electronic patient records will be introduced on a phased basis.	• Phased implementation of the electronic health-care record in line with the National Health Information Strategy	Ongoing	DoHC/health boards/Health Information and Quality Authority
119 A national secure communications infrastructure will be developed for the health services.	• Health services secure network	2004	DoHC/health boards/Health Information and Quality Authority
120 Information system development will be promoted as central to the planning process.	• Enhanced planning protocols in place	2002	DoHC/health boards
121 Health information legislation will be introduced.	• Bill published	2002	DoHC

CHAPTER 8

Making change happen

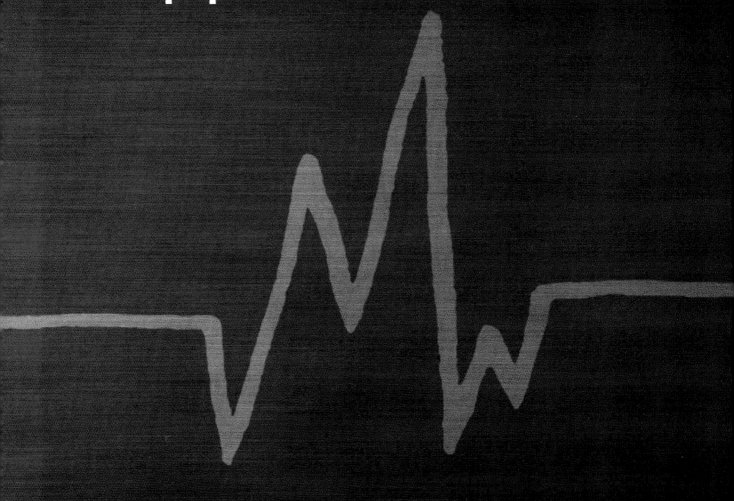

Introduction

The Strategy sets out an ambitious programme of development and reform for the health system. The various initiatives have at their core the guiding principles of *equity, people-centredness, quality* and *accountability*. They are aimed at achieving the goals of *better health for everyone, fair access, appropriate* and *responsive care delivery* and *high performance*.

Many of the actions required for implementation have been referred to already. These are summarised in Chapter 7. The aim is to ensure that responsibility for delivering on various aspects of the Strategy is made explicit and that implementation is achieved nationally in a consistent, effective and timely manner.

The approach to implementation makes clear not just how change will be implemented, but also how outcomes will be monitored and evaluated over time. Ongoing measurement and reporting of progress against the targets set out in Chapter 7 will be an essential part of the implementation process. This will ensure that:

- those responsible for implementation are accountable for the progress they are making

- the return on the increased investment in health that will flow from this Strategy is measured

- those charged with the planning, development and delivery of services can make informed choices on the continuing direction for consolidation, improvement and change.

Implementation is about the steps required to put each aspect of the strategy into operation. The Action Plan sets out who is responsible for each key element of the Strategy, how it will be implemented, and by when. **Monitoring and evaluation** is concerned with the means by which progress in delivering targets is monitored and the quality and effectiveness of the services are evaluated.

Implementation

The approach to implementing the Strategy is set out below. It takes account of two particularly important considerations:

- the inter-sectoral nature of the issues that have an impact on health

- the need to engage with and encourage the participation of health services staff, communities, voluntary organisations, patients, clients and users in progressing the reforms set out.

The approach to implementation will:

- make explicit the responsibilities and tasks of relevant sectors, organisations and key individuals

- have clear political leadership

- reflect the valid expectations of users, voluntary and community interests and staff to be involved in re-shaping the health system

- allow for responsive innovation in addressing locally identified priorities and needs.

Implementing the Strategy across all sectors

Managing the inter-sectoral nature of health represents a significant challenge to developing a successful implementation framework. To achieve this:

- A Cabinet Sub-Committee on Implementation of the Health Strategy chaired by An Taoiseach will be established. Membership of the Sub-Committee will include the Ministers for Health and Children; Finance; Education and Science; Environment and Local Government; Social, Community and Family Affairs; and other Ministers as issues of relevance to them arise. The Cabinet Sub-Committee will oversee progress in implementing the Strategy and review selected initiatives under the Strategy as it sees fit.

- The Cabinet Sub-Committee will be supported in its work by an Inter-Departmental Group of senior officials drawn from the relevant departments and chaired by the Secretary General of the Department of Health and Children. It will review the implementation and impact of the Strategy on a continuing basis. It will focus in particular on high-priority cross-sectoral issues affecting health, such as accident prevention, tobacco use, alcohol and illicit drug misuse, air pollution, transport and water quality. With the support of the Committee, health proofing will be built into all public policy formulation and will feature in the strategy statements and business plans of all Government departments.

- As indicated in Chapter 4, a new Population Health Division will be established within the Department of Health and Children. The Division will ensure a focus for population health within the department, liaise with all Government departments on health proofing policies, develop legislation requiring that future Government decisions incorporate health proofing, facilitate health impact assessments locally, regionally and nationally and assess the impact and effectiveness of population health initiatives undertaken.

- At health board level, a population health function will be established in each of the health boards to support the boards' involvement with external agencies, to ensure that health proofing and health impact assessments are carried out locally and to develop and formulate policy for population health at a local level.

Implementing the Strategy in the health system

- A National Implementation Team will be established within the Department of Health and Children to drive the implementation of this Strategy within the health system at national level. It will co-ordinate and monitor actions within the Department, at Government and inter-departmental level and within the health boards and other agencies in the health services. This Unit will service the Cabinet Sub-Committee and the Inter-Departmental Group of senior officials.

- The National Implementation Team will prepare an annual report to the Cabinet Sub-Committee on the progress achieved in implementing each key aspect of the Strategy, and identifying the next steps to be taken in the coming years. This report will be submitted to the Joint Oireachtas Committee on Health and Children, and made widely available.

- A National Steering Group, to include a number of people outside the health sector who have practical experience of change management, will be established to work with the Department and health agencies. It will oversee and report to the Minister for Health and Children on the implementation of the Strategy. The National Steering Group will provide expertise and hands-on experience in achieving the momentum needed for the changes set out in the Strategy.

Dedicated arrangements will also be required within each of the health boards to co-ordinate and monitor the local level actions required to achieve the goals set out in the Strategy. There will be significant challenges to organisations, staff and managers within the system. Change of the level envisaged will require careful management and will involve significant development of the system's capacity and capability to achieve it. To support this an Implementation Team will be established in each health board with responsibility for driving the detailed implementation of the Strategy at local level. The boards may also decide to take joint action on aspects of the implementation process, either through the HeBE or by other means. The core purpose of the Team will be to support staff, managers and frontline services to improve health and health care by implementing the developments and initiatives set out in this Strategy. The Implementation Teams will:

- lead implementation of the Strategy at health board level

- work closely with the National Steering Group in achieving 'quick wins' and early implementation of change at local level, through co-operation with the key stakeholders

- take the lead on organisation development and modernisation by

  - promoting excellence in services and spreading best practice throughout the system

  - enhancing individual and organisational leadership abilities

  - supporting policy development and implementation at health board level

- provide input and support to the work of the Health Information and Quality Authority and the National Hospitals Agency in

  - spreading best practice,

  - establishing realistic regional and local targets for the development and improvement of services

  - implementing risk management and safe system strategies

  - focusing on improvements in high priority areas of service

- facilitate resource allocation in a structured and systematic way to match specific goals and targets proposed within the Strategy.

Involvement of wider stakeholders

The central contribution of staff, users, communities and voluntary organisations in shaping this Strategy will be mirrored by a continuing key role for all stakeholders in its implementation over the next seven years.

- The partnership arrangements in place nationally and in each of the health boards will be used as a vehicle for the involvement of staff and staff groups in the implementation of the Strategy at national and local levels. The partnership structures will be invited to work alongside the National Steering Group and the Implementation Teams in each health board. A central focus of partnership will be to explore ways of achieving organisational change and new, more flexible forms of work organisation.

- A broadly based National Consultative Forum will be convened annually to consider progress reports on the implementation of the Strategy and to comment on priorities in the light of progress and emerging trends. The Forum may review the annual reports submitted to the Cabinet Sub-Committee and any other reports on health and health care it sees as relevant.

All-Ireland and international dimensions

In implementing the Health Strategy, the scope for co-operation at a North/South and international level will be utilised to the full.

All-Ireland dimension

The Department of Health and Children has for many years maintained co-operative relations and contacts with the Department of Health, Social Services and Public Safety (DHSSPS) in Northern Ireland. These arrangements were primarily conducted on an informal basis. In addition to this, however, there existed strong working relationships between individuals, health professionals and local/regional health authorities on both sides of the border – of which Co-operation and Working Together (CAWT) is an excellent example – all of whom identified the value of working together in the field of health.

The Good Friday Agreement represented a watershed in co-operation between North and South at the highest political and administrative level. Following the identification of health in the Agreement as one of the areas for North/South co-operation and implementation, the mandate that was entrusted to the Departments – South and North – was to seek opportunities for joint co-operation in five health operational areas. These are:

- Accident and emergency planning

- Planning for major emergencies

- High technology equipment

- Cancer research

- Health promotion.

In addition, the Agreement provided for the establishment of six Implementation Bodies of which one was to be on Food Safety. The Food Safety Promotion Board was subsequently established.

The establishment under the Agreement of the North-South Ministerial Council (NSMC) has provided a significantly greater focus, momentum and authority for developing mutual interests in the field of health through co-operative and joint action. Work in the co-operation areas is being taken forward on a structured basis by designated officials in the two Departments and in conjunction with local agencies and interests. In addition, significant research has been conducted to identify obstacles to cross-border mobility and potential areas for service-based co-operation.

The value of existing co-operation arrangements is recognised, such as those in the area of health promotion, and joint services or training initiatives at local level. There are, however, significant obstacles and challenges to co-operative action between the North and South. Some of these relate to established practices, such as professional accreditation and funding arrangements. Other challenges and opportunities now presenting would involve taking co-operation to the level of planning and delivering certain high-cost acute hospital services which require a significant population base for sustainability.

The Department of Health and Children shares the views on the need to explore and pursue the potential for cross-border co-operation in hospital services, expressed in the Report of the Northern Ireland Acute Hospitals Review Group (2001). Furthermore, it recognises the challenges and opportunities attending cross-border co-operation in health services in Ireland which were set out in the 2001 Report of the Centre for Cross-Border Studies on the subject. The Department is committed to exploring and developing opportunities for co-operation which:

- safeguard or improve public health

- provide greater access to services for patients

- make good economic sense

- are sustainable

- involve a significant mutual benefit.

Accordingly, during the currency of this Strategy, the Department of Health and Children, working with the DHSSPS, will:

- continue on-going contacts and work to develop initiatives in the five areas of co-operation designated under the Good Friday Agreement (accident and emergency planning, planning for major emergencies, high technology equipment, cancer research and health promotion)

- identify further areas for co-operation

- commission research or evaluation to expand the evidence base for co-operative measures and best practice

- address, to the greatest possible extent, the identified obstacles to cross-border mobility and co-operation

- examine and, where feasible, develop joint planning and delivery of specialised acute hospital services which require the critical mass represented by the population of the island as a whole.

Both in conjunction with the DHSSPS and independently, the Department will strengthen its relationships and contacts with the relevant interested agencies, particularly CAWT.

International dimension

The protection, improvement and monitoring of public health have been long established as matters of particular international importance and concern. The need for close co-operation in the field of health is heightened by the emergence of new threats to health, technological advancement in the field of health and the ongoing search for most effective and efficient systems for delivering quality care. Accordingly, Ireland has for many years played its full part in a number of key international governmental bodies concerned with health issues including the European Union, the World Health Organisation and the Council of Europe. In these fora, the Department has contributed to, and learned from, international thinking, trends, experience and policy in relation to health.

During the course of the period of implementation of the Health Strategy, the Department will maintain full engagement with, and involvement in, the work of these key international bodies. The aim of the Department of Health and Children will be to:

- discharge Ireland's international responsibilities in the field of health

- contribute to international deliberations and policy formation

- learn from experiences and trends in other countries with a view to achieving best possible organisation and delivery of services.

Monitoring and evaluation

In addition to implementation, it will be important to put in place a system to monitor progress and systematically evaluate the quality and effectiveness of services being delivered. Monitoring and evaluation must become intrinsic to the approach taken by people at all levels of the health services. The arrangements to support these functions will be strengthened, as described below.

The use of a formal organisational function for monitoring and evaluation has been introduced in the Eastern Regional Health Authority (ERHA). This emphasis now needs to be mirrored within the Department of Health and Children and in each of the health boards so that we can develop a stronger focus on monitoring and evaluation throughout the system. A formal monitoring and evaluation function will be established within the Department and by each health board region. As in the case of the ERHA, the function at health board level will be to monitor progress against targets and to evaluate outcomes over the medium to long term.

Monitoring standards

The detailed standards against which progress will be measured will reflect targets set out in Chapter 7. These high-level monitoring standards will be set at a level that will be challenging but attainable. The standards selected will be based on robust evidence rather than on the basis of information gathering convenience and, where possible, will facilitate international comparison on the basis of WHO guidelines.

Performance indicators for service planning, monitoring and evaluation will be further developed, based on information derived directly from operational service delivery, combined with data on population health. This work will be informed by national and international research. A national set of key performance indicators will be developed jointly between the Department and the health boards, with advice from the Health Information and Quality Authority and, where relevant, the National Hospitals Agency. These indicators will be relatively small in number and will represent the key pieces of information required for communication of achievement between the health boards and the Department. Individual agencies will supplement these with specific performance indicators required by local management.

When combined with basic information on finance and activity, good performance indicator information should enable:

- managers to judge that service delivery is effective and quickly identify any difficulties arising

- policy makers to judge how well policy is being implemented

- evaluation and review of services and policy, thus informing future developments

- better communication of achievements, understanding of actions required, and participation in management across professional boundaries

- the public to be better informed.

The results and analysis of these performance indicators will be made available to the public in a way that will assist them in contributing to policy formation and coming to a better understanding of the health-related services available to them. Information systems will be put in place from which performance indicators can be derived automatically, without disruption to service delivery.

Evaluation

In tandem with the ongoing monitoring of performance within the health services described above, there is a need for a more focused and in-depth assessment of the quality, equity, and patient-centredness of particular services through a series of formal evaluations. While many local and national policy and service reviews and customer service initiatives are being undertaken around the country, a more systematic approach to the evaluation of services on a national basis is now needed.

At national level, this will be done externally by the Health Information and Quality Authority, as discussed in Chapter 5. At local level, the monitoring and evaluation function to be established in each health board region will carry out this function.

The Department of Health and Children will, as part of the service planning process, require each health board to specify the formal evaluations to be undertaken by their respective monitoring and evaluation units. In the case of the eastern region, the service areas selected for review will be identified by the Eastern Regional Health Authority rather than the three Area Health Boards in the region.

External monitoring and evaluation

The Health Information and Quality Authority will have a specific remit in relation to carrying out formal independent evaluations of services at national level. The services to be reviewed will be selected in consultation with service providers, users and other stakeholders. The Authority will be charged with developing and managing an ongoing monitoring and evaluation programme which will include responsibility for the initial determination of standards, performance indicators, agreed data dictionaries and definitions, minimum data sets and resource requirements.

This responsibility will complement the Authority's remit for the overall development of information management within the health system that are also described in Chapter 5 of this Strategy.

The Authority will harness the contribution of the new National Hospitals Agency in developing and monitoring standards for the acute hospital sector. This will also provide a framework for evaluating the role and impact of third party agencies such as the professional, regulatory and training bodies on acute hospital service delivery.

The Health Information and Quality Authority will also contribute to the evaluation of services through its important role in the overall quality agenda which will involve the introduction of formal accreditation programmes that incorporate formal quality assessments, the development and dissemination of best practice standards, and the introduction of formal patient safety and adverse incident reporting systems. It will liaise with the proposed agency dealing with claims of clinical negligence.

Monitoring and evaluating other sectoral inputs

At a national level a formal mechanism for monitoring and evaluating the impact of the various non-health sectors on overall population health status, based on their explicit responsibilities and targets, will be developed through the introduction of a Government-wide system of health impact assessment.

The Health Information and Quality Authority will have a key role in developing and implementing this tool at a national level and for supporting and facilitating its use at Department of Health and Children and local health board level.

Developing monitoring and evaluation capacity

The determination and agreement of standards, definitions, data-sets, targets and reporting requirements will not in themselves achieve a robust monitoring and evaluation culture within the health services or the wider health system. Within the health services, major effort will be required to develop capacity and capability to support that culture.

This is why, rather than exercising a simple inspectorate approach from its establishment, the Health Information and Quality Authority will have an important role in working with agencies on developing standards and identifying and meeting resource requirements in a supportive and developmental manner. In developing a monitoring and evaluation culture, it will be essential to dedicate substantial resources to this capacity and capability building exercise. In particular, this will mean supporting agencies individually and through HeBE in:

- making the major investment required in information and communication systems throughout the services

- addressing the major programme of human resource development to go along with that. If a successful and effective monitoring and evaluation culture is to be achieved, a supportive rather than policing approach must dominate.

Framework for implementation, monitoring and evaluation

National level

Implementation

- Cabinet Sub-Committee on Implementation of Strategy, chaired by An Taoiseach

- Inter-Departmental Committee to support the Cabinet Sub-Committee and review the cross-sectoral impact of the Health Strategy

- Dedicated National Implementation Team in Department of Health and Children to drive implementation of the Strategy within the health system and to prepare published annual progress report for the Cabinet Sub-Committee and the Joint Oireachtas Committee on Health and Children

- National Steering Group including external expertise in change management to identify approaches for implementation and to help create momentum for change.

Monitoring and evaluation

- Dedicated monitoring and evaluation function within the Department of Health and Children

- Department and health boards to agree a key set of nationally applicable performance indicators. (Individual agencies to supplement these as required with more detailed local indicators)

- New division of population health in the Department of Health and Children to facilitate health impact assessment, promote health proofing of all Government decisions and ensure a population health focus at national level.

Health boards/local level

Implementation

- Implementation Teams to implement Strategy at local level, working with local stakeholders and the National Steering Group

- Dedicated population health function in each health board, headed by senior manager with responsibility for liaison between agencies and health impact assessment.

Monitoring and evaluation

- Dedicated monitoring and evaluation function within each health board to review selected services as specified in service plan

- Performance management systems to be introduced.

Wider stakeholders

- National Forum of all stakeholders to review implementation reports of the Department's Health Strategy Unit and reports on monitoring and evaluation

- Further development of partnership structures for staff involvement in implementation of Health Strategy at local and national level.

External assessment of progress

- Health Information and Quality Authority to:

  - Carry out independent evaluation of selected service areas each year

  - Work with agencies to develop standards, methods and targets against which to evaluate services

  - Drive information developments in line with the National Health Information Strategy

  - Pursue national quality agenda, including accreditation, best practice guidelines and risk management

  - Develop health impact assessment tools for national and local application

  - Oversee health technology assessment.

Appendices

Appendix 1

The consultation process for the Health Strategy

Background

The Minister for Health and Children decided to consult widely in preparing the Health Strategy. Colgan and Associates were appointed as consultants in February, 2001 to design, plan, implement and report on the consultation programme.

The main objective of the consultation process was to gather the views of members of the public, service users, service providers, staff and management of the health services and to channel these views into the development of the Health Strategy.

A separate report providing full details of the consultation process and its findings, *Your Views about Health*, is available from the Department of Health and Children.

Structures for preparing the new Strategy

A number of structures were set up to prepare the new Strategy. The preparation was overseen by a Steering Group representing the Department of Health and Children, the Department of the Taoiseach, the Department of Finance and the health boards. The Steering Group had overall responsibility for the consultation process.

A Project Team comprising officials of the Department of Health and Children and the health boards was established to work to the Steering Group and produce the Strategy document.

The Minister established a National Health Strategy Consultative Forum representative of key stakeholders to support the Steering Group by providing advice on the key themes and direction of the Strategy and on the process for its preparation. It proved to be a valuable means of discussion that underpinned the entire consultation process.

In addition to the plenary sessions, the Forum was divided into eight working groups to deal with specific issues: funding, eligibility, delivery systems/human resources, population health, quality, voluntary/statutory interface, e-health and futures in health care.

Consulting the stakeholders

The public

In view of restrictions on travel in the early part of 2001 due to foot-and-mouth disease, the main means of consulting with the general public was through the consultation pack *Your Views about Health*. Members of the public and organisations were invited, by means of a questionnaire, to describe their experiences of the health services and to give their views on future change.

Over 1,500 submissions were received from members of the public.

The Department of Health and Children also commissioned Irish Marketing Surveys to carry out market research. This research included a quantitative and qualitative survey involving a nationally representative sample of 2,000 adults.

Organisations

A number of organisations participated in the process by completing the questionnaire *Your Views about Health*, referred to above. Others submitted independent submissions setting out their views in detail. A number of health boards arranged workshops for locally-based organisations.

Over 300 submissions were received from organisations.

Health services personnel

Extensive and detailed consultation was undertaken in each of the ten health board areas. In addition, a number of health services staff completed the questionnaire *Your Views about Health*. Consultation also took place with staff in the Department of Health and Children.

People living in poverty

In the case of people living in poverty, a separate consultation process was undertaken through the National Anti-Poverty Strategy (NAPS).

Links with the development of the Strategy

The material contained in the questionnaires and in submissions fed into the process of developing the Strategy in a number of ways:

* The material was read and indexed and made available to the relevant working groups involved in developing the Strategy.

* Reports on the content were prepared for the Steering Group.

* An overview of the findings was presented to the National Consultative Forum in July, 2001.

Key themes emerging from the consultation process

A whole-system approach to health

High priority is given to the promotion of health and prevention of illness in a way that empowers individuals and communities to take responsibility for their lives and their health and which provides the supports they need for that task. There is consensus that health promotion must be viewed broadly, encompassing education, housing, income support, provision for leisure, mental health, as well as complex structural issues such as poverty and marginalisation. The feedback also underscores the strategic and long-term benefits of giving children and young people the information, facilities and supports needed to optimise their health and well-being.

Going beyond 'more'

The need for more investment at all levels is a theme that emerges throughout the consultation process. Linked with this need for more resources, however, is the need for strategic change around how the health system is experienced by the public. The changes envisaged centre on fairness, equity of access, quality of care and quality of people's experience of the health system, and the provision of holistic and seamless services.

Towards a holistic and seamless service

A strong strategic focus is on a health system that is responsive to the whole person and his or her well-being. Such a system envisages full integration of services that place the person at its centre. There is a clear understanding that existing system rigidities – in attitudes, contractual arrangements, service delivery systems and boundaries between agencies and funding mechanisms – must be addressed if the new person-centered ethos is to permeate the health system.

A focus on community

There is a strong focus on providing care in the community. There are numerous proposals for developing a new model for delivering health care in the community, the availability of a wider range of services, developing the role of the general practitioner, and improved linkages within and between services.

The focus on community is strongly evident in the priority given to providing services in the community to vulnerable groups such as older people and people with disabilities. The need for rural transport is highlighted consistently.

A fair health system

One of the key findings from the consultation process is that there is a strong will to change what is perceived to be an inequitable system, particularly in the case of access to hospital treatment and specialist care. There is also concern about geographic disparities and access to services for vulnerable and/or marginalised groups such as older people, people with mental health difficulties, the homeless and ethnic minorities.

Delivering high quality of care, treatment and support

The future development of the health system must place a very high premium on the quality of service provided.

Respectful relationships

The theme of respectful relationships is evident in the consultation process. Reported experiences of disrespect or poor communication make a strong and lasting impression. Strategies to address this issue include increasing staffing levels so as to remove some of the pressure on staff, training and development programmes for health service personnel in customer services, effective complaints and appeals procedures, anti-ageism, disability awareness programmes and culturally sensitive information services and practices.

There are two significant strands to this theme. One is mutual respect in the relationships between the groups who make up the health system – service providers, users, advocacy groups, policy makers, funders, staff and employers. The second is the need for supporting the staff in the health services through a human resources strategy that would place a high priority on promoting the well-being of health service personnel.

Full details of the messages from the consultation process are contained in the report on consultation *Your Views about Health*.

Appendix 2

Recent Strategies and Policy Documents

1 Cancer Services in Ireland: A National Strategy (1996)

Actions 5, 12 and 56

The National Cancer Strategy was published in 1996 and was followed by a 3-year action plan in 1997. The main elements of the Strategy involved:

*   reorganisation of cancer treatment services based on principles of best practice, patient-centredness and equity of access throughout the country. This involved organising services around three supra-regional centres and regional centres based in other health board areas

*   establishing screening and early detection programmes of proven value

*   using health promotion activities to emphasise the importance of healthy lifestyles

*   further developing specialist palliative care services

*   facilitating greater co-ordination of cancer research.

Since 1997, major progress has been made in implementing the National Cancer Strategy. The National Cancer Forum has been established to advise on the implementation of the Strategy. Regional directors of cancer services in each health board area were appointed to prepare regional cancer plans and to oversee their implementation. The first phase of a national programme of screening for breast cancer is in place and the National Cervical Screening Programme was launched in 2000. Specific cancer research funding has been provided and a cancer consortium involving Ireland, Northern Ireland and the National Cancer Institute (USA) has been established to develop joint cancer research projects, scholar exchange programmes and a range of other collaborative activities.

2 Best Health for Children (1999)

Actions 8, 14 and 27

Best Health for Children involved a co-ordinated partnership approach by the health boards to protecting and promoting children's health. The initial part of *Best Health for Children* is concerned with promoting health in younger children and, in particular, the role of screening and surveillance and the development of parenting, education and support.

3 The National Health Promotion Strategy 2000-2005

Action 5

This strategy recognises the need to improve the health and social gain of those who are disadvantaged or from lower socio-economic groups by developing sensitive and appropriate health promotion programmes to meet their needs. Key priorities are to

- focus on the link between health promotion and the determinants of health

- provide information and data on socio-economic and environmental factors, lifestyle behaviours and health status

- identify the prerequisites needed at a national and regional level to support and sustain health promotion

- emphasise the role for inter-sectoral and multi-disciplinary approaches in the planning, implementation and evaluation of health promotion initiatives.

The National Health Promotion Strategy outlines three major strands for the future development of health promotion

- the establishment of a new National Health Promotion Forum under the Chairmanship of the Minister

- the provision of more comprehensive and reliable data

- a need for greater inter-sectoral and multi-disciplinary approaches.

The new National Health Promotion Forum will provide an effective platform to tackle inter-sectoral approaches to the major determinants of health which are set out in detail in the Strategy. The Strategy informs the future direction and focus for the Department's Health Promotion Unit and the health boards for the next five years. It also provides a resource and guide for relevant partners, statutory and non-statutory, concerned with promoting positive health in the new millennium.

4 Towards a Tobacco-Free Society (2000)

Action 6

The Minister for Health and Children established a policy review group to carry out a fundamental review of smoking and health policy. The Government approved the publication of the report of the group, *Towards a Tobacco-Free Society,* and the preparation of a new Bill to implement its recommendations. The report sets out Government policy on reducing the incidence of smoking. The Government approved the drafting of the Public Health (Tobacco) Bill and agreed to give the Bill priority in the Government's legislative programme. The text of the Bill was published in August 2001.

5 The Health of Our Children (2001)

Actions 8, 9, 14 and Chapter 6

The Second Annual Report of the Chief Medical Officer of the Department of Health and Children is concerned with children's health in Ireland. The report acknowledges the very important contribution of services that are being provided by way of cure and rehabilitation for children with health needs. However, it argues for greater emphasis on prevention and health promotion in our approach to children's health.

In preparing a new health strategy the report calls for specific consideration to be given to eligibility for services for children, a national strategy to prevent accidents in childhood and measures to reduce the availability and consumption of tobacco, alcohol and illicit drugs by children.

The report also reviews progress in relation to many of the issues highlighted in the First Annual Report of the Chief Medical Officer including cancer, cardiovascular disease, communicable disease and in particular health inequalities.

6 Cardiovascular Health Strategy (1999)

Actions 5, 13 and 56

The Cardiovascular Health Strategy, *Building Healthier Hearts*, was launched in July 1999. It addressed the common aspects of prevention of cardiovascular disease, as well as the treatment and rehabilitation of patients with coronary heart disease. The following overall aims were identified:

- to reduce the risk factor profile in the general population

- to detect those at high risk

- to deal effectively with those who have clinical disease

- to ensure the best survival and quality of life outcome for those who recover from an acute attack.

The Department of Health and Children has set a medium-term objective to bring our levels of premature deaths from cardiovascular disease into line with the EU average at a minimum, and as a long-term objective to reduce our rates to those of the best performers in the EU. The Cardiovascular Health Strategy, which contains 211 recommendations, is designed to achieve these objectives systematically. Implementation of the recommendations will require substantial developments in health promotion (which is much broader than the health services), primary care, pre-hospital care, hospital care, cardiac rehabilitation and the audit and evaluation of services.

7 Our Children – Their Lives, The National Children's Strategy (2000)

Actions 8, 14 and Chapter 6

The National Children's Strategy sets out a common vision to work towards:

> *An Ireland where children are respected as young citizens with a valued contribution to make and a voice of their own; where all children are cherished and supported by family and the wider society; where they enjoy a fulfilling childhood and realise their potential.*

Six principles are identified to guide all actions to be taken: actions should be child-centred, family-oriented, equitable, inclusive, action-oriented and integrated.

The Strategy proposes a more holistic way of thinking about children, a 'whole child' perspective, which reflects contemporary understanding of childhood. This perspective is used together with the outcome of the consultation to set three national goals for children:

- Children will have a voice in matters which affect them and their views will be given due weight in accordance with their age and maturity

- Children and their lives will be better understood; their lives will benefit from evaluation, research and information on their needs, rights and the effectiveness of services

- Children will receive quality supports and services to promote all aspects of their development.

The new structures being put in place to implement the Strategy include:

- a cabinet committee on children chaired by the Taoiseach

- the National Children's Office to support the Minister for Children in her role of co-ordinating the implementation of the Strategy

- a National Children's Advisory Council

- an Ombudsman for Children.

8 Adolescent Health Strategy (2001)

Action 14 and Chapter 6

The Adolescent Health Strategy is based on the deliberations of a sub-committee of the national conjoint child health committee, which was appointed by health board CEOs to make recommendations on a number of issues pertaining to adolescent health. The first part of the strategy highlights:

* the need to tackle inequalities

* a need to refocus attention from health-related lifestyle behaviour and the concept of risk to a 'whole-child perspective'

* issues of mental health which have wide ranging impacts on other health issues

* the need for improved data collection methods.

The second part introduces the concept of the adolescent-friendly health service, the key elements of which are:

* accessibility of services

* flexibility in service delivery

* ensuring staff have appropriate skills and training

* providing quality information on health issues

* partnership working involving adolescents, staff, parents/carers and service providers.

9 Report of the Review Group on Child and Adolescent Psychiatric Services (2001)

Actions 14, 25 and Chapter 6

A working group to advise the Minister for Health and Children on the development of child and adolescent psychiatric services was established in June 2000. Its first report was published in March 2001 and includes recommendations on how services should be developed in the short, medium and long term to meet the needs of those under the age of 18. It analysed two specific areas – the organisation of services for the treatment of Attention Deficit Hyperactivity Disorder/Hyperactivity Kinetic Disorder (ADHD/HKD) and the provision of child and adolescent psychiatric in-patient units.

The report emphasises that the treatment of ADHD/HKD is an integral component of the provision of a comprehensive child and adolescent psychiatric service. It recommends that priority should be given to the recruitment of the required expertise for the completion of existing consultant-led multi-disciplinary teams and calls for closer liaison with the education system and other areas of the community health services.

The report also recommends that a total of seven child and adolescent in-patient psychiatric units for children ranging from 6-16 years should be developed throughout the country. It is envisaged that the focus of the centres will be the assessment and treatment of psychiatric, emotional or family disorders.

10 National Drugs Strategy (2001)

Action 22

The National Drugs Strategy was prepared by the Department of Tourism, Sport and Recreation and launched in May 2001. Its overall aim is to provide an effective, integrated response to the problems posed by drug misuse. Three basic principles underpin the strategy:

- the response to the drug problem must take account of the different levels of drug misuse which are being experienced around the country. The use of illicit drugs, particularly cannabis and ecstasy, is a nation-wide phenomenon. However, heroin abuse, in view of its public health implications and close association with crime, is the primary focus of the National Drugs Strategy

- the need to ensure that all programmes and services which respond to the drug problem are delivered in a coherent and integrated manner

- the need to encourage communities experiencing the highest levels of drug misuse to participate in the design and delivery of the response to the problem in their areas.

Arising from these principles, the key objectives are:

- to reduce the number of people turning to drugs in the first instance through comprehensive education and prevention programmes

- to provide appropriate treatment and aftercare for those dependent on drugs

- to have appropriate mechanisms at national and local level aimed at reducing the supply of illicit drugs

- to ensure that an appropriate level of accurate and timely information is available to inform the response to the problem.

11 Report of the National Advisory Committee on Palliative Care (2001)

Action 31

Palliative care is the continuing active total care of patients and their families at a time when the medical expectation is no longer a cure. It responds to physical, psychological, social and spiritual needs, and extends to support in bereavement.

The National Advisory Committee on Palliative Care comprised representatives from the medical and nursing profession working in palliative care, hospice administrators, representatives of the Irish Hospice Foundation, the Irish Cancer Society and the Department of Health and Children.

The report describes the components of a comprehensive palliative care service and acts as a blueprint for its development. Among the report's recommendations are that each region should have a specialist palliative care unit. Such units would act as a specialist resource for the delivery of palliative care services in the hospital and in all care settings across the region. The report makes recommendations on estimated bed number requirements for these units. There are also comprehensive recommendations on how palliative care services in all settings should be staffed.

The report underlines the particular needs of specialist palliative care settings in relation to physical structure and environment. It recommends that an expert group on design guides for specialist palliative care settings be established.

12 National AIDS Strategy (2000)

Action 33

The report of the National AIDS Strategy Committee, AIDS Strategy 2000 was launched in June 2000.

It comprises the reports of four sub-committees of the National Committee:

- Surveillance

- Education and Prevention

- Care and Management

- Discrimination.

In the report each of the sub-committees examines progress made since 1992 and makes recommendations for future action, which have been endorsed by the National Committee. An important point to emerge from the reports is that HIV/AIDS should now be dealt with in the wider context of sexual health and other sexually transmitted infections.

The introduction of routine antenatal testing for HIV in 2000 means that where a pregnant woman tests positive for HIV she can avail of treatments that greatly improve the outcome for herself and her baby. One of the challenges for the future is to have as high an uptake as possible for this programme.

13 Programme for Prosperity and Fairness (2000)

Action 37

The Programme for Prosperity and Fairness (PPF) is the fifth national agreement between the social partners, and follows on from the Programme for National Recovery, the Programme for Economic and Social Progress, the Programme for Competitiveness and Work, and Partnership 2000.

The PPF aims to:

- keep the economy competitive in a rapidly changing world

- provide a strong basis for further economic prosperity

- improve the quality of life and living standards for all

- bring about a fairer and more inclusive Ireland.

The PPF is dependent upon achieving an average annual GNP growth rate of about 5.6 per cent over the period of the Agreement and a goal of maintaining significant budgetary surpluses in each year.

The PPF recognises the need to provide quality health care services for people who are ill or who have disabilities. Emphasis is placed on improving quality of life through targeted health promotion and preventive strategies. Measures will include:

- major capital investment to increase the capacity of the health services, both hospital- and community-based

- the development of the Health Promotion Strategy (published in July 2000) targeted at areas such as smoking, healthy eating, and lifestyle changes

- the expansion of treatment and rehabilitation services for drug misusers

- enhanced services for particular target groups such as women, people with disabilities, older people and travellers

- the development of new models to explore ways of moving further towards the provision of 24-hour seven-day primary care.

14 Making Knowledge for Health – National Health Research Strategy (2001)

Action 73

The National Health Research Strategy proposes a thriving research culture supported by two complementary but distinct pillars:

- establishment of a research and development function within the health services

- enhanced support for science for health.

It emphasises that we are on the eve of one of the most remarkable transformations of the understanding of the human body and of health and disease. Knowledge will become available as a consequence of the mapping of the human genome and other discoveries. This transformation in knowledge will generate much more effective means to protect health and combat disease.

Making Knowledge Work for Health is the result of intensive consultation over a two-year period involving health providers, the universities and third-level colleges, the research community, the voluntary sector and the health-care industry. Its proposals reflect a consensus on how the health service should create, transfer and apply knowledge to promote health, combat disease and make services more effective. It develops the thinking of the White Paper on Science, Technology and Innovation (1996) and the Technology Foresight Report of the Irish Council for Science, Technology and Innovation (1999) in the context of the health services.

The analysis and proposals in the document are central to supporting a knowledge-based approach to health, guaranteeing better quality services to patients, ensuring more effective delivery of health services and creating a high-quality training environment for young health professionals. These are cross-cutting issues that are relevant to all aspects of the new Health Strategy. (Further details of the National Health Research Strategy are contained in Chapter 4.)

15 National Development Plan 2000-2006 (1999)

Chapters 3 and 5

The National Development Plan (NDP) involves an investment of over £40 billion (€52 billion) of public, private and EU funds (in 1999 prices) over the period 2000-2006. It is the largest and most ambitious investment plan ever drawn up for Ireland. The plan will involve significant investment in health services, social housing, education, roads, public transport, rural development, industry, and water and waste services. Unlike previous plans most of the public funding for this plan (about 90 per cent) will be provided from domestic sources, mainly from the Exchequer. The contribution from the EU will total £4.7 billion (€6 billion)

The NDP will involve a total capital investment of £2 billion (€2.5 billion) in the health sector. The priorities for this investment are:

- to provide facilities for persons with an intellectual disability

- to develop a range of facilities for older people

- to address major needs in the provision of modern accommodation for people with a mental illness and people with a physical disability

- to provide a comprehensive, quality and accessible acute hospital infrastructure

- to address child care needs

- to maximise the potential of information and communication technology (ICT) in the health care sector.

16 National Health Information Strategy (forthcoming)

Action 115

In April 2000, the Minister for Health and Children announced the development of a National Health Information Strategy (NHIS) to provide a blueprint for gathering and using information for health. The aim is to produce a strategy that will guide the development of a co-ordinated and integrated health information system over the next 5-7 years, and that is responsive to the health information needs of stakeholders - the public, patients, carers, health professionals, service managers and policy makers. The NHIS will support and complement this Health Strategy.

Appendix 3

Health agencies

Statutory bodies and non-statutory organisations

Body	Function
An Bord Altranais (Nursing Board)	The regulatory body for the nursing profession. Its main functions are to maintain a register of nurses and to provide for the education and training of nurses and student nurses
An Bord Uchtála (Adoption Board)	Makes Adoption Orders and registers voluntary adoption societies
Board for the Employment of the Blind	Provides employment for a number of blind and visually impaired people
Bord na Radharcmhastóirí (Opticians Board)	The regulatory body for opticians. The board's main functions include the training and registration of ophthalmic and dispensing opticians and regulating the practice of optics
Breastcheck	Responsible for the National Breast Screening Programme that aims to reduce breast cancer related deaths in women
Comhairle na Nimheanna (Poisons Council)	Advises the Minister for Health and Children on the control of poisons
Comhairle na nOspidéal	The statutory body responsible for regulating the number and type of consultant and senior registrar appointments and for specifying the necessary qualifications for these posts
Dental Council	The regulatory body for the dental profession. Its functions include maintaining a register of dentists and dental specialists, ensuring that the standards of dental training are maintained and inquiring into the fitness of a dentist to practice on specific grounds
Drug Treatment Centre Board	Provides a range of programmes for the treatment of drug addiction
Food Safety Authority of Ireland	Provides advice on issues relating to safety, nutrition, food law and other matters regarding the processing and sale of food
Food Safety Promotion Board	A North/South institution which promotes food safety awareness. It also supports north/south scientific co-operation, promotes links between institutions working in the field of food safety and promotes specialised laboratory services
General Medical Services (Payments) Board	Administers payments to doctors and pharmacists under the GMS scheme
Health Research Board	Provides advice on health research and related matters
Health Services Employers Agency (HSEA)	A statutory agency representing health service employers. Its functions include the promotion and support of value for money, efficiency and effectiveness in employment practice and the negotiation of industrial relations issues with health unions
Hospitals Trust Board	Administers the Hospitals Trust Fund
Institute of Public Health (IPH)	A cross-border body established by the Department of Health and Children and the Department of Health, Social Services and Public Safety (NI). The IPH is concerned with tackling health inequalities, strengthening partnerships and networking nationally and internationally, contributing to public health information and surveillance and strengthening public health capacity
Interim Special Residential Services Board	Advises the Ministers for Health and Children and Education and Science on matters relating to children in respect of whom child detention or special care orders have been made by the courts

Irish Blood Transfusion Service	Organises and administers the national blood transfusion service including the processing and supply of blood and blood products to Irish Hospitals. It also operates the National Haemovigilance Office, the Irish Unrelated Bone Marrow Registry and the National Tissue Bank
Irish Medicines Board	The authority responsible for the licensing of human and veterinary medicines and the approval of clinical trials. It also acts as an advisory body to the Minister in relation to safety, control and regulation of medicines generally
Medical Council	The statutory body for the medical profession. Its functions include administering the General Register of Medical Practitioners, ensuring that the standards of medical training are maintained and inquiring into the fitness of a doctor to practise on specific grounds
National Cancer Registry Board	A statutory body established to collect and analyse data and to report on cancer incidence and mortality in Ireland
National Children's Advisory Council	Advises the Minister for Health and Children on all aspects of children's lives, on better delivery and co-ordination of services to children, contributes to monitoring and evaluation of implementation of the National Children's Strategy, undertakes and advises on research and advises on the development of mechanisms to consult with children
National Children's Office	Responsible for the implementation of the National Children's Strategy. It provides advice to the Minister for Health and Children, develops measures to further the goals of the strategy and is responsible for fulfilling Ireland's commitments under the United Nations Convention on the Rights of the Child
National Council for the Professional Development of Nursing and Midwifery	The body responsible for the continuing education and professional development of nurses and midwives
National Council on Ageing and Older People	Advises the Minister for Health and Children on all aspects of ageing and older people
National Disease Surveillance Centre (NDSC)	Ireland's specialist centre for surveillance of communicable diseases. The aim of NDSC is to improve the health of the Irish population by the collation, interpretation and provision of the best possible information on infectious diseases. This is achieved through surveillance and independent advice, epidemiological investigation, research and training
National Social Work Qualifications Board	A statutory body which assesses the suitability of social work education and training and advises the Minister for Health and Children on standards which should apply
Office for Health Gain (OHG)	A body established by health board chief executive officers to facilitate health boards and others working to achieve health gain in response to the 1994 health strategy
Office for Health Management (OHM)	A body established to implement the national strategy for management development for the health and personal and social services in Ireland. Its main function is to facilitate management development for the health services by acting as a central resource and commissioning body
Office of Tobacco Control/Tobacco Control Agency (proposed)	Established on an administrative basis pending legislation. The Public Health (Tobacco) Bill provides for the establishment of a Tobacco Control Agency to advise the Minister on tobacco control measures, to monitor and co-ordinate the implementation of such measures and to advise the Minister on the control and regulation of the manufacture, sale, marketing and smoking of tobacco products
Pharmaceutical Society of Ireland	The professional body for the pharmaceutical profession. Its chief functions relate to the education, examination and registration of pharmaceutical chemists
Postgraduate Medical and Dental Board	Promotes and co-ordinates postgraduate medical and dental education and advises the Minister for Health and Children on all matters relating to such education
Pre-hospital Emergency Care Council	Responsible for the recognition of institutions for the education and training of emergency medical technicians
Social Services Inspectorate (SSI)	Established in 1999 by the Department of Health and Children as an independent body to inspect social services provided by health boards. To date the SSI has focused on child care services
Women's Health Council	Advises the Minister for Health and Children on all aspects of women's health

Health boards

Health boards were established under the Health Act, 1970 for the administration of the health services in the State. Health boards replaced local authorities in fulfilling this role. There are currently ten health boards established: three area health boards located in the eastern region under the aegis of the ERHA and seven regional health boards covering the rest of the country.

Eastern Regional Health Authority (ERHA)

The ERHA plans, commissions, monitors and evaluates health and personal social services in the eastern region, covering counties Dublin, Wicklow and Kildare, from the three area health boards and other providers located in the region. The three area health boards in the region are responsible for the provision of health and personal social services in their area:

East Coast Area Health Board	South-eastern Dublin and the eastern portion of Wicklow
Northern Area Health Board	Dublin city and county north of the River Liffey
South Western Area Health Board	Dublin inner city area south of the River Liffey, South Dublin, Kildare and the Baltinglass area of Wicklow

Regional health boards

The seven regional health boards are responsible for providing or arranging the provision of health and personal social services in the following counties:

Midland Health Board	Laois, Offaly, Longford and Westmeath
Mid Western Health Board	Clare, Limerick and Tipperary North Riding
North Eastern Health Board	Cavan, Monaghan, Meath and Louth
North Western Health Board	Donegal, Sligo and Leitrim
South Eastern Health Board	Wexford, Carlow, Kilkenny, Waterford and Tipperary South Riding
Southern Health Board	Cork and Kerry
Western Health Board	Galway, Mayo and Roscommon

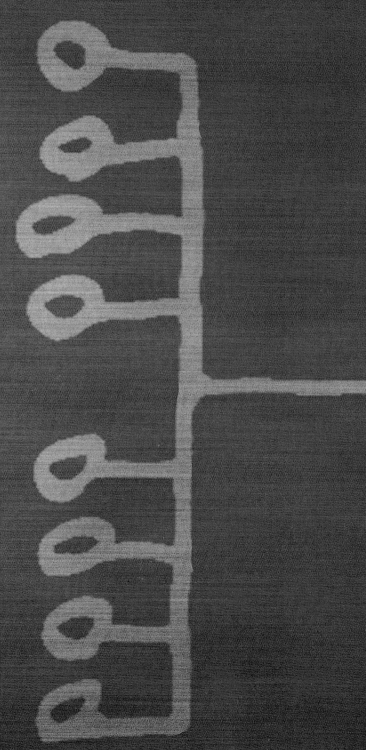

Glossary of terms

Acute hospital: A hospital providing medical and surgical treatment of relatively short duration. All, except district hospitals, are consultant-staffed. District hospitals are classified as acute where the average length of stay is less than 30 days

Advanced nurse practitioner/ advanced midwife practitioner: Advanced nursing and midwifery practice is carried out by autonomous, experienced practitioners who are competent, accountable and responsible for their own practice. They are highly experienced in clinical practice and are educated to masters degree level (or higher)

Advocacy service: Assigns someone who represents and defends the views, needs and rights of an individual who is not in a position to or does not feel able to do this for him or herself

Alternative medicine: A broad range of healing resources that encompasses health systems and practices, that are seen as alternative to conventional medicine or health care, as well as the theories and beliefs that underlie them

Autologous transfusion: A transfusion in which the donor and recipient are the same person and which uses pre-deposited blood and blood products

Bed designation: The assigning of beds in public hospitals for sole use by public or private patients

Capital funding: Money allocated for spending on assets, such as buildings or equipment, which will be used for more than one year

Care plan: A plan formulated by a health professional in consultation with individual patients, their families and other appropriate professionals that describes what kind of services and care that person should receive

Casemix: A method of quantifying hospital workload by describing the complexity and resource-intensity of the services provided. This differs from a simple count of total patients treated or total bed days used

Childcare: Describes day-care facilities and services for pre-school children and school-going children out of school hours

Child care: The services under the remit of the Department of Health and Children for children who require care and protection from the State

Clinical audit: The systematic, critical analysis of the quality of care, including the procedures used for diagnosis and treatment, the use of resources and the resulting outcome and quality of life for the patient

Clinical nurse specialist / Clinical midwife specialist: A nurse or midwife specialist in clinical practice who has undertaken formal recognised post-registration education relevant to his or her area of specialist practice at higher diploma level. Such formal education is underpinned by extensive experience and clinical expertise in the relevant specialist area

Clinical pathways: A method used in health care to organise, evaluate and limit variations in patient care. This method integrates the components of the care plan into one which addresses the needs and services provided to the whole patient

Consultant-led service: A service supervised by consultants who lead and advise teams of doctors in training and other staff in the delivery of care to their patients

Consultant-provided service: A service delivered by consultants, working in teams, who have a substantial – and direct - involvement in the diagnosis, delivery of care and overall management of patients

Council of Europe: An intergovernmental organisation, of which Ireland is a member. The Council of Europe is concerned with the protection and promotion of human rights and democracy throughout Europe, and with strengthening political, social, legal and cultural co-operation among its member states

Day patient: A person admitted to hospital for treatment on a planned (rather than an emergency) basis and who is discharged on the same day

Defibrillation: The use of a carefully controlled electric shock, administered either through a device on the exterior of the chest wall or directly to the exposed heart muscle, to restart or normalise heart rhythms

Diagnostic: Pertaining to the determination of the nature of a cause of disease

Discharge planning: The active planning of discharge and post-discharge services for in-patients

Elective treatment: A planned or non-emergency admission or procedure that has been arranged in advance. This differs from emergency treatment that is urgently required

Eligibility: Refers to whether or not a person qualifies to avail of services, either without charge (full eligibility) or subject to prescribed charges (limited eligibility)

Entitlement: A right granted by law or contract, especially to benefits or services

Environmental health: Comprises those aspects of human health and disease that are determined by factors in the environment. It also refers to the theory and practice of assessing and controlling factors in the environment that can potentially affect health

Evidence-based practice: Practice which incorporates the use of best available and appropriate evidence arising from research and other sources

Gross domestic product (GDP): The total output produced in the Irish economy regardless of the residence of the owners of production. It includes output by foreign-owned producers located in Ireland, but does not include output by Irish-owned producers located abroad

Gross national product (GNP): The total income earned by residents of a country irrespective of where that income is generated. It is equal to GDP plus income earned abroad by Irish residents, less income earned in Ireland by foreign residents

Health and personal social services: Services provided by public, private and voluntary agencies that are aimed directly at improving health status

Health system: The term used to describe agencies that provide health services or whose actions have an impact on health

HESSOP Report: The Health and Social Services for Older People report conducted by the National Council for Ageing and Older People. Older people were consulted on their service needs and their use and experiences of current services

Hospital in-patient enquiry (HIPE): A health information system that collates data about each in-patient and day care hospital discharge, including diagnostic and treatment information and length of stay

Interdisciplinary or multidisciplinary approach: The term used to describe professionals from more than one discipline working together in a co-ordinated way

Intersectoral or multi-sectoral issues: The term used to describe policy issues that involve more than one department or agency and may require a co-ordinated approach

In-patient: A person admitted to hospital for treatment or investigation who stays for at least one night

Key worker: A designated person assigned to an individual or family who acts as a liaison with outside agencies, co-ordinates social and health services and acts as a resource person for their clients

Morbidity Rate: The number of ill people in a given population in a particular time period

Mortality Rate: The number of deaths in a given population in a particular time period

Multi-annual budgeting: A system of budgeting where money is allocated for a project for more than one year. In effect a budget is agreed for each year over the lifetime of a project and the agreed level of funding is guaranteed for this period. A multi-annual budget (MAB) is a budget for a project covering more than one year

National Anti-Poverty Strategy, 1997: A 10-year Government programme for reducing poverty through a range of targets focusing on global poverty, educational disadvantage, unemployment, income adequacy and rural/urban development. The Programme for Prosperity and Fairness committed the Government to setting targets in the area of health, housing and accommodation

National Development Plan 2000-2006: The plan sets out a coherent strategy for development in the areas of infrastructure, education and training, the productive sector and the promotion of social inclusion. It includes a framework for the promotion of a more balanced regional development. It will involve an investment of £40 billion (€52 billion) over the period 2000-2006 of public, EU and private funds. A total of £2 billion (€2.5 billion) has been allocated to the health sector

National psychiatric in-patient reporting system (NPIRS): A database with details of all discharges from public in-patient units for persons with mental illness

Out-of-hours service: Services provided outside 'traditional' business hours, i.e. before 9am and after 5pm on weekdays and all services provided during weekends and bank holidays

Out-of-pocket: Funding for a service that is received through direct payments to the service provider by users

Out-patient: A patient who attends a hospital clinic for treatment and is not admitted to the hospital

Palliative care: The active total care of patients whose condition is no longer responsive to curative treatment

Personal public service number (PPSN): Unique personal reference number for the public service, including social welfare, tax, education and health service eligibility

Primary care: An approach to care that includes a range of services designed to keep people well, from promotion of health and screening for disease to assessment, diagnosis, treatment and rehabilitation as well as personal social services. The services provide first-level contact that is fully accessible by self-referral and have a strong emphasis on working with communities and individuals to improve their health and social well-being

Public Private Partnerships (PPP): An agreement between a public authority and a private sector business for the purpose of designing, building and possibly operating a capital development or service which is traditionally provided by the public sector. The use of PPPs in the health sector will be used to help accelerate capital provision, yield long-term value for money for the Exchequer and ensure quality public services

Purchasing power parity: The adjustment made between the currencies of different countries to reflect differences in exchange rates. The purchasing power parity (PPP) rate enables more valid comparisons to be made between relative prices when these are measured in a common currency. Health spending comparisons are often expressed in US$, in PPP terms

Risk management: The prevention and containment of liability by careful and objective investigation and documentation of critical or unusual patient care incidents

Secondary care: Specialist care that is typically provided in a hospital setting

Service agreement: A formal agreement between a health board and a voluntary agency in which the board provides funding in exchange for an agreed level and type of service

Shared care: Continuing care for those with on-going needs which is usually provided by both primary and secondary care providers

Social capital: Those stocks of social trust, norms and networks that people can draw upon to solve common problems. These include organised supports such as parish and neighbourhood associations, sports clubs and co-operatives and less formal supports such as close neighbours and extended family

Social, Personal and Health Education (SPHE): Introduced in the late 1990s to drive all school programmes relating to lifestyle choices. SPHE has formed part of the Primary School Curriculum since 1999 and is being introduced on a phased basis at junior cycle level from October 2000. All post-primary schools will have a programme in place by September 2003

Specialist services: Care delivered by consultants and other specialist health care professionals in a hospital or community setting

Strategic Management Initiative (SMI): The initiative launched by the Government in 1994 to reinvigorate the management and performance of the public service

Telemedicine: Rapid access to shared and remote medical expertise by means of telecommunications and information technologies, no matter where the patient or relevant information is located

Tertiary care: Very specialised care, normally confined to a small number of locations

Triage: The initial rapid assessment of patients in order to direct them to the service appropriate to their needs

Value for money (VFM): Examinations carried out by the Comptroller and Auditor General (C&AG) that aim to establish whether resources have been acquired, used or disposed of economically and efficiently. Examinations can also investigate whether public bodies have appropriate systems, practices and procedures for evaluating the effectiveness of their activities

vCJD: variant Creutzfeldt-Jakob Disease

Whole-time equivalent numbers: A measure of the number of people working in an organisation which takes into account the number of hours worked by both full and part-time staff and expresses this in terms of the number of people working full-time that it would take to carry out the same work. In its simplest form two part-time workers are deemed to be equivalent to one whole-time equivalent

References

Acute Hospitals Review Group Report (2001). Belfast: Department of Health, Social Services and Public Safety.

Addressing health inequalities. *A Combat Poverty Agency submission to the Western Health Board Initiative 'Developing Acute Hospitals in the New Century'* (2000). Dublin: Combat Poverty Agency.

Adolescent Health Strategy (2001). Dublin: National Conjoint Child Health Committee

Annual Report of the Chief Medical Officer 1999 (2000). Dublin: Department of Health and Children.

Bacon P. and Associates (2001). *Current and Future Supply and Demand Conditions in the Labour Market for certain Professional Therapists.* Dublin: Department of Health and Children.

Balanda K. and Wilde, J. (2001). *Inequalities in Mortality – A report on All-Ireland Mortality Data* (1989-1998). Dublin: The Institute of Public Health in Ireland.

Central Statistics Office (2001). Data supplied to the Department of Health and Children.

Child Care Act (1991). Dublin: Stationery Office.

Children Act (2001). Dublin: Stationery Office.

Clinical Governance (2000). Dublin: The Office for Health Management.

Daly, A. and Walsh, D. (1999). *Activities of Irish Psychiatric Services Report 1999* Dublin: Health Research Board.

Deloitte and Touche (2001). *Audit of the Irish Health Service for Value for Money.* Dublin: Department of Health and Children

Denyer, S., Thornton, L and Pelly, H. (1999) *Best Health for Children – Developing a partnership with Families* (1999). Manorhamilton: National Conjoint Child Health Committee, Health Board Chief Executive Officers.

Department of Community Health and General Practice. (2001). *Inequalities in health in Ireland- hard facts.* Dublin: Trinity College.

Department of Finance (1999). *The National Development Plan 2000-2006.* Dublin: Stationery Office.

Department of Health. (1984). The Psychiatric services - *Planning For The Future.* Dublin: Stationery Office.

Department of Health (1988). *The Years ahead: A Policy for the Elderly. Report of the Working Group on the Services for the Elderly.* Dublin: Stationery Office.

Department of Health. (1990). *Needs and abilities- Report of the Review Group on Mental Handicap Services.* Dublin: Stationery Office.

Department of Health (1994). *National Breastfeeding Policy for Ireland.* Dublin: Department of Health.

Department of Health (1994). *Services for People with Autism.* Dublin: Stationery Office.

Department of Health (1994). *Shaping a Healthier Future: A strategy for effective healthcare in the 1990's.* Dublin: Stationery Office.

Department of Health (1995). *Developing a policy for women's health-A discussion document.* Dublin: Stationery Office.

Department of Health (1996). *A Strategy for Equality- Report of the Commission on the Status of People with Disabilities.* Dublin: Stationery Office.

Department of Health (1996). *National Cancer Strategy.* Dublin: Stationery Office.

Department of Health (1996). *Report of the Department of Health Cervical Screening Committee.* Dublin: Stationery Office.

Department of Health (1996). *The National Alcohol Policy.* Dublin: Stationery Office.

Department of Health (1996). *Towards an independent Future-Report of the Review Group on Health and personal Social Services for People with Physical and Sensory Disabilities.* Dublin: Stationery Office

Department of Health and Children (1998). *Adding years to life and life to years. A Health Promotion Strategy for Older People.* Dublin: Stationery Office.

Department of Health and Children (1998). *Report of the National Task Force on Suicides.* Dublin: Stationery Office.

Department of Health and Children (1999). *Building Healthier Hearts. National Cardiovascular Health Strategy.* Dublin: Stationery Office.

Department of Health and Children (1999). *Children First. National Guidelines for the Protection and Welfare of Children.* Dublin: Stationery Office.

Department of Health and Children (1999). *Health Statistics.* Dublin: Stationery Office.

Department of Health and Children (1999). *Proposal for a National Environmental Health Action Plan.* Dublin: Stationery Office.

Department of Health and Children (1999). *White Paper on Health Insurance.* Dublin: Stationery Office.

Department of Health and Children (2000). *A Plan for Women's Health 1997-1999.* Dublin: Stationery Office.

Department of Health and Children (2000). *AIDS Strategy 2000: Report of the National AIDS Strategy Committee.* Dublin: Stationery Office.

Department of Health and Children (2000). *National Children's Strategy: Report of the Public Consultation.* Dublin: Stationery Office.

Department of Health and Children (2000). *National Health Promotion Strategy, 2000-2005.* Dublin, Stationery Office.

Department of Health and Children (2000). *National Strategy on Youth Homelessness.* Dublin: Stationery Office.

Department of Health and Children (2000). *Public Health Information System, version 4.* Dublin: Department of Health and Children.

Department of Health and Children (2000). *The National Children's Strategy – Our children their lives.* Dublin, Stationery Office.

Department of Health and Children (2000). *Towards a tobacco-free society: The Report of the Tobacco-Free Policy Review Group.* Dublin: Stationery Office.

Department of Health and Children (2000). *Intensive Care Units. Disturbed Mentally Ill. (Draft Report)* unpublished.

Department of Health and Children (2001). *Effective Utilisation of Professional Skills of Nurses and Midwives.* Dublin: Department of Health and Children.

Department of Health and Children (2001). *First Report of the Review Group on Child and Adolescent Psychiatric Services .* Dublin: Stationery Office.

Department of Health and Children (2001). *Public Health (Tobacco) Bill. No. 46.* Dublin: Stationery Office.

Department of Health and Children (2001). *Your Views about Health. Report on Consultation.* Dublin: Stationery Office.

Department of Health and Children (2001). *Primary Care: A New Direction.* Dublin: Stationery Office.

Department of Health and Children. *Guidance for Best Practice on Recruitment of Oversea's Nurses and Midwives* – in press.

Department of Health and Children: (2001) *Making Knowledge Work for Health a Strategy for Health Research.* Dublin: Department of Health and Children.

Department of Justice, Equality and Law Reform (2001) *Report of the Group to review the structure and organisation of Prison Health Care Services.* Dublin: Stationery Office.

Department of Social, Community and Family Affairs (1996). *National Anti-poverty Strategy-Sharing in progress.* Dublin: Stationery Office.

Department of Social, Community and Family Affairs (2001). *White Paper on Supporting Voluntary Activity.* Dublin: Stationery Office.

Department of the Environment and Local Government (2000). *Homelessness – an integrated strategy.* Dublin: Stationery Office.

Department of the Taoiseach (2000). *The Programme for Prosperity and Fairness.* Dublin: Stationery Office.

Department of Tourism, Sport and Recreation (2001). *Building on Experience. National Drugs Strategy 2001-2008.* Dublin: Stationery Office.

Dixon M. and Baker A. (1996). *A management development strategy for the health and personal social services in Ireland.* Dublin: Department of Health and Children.

Employment Equality Act (1998). Dublin: Stationery Office.

Equal Status Act (2000). Dublin: Stationery Office.

EU Directive 2000/EC of the European Parliament and of the Council Amending Council Directive 93/104/Ec concerning certain aspects of the organisation of working time to cover sectors and activities excluded from that Directive.

European Home and Leisure Accident Surveillance System report for Ireland 1998 (1999). Dublin: Department of Health and Children.

Eurostat (1999). *Key figures on health Pocketbook - 1999 Edition. Luxembourg: Office for Official Publications of the European Communities*

Food Hygiene Act (1998). Dublin: Stationery Office.

Food Safety Authority of Ireland Act (1998). Dublin: Stationery Office.

Foster Care – a Child Centered Partnership – Report of the Working Group on Foster Care (2001). Dublin: Stationery Office.

Friel S., Nic Gabhainn S. and Kelleher C. (1999). *The National Health and Lifestyle Surveys: survey of lifestyle attitudes and nutrition and the Irish health behavior in school-aged children* (SLAN and HBSC) Galway: Centre for Health Promotion Studies; National University of Galway.

Guidelines on good practice and quality assurance in mental health services (1998). Dublin: Department of Health and Children.

Health (Amendment) (No. 3) Act (1996). Dublin: Stationery Office.

Health (Eastern Regional Health Authority) Act (1999). Dublin: Stationery Office.

Health (Miscellaneous Provisions) Act (2001). Dublin: Stationery Office.

Health (Nursing Homes) Act (1990). Dublin: Stationery Office.

Health Act (1970). Dublin: Stationery Office.

Health Research Board (2000). *Making Knowledge for Health – Towards a strategy for Research and Innovation for Health.* Dublin: Health Research Board.

Irish Medicines Board Act (1995). Dublin: Stationery Office.

Kumar S. (1999). *Health in Development.1999 World Health Assembly 52nd.* World Health Organisation.

Medicinal Products (Prescriptions and Control of Supply) Regulations S.I. No. 256/1996. Dublin: Stationery Office.

Medicinal Products (Prescriptions and Control of Supply) (Amendment) Regulations S.I. No. 309/1996. Dublin: Stationery Office.

Medicinal Products (Prescriptions and Control of Supply) (Amendment) Regulations S.I. No. 271/1999. Dublin: Stationery Office.

Mental Health Act. No. 25 (2001). Dublin: Stationery Office.

Mental Health Treatment Act (1945). Dublin: Stationery Office.

Mid Western Health Board (2000). *Irish Cervical Screening Programme.* Limerick: Mid Western Health Board.

Mulvany, F. (2000) *National intellectual Disability Database Annual Report (1998/1999).* Dublin: Health Research Board.

National Cancer Registry Board (1998). *Cancer in Ireland, 1997. Incidence and Mortality.* Cork: National Cancer Research Board.

National Council on Ageing and Older People (1999). *An Action Plan for Dementia.* Dublin: National Council on Ageing and Older People.

Nolan B. and Callan T..(1994). *Poverty and Policy in Ireland.* Dublin: Economic and Social Research Institute.

Nolan B. and Wiley M. (2000). *Private Practice in Irish Public Hospitals.* Dublin: Economic and Social Research Institute.

North Eastern Health Board (2001) *Men Talking.* Kells, Co Meath: Department of Public Health.

Report of the Commission on Nursing: a blueprint for the future (1998). Dublin: Stationery Office.

Report of the Expert Group on Various Health Professions (2000) Dublin: Expert Group on Various Health Professions.

Report of the Forum on Medical Manpower (2001) Dublin: Department of Health and Children.

Report of the National Advisory Committee on Palliative Care (2001) Dublin: Department of Health and Children.

Report of the Review Group on Ambulance Services (1993) Dublin: Department of Health.

Report of the Sub-Group to The National Cancer Forum (2000) Dublin: Department of Health and Children.

Report of the Working Group on Ambulance Service Review (2001) Dublin: Working Group on Ambulance Service Review.

Report on the Men's Health Conference (1999). Bundoran, Co. Donegal: North Western Health Board.

Saskatchewan Commission on Medicare. (2000). Government of Saskatchewan [Online], Available: www.health.gov.sk.ca/commission.html (June, 2001).

Scallan, E., Staines, A., Fitzpatrick P., Laffoy, M. and Kelly, A. (2001). *Injury in Ireland.* Dublin: Department of Public Health Medicine and Epidemiology, University College Dublin.

The Health of our Children-Annual Report of the Chief Medical Officer (2000) Dublin: Department of Health and Children.

The Nursing and Midwifery Resource Interim Report of the Steering Group (2000) Dublin: The Department of Health and Children.

The Office of the Comptroller and Auditor General (1997). *Value for Money Report – Emergency Ambulance Services.* No. 20 Dublin: Stationery Office.

The Protection of Persons Reporting Child Abuse Act (1998). Dublin: Stationery Office.

The Report of the National Joint Steering Group on the Working Hours of Non Consultant Hospital Doctors (2001). Dublin: Department of Health and Children.

Us Men, Our Health (2000). Galway: The Western Health Board.

Wiley M. (2001). *Critique of shaping a healthier future: A strategy for effective healthcare in the 1990's.* Dublin: Economic and Social Research Institute.

World Health Organisation (1999). *Health 21-Health for All in the 21st Century. An Introduction.* Copenhagen: World Health Organisation.